Balancing Work and Caregiving for Children, Adults, and Elders

D1512062

FAMILY CAREGIVER APPLICATIONS SERIES

Series Editors

David E. Biegel, *Case Western Reserve University*
Richard Schulz, *University of Pittsburgh*

The **Family Caregiver Applications Series** is an interdisciplinary book series focusing on the application of knowledge about family caregiving, both within and across dependent populations, extending into the practice and policy arenas. The volumes are well-grounded theoretically and empirically, advance existing knowledge in the field, and are state-of-the-art works designed to fill existing gaps in the literature.

Advisory Board Members

Volumes in This Series:

1. **Family Caregiving in Chronic Illness: Alzheimer's Disease, Cancer, Heart Disease, Mental Illness, and Stroke**
   David E. Biegel, Esther Sales, and Richard Schulz

2. **Grandmothers as Caregivers: Raising Children of the Crack Cocaine Epidemic**
   Meredith Minkler and Kathleen M. Roe

3. **Balancing Work and Caregiving for Children, Adults, and Elders**
   Margaret B. Neal, Nancy J. Chapman, Berit Ingersoll-Dayton, and Arthur C. Emlen

Family Caregiver Applications Series
Volume 3

Balancing Work and Caregiving for Children, Adults, and Elders

Margaret B. Neal
Nancy J. Chapman
Berit Ingersoll-Dayton
Arthur C. Emlen

Published in cooperation with the
Center for Practice Innovations,
Mandel School of Applied Social Sciences
Case Western Reserve University

SAGE Publications
International Educational and Professional Publisher
Newbury Park London New Delhi

For information address:

SAGE Publications, Inc.
2455 Teller Road
Newbury Park, California 91320

SAGE Publications Ltd.
6 Bonhill Street
London EC2A 4PU
United Kingdom

SAGE Publications India Pvt. Ltd.
M-32 Market
Greater Kailash I
New Delhi 110 048 India

Printed in the United States of America

Library of Congress Cataloging-in-Publication Data

Main entry under title:

Balancing work and caregiving for children, adults, and elders/
    Margaret B. Neal . . . [et al.].
        p. cm. –(Family caregiver applications series; v. 3)
    Includes bibliographical references and index.
    ISBN 0-8039-4281-8. —ISBN 0-8039-4282-6 (pbk.)
    1. Work and family. 2. Caregivers. I. Neal, Margaret B.
II. Series.
HD4904.25.B34   1993
306.87—dc20   92-35345

93 94 95 96   10 9 8 7 6 5 4 3 2 1

Sage Production Editor: Diane S. Foster

Contents

IV. IMPLICATIONS AND RECOMMENDATIONS

Series Editors' Foreword

Many individuals who are caregivers to children, disabled adults, or elderly members of their family are also employed. This combination of employment and caregiving responsibility can be a source of strain for the caregiver and a source of concern to employers who may fear loss of worker productivity and availability.

This volume presents results of an empirical study of caregiving and work and discusses policies, benefits, and services that need to be enhanced or developed to address the needs of employed caregivers. It is based upon a survey of almost 10,000 employees of 33 businesses and agencies in a large metropolitan area. The volume addresses fundamental questions including: Why have work and family issues become so important in the Unted States in the last decade? Does caregiving have an impact on employee absenteeism and stress? How do caregivers juggle their work- and family- related responsibilities? and How have employers responded to meet the special needs of family caregivers?

While the challenges individuals face in combining work and caregiving are widely discussed in the literature, this book extends the existing literature in a number of unique and important ways. First, the research is based on a large sample of caregivers and noncaregivers and is therefore able to isolate the effects of caregiving per se. Second, this is the first major study of caregiving and work in which the full range of caregiver types is examined, including individuals whose primary responsibility is caring for a young child, disabled adult, or elderly individual, as well as those who occupy multiple caregiving roles. This enables the authors to make important comparisons between individuals with few caregiving demands with those who must provide care to several different individuals simultaneously. Finally, the authors capture the qualitative perspectives of individual respondents through narrative descriptions of individual cases.

Other strengths of this volume include its well-conceptualized theoretical framework, multivariate data analytic techniques, and the extensive discussion of the implications of this research for public policy and service delivery. We believe that this volume addresses a vital public policy issue that can be expected to become even more important in the decades ahead. As such, this book should be of interest and of great value to a broad audience of policymakers, researchers, service providers, and students.

David E. Biegel
Richard Schulz
Series Editors

Preface

This book focuses on employees who have responsibility for the care of one or more of three groups of dependents—children, adults with disabilities, or elders. The impact of these informal caregiving responsibilities on both employees and their work is examined, as are the programs and policies that have been developed to ease the negative effects of combining paid work and caregiving. To address the lack of integrated information about the three groups of caregivers, this book presents and synthesizes relevant research about them. Indeed, the caregiving literature with regard to care for adult dependents has been further fragmented by the type of disability, including such categories as chronic mental illness, physical illness, or developmental disability. The book describes and analyzes the full range of work schedule policies, benefits, and workplace-based programs developed for each of these caregiver groups. It also makes recommendations concerning both national and local policies that pertain to employers, community services, and families themselves. Its purpose is to inform policy and practice regarding employees who are family caregivers.

This book is the work of four individuals with different yet overlapping interests who joined in looking at the commonality of caregiving in the context of employment. Academic research is typically conducted along disciplinary lines and according to stages of human development, such as childhood, adulthood, and aging. This book cuts across those traditional lines to examine informal caregiving and its personal as well as organizational effects for employees who care for dependents across the life-span. By focusing on comparative issues of caregiving in relation to work and family, we hope to speak to several disparate audiences:

experts in the fields of family studies, work performance, child care, adult care, and elder care, and professionals in human resource policy relating to employee benefits and services. Our audiences should include employers concerned about the well-being of their employees as well as policymakers and citizens concerned about the well-being of three generations.

Although all four authors participated in all parts of the collaborative effort that this book represents, each took primary responsibility for particular chapters. Margaret B. Neal provided much of the integrative work of the book, including Chapters 1, 7, and 11, as well as the chapter on workplace policies and benefits (Chapter 8). Nancy J. Chapman focused on issues of multiple role occupancy (Chapters 1 and 6) and on the conceptual framework and methodology (Chapter 2) and shared with Margaret B. Neal the major effort of data analysis (Chapters 3 through 6). Berit Ingersoll-Dayton took responsibility for developing the chapters on care for adults with disabilities and elders (Chapters 4 and 5) and on workplace services for caregivers (Chapter 9). Arthur C. Emlen's long-term interest in children and child care is reflected in his work in Chapter 3, while his development of needs assessment techniques for businesses is described in Chapter 10.

A word about language. In different fields of endeavor, words take on special meanings that are unfamiliar to others and make it difficult to undertake a comprehensive discussion of common issues. For some, the term *dependent care* refers to care of elders. For others, it refers to care of children. And for others, this term refers only to the care of those who are claimed as financial dependents for income-tax purposes. We, however, use the term *dependent care* generically to encompass child care, elder care, and care of adults with disabilities. Our focus includes those who are financially dependent on the employee, but also, in the case of adults and elders, those who are not. Similarly, in the field of elder care, the term *caregivers* refers to those individuals who have informal, unpaid caregiving responsibilities. In the child care field, however, the term *caregivers* refers to persons other than the employee who provide supplemental child care, often on a paid basis. Consequently, in this book we try to speak generically of "caregiving responsibilities," which include providing direct personal care as well as finding and managing supplemental care in the community. Finally, we occasionally use the term *family care* in lieu of dependent care, although it should be noted that the recipients of care are not always family members.

As in all efforts of this magnitude, thanks are owed to many individuals and organizations. The Meyer Memorial Trust provided funding for the original study on which this book is based, "Work and Elder Care: Supporting Families in the Workplace" (Grant Number 86064020). The staff of the research project included Patricia Ebert, Wendy Lebow, Pamela Sievertson, Janet Langbecker, and Darey Shell. Furthermore, we gratefully recognize the contributions of Paul E. Koren, Research Associate at the Regional Research Institute for Human Services at Portland State University, who helped to develop the employee survey method that was adapted for use in our research. We also thank the 33 employers who allowed us to survey their employees.

In the preparation of the book itself, our invaluable support staff included Susan Wladaver-Morgan, who provided thoughtful and careful editing, and Julia Morgan, who provided not only research, clerical, and word-processing assistance, but also humor and moral support. We have very much appreciated conversations, insights, and support from our colleagues, including Maria Talbott, David L. Morgan, Nancy Perrin, Elizabeth Kutza, Nohad Toulan, Alan Cabelly, Doreen Grove, Randy Boose, Pat Hogan, Paula Carder, Jennifer Gregorio, and Sue Reggiani. Many thanks, too, to our book series editors, David E. Biegel and Richard Schulz, for their encouragement and their comments on earlier drafts of the manuscript.

Finally, we wish to thank the employees who responded to our survey, especially those who took the time to write comments on the backs of their survey instruments. It is their comments that begin each chapter and that so ably, and sometimes quite poignantly, serve as illustrations throughout the book. And last, but certainly not least, we wish to publicly thank our own families, who supported us as we juggled our diverse work and family responsibilities while completing this book.

PART I

Introduction

1

Dependent Care as a Corporate, Family, and Community Concern

I am a single parent who gets no child support. . . . My child is very dependable and can and does care for himself, but has been a latchkey child since age 9. . . . I only hope 9 through 13 has not left a permanent scar emotionally for my child. I grew up in an era where mom was always there, this day and age does not allow such luxury or comfort.

Interest in the relationship between employees' work and home lives has grown dramatically in the past decade. While home and work have traditionally been viewed as separate spheres, their interdependence is increasingly recognized. Crouter (1984) described this interrelationship between work and family as having important "spillover" effects, both positive and negative, from one sphere to the other.

The problem of balancing work and family responsibilities has long been identified for employees who have young children. More recently, attention has also been directed to employees who have responsibilities for other family members requiring assistance, particularly elderly persons. As Carter and Piktialis (1988, p. 53) noted, "Few . . . would dispute that elder care is becoming a complex and often anxiety-provoking issue for the employees of many U.S. corporations, much as child care emerged as an urgent issue several years ago."

To date, few if any published studies, with the exception of one by the authors (Neal, Chapman, Ingersoll-Dayton, Emlen, & Boise, 1990), have compared employees with responsibilities for dependents of the different age groups: children, adults, and elders. Similarly, few researchers have examined the differential impact on employees of caring for these different groups. Knowledge of the nature and effects of employees'

3

dependent-care responsibilities is crucial. Public and corporate policy-makers, human resource managers, and health and social service providers alike will need this information as they attempt to design policies and programs to ease the conflict between family and work roles.

WHY THE CURRENT INTEREST
IN WORK-FAMILY ISSUES?

Several interrelated demographic, social, and economic trends in the United States are affecting both the need for and the availability of family caregivers to assist dependent family members. These trends have resulted in changes in the composition of the American population, the American family, and the American work force. They point toward important consequences: increasing demand for informal care for dependents, decreasing availability of informal caregivers, and a smaller work force.

Increasing Demand for Informal Care

The increasing demand for informal care derives first from gains in longevity due to scientific and technological advances. The American population is aging. In 1980, 11% of the U.S. population was 65 years of age or older, but by the year 2000 this segment of the population is expected to comprise 13% of our population; and by 2050, 20% of Americans are expected to be age 65 or older. Furthermore, among the elderly, it is the segment that is oldest, frailest, and most likely to need care—those 85 and older—that is growing fastest (Subcommittee on Human Services, 1987).

A second reason for the growing demand for informal care is the increase in the number of adults with disabilities as people survive what in the past were often fatal injuries and diseases, again due to advancing medical knowledge and technology. For example, Trieschmann (1980) stated that with advances in medical science, some persons with spinal cord injuries may achieve a normal life expectancy. Based on 1980 census statistics (U.S. Bureau of the Census, 1983), 8% of the population between the ages of 16 and 64 have a physical, mental, or other health problem that limits or prevents their ability to work. Disability can be measured in a variety of ways; thus estimates of prevalence can vary widely. For example, 20.6% of the population over the age of 15 is "limited in ability to perform selected physical functions," 7.5% have a "severe functional limitation," 8.8% are "unable to perform their major activity" (ability to care for self, to work, or to attend school), and 19.1% have suffered from a mental disorder during the previous 6 months (including substance abuse and cognitive impairment) (Kraus & Stoddard, 1989, pp. 2-4, 7). The inconsistent measures make assessment of trends in prevalence of disability particularly difficult. Work disability appears to have declined very slightly from 1981 to 1988 (from 9.0% to 8.6%), but severe work disability has been virtually constant over the same time period (about 4.8%) (Kraus & Stoddard, 1991).

Third, changes in the reimbursement and financing of health care now place less emphasis on institutional care and more on community-based care for individuals who are frail or who have disabilities. These policies require earlier hospital discharges and more complex home-care regimens (Akabas, 1990; Ontario Women's Directorate, 1990; Subcommittee on Human Services, 1987; U.S. Department of Labor, 1986). As noted by the Ontario Women's Directorate (1990), this trend means that such individuals need greater direct support from their families and communities. At the same time, however, the declining fertility rate is decreasing the demand for child care. Overall, then, we have a change in the balance of demand for care, away from children and toward adults and elders.

Decreasing Availability of Informal Caregivers

Several social and economic trends point toward the loss of people available to provide care for dependents (Subcommittee on Human Services, 1987). First, the declining fertility rate means that there will be fewer adult children to care for the growing elderly population. In the mid-1950s, the fertility rate of American women peaked at about 3.5 children, followed by a steady decline to a low of 1.7 children in 1976. Since 1976, the rate has slowly risen to about 1.9 children (National Center for Health Statistics, 1990). The percentage of women who were childless rose for all age groups from 1976 to 1988 (U.S. Bureau of the Census, 1989a). At the same time, more of the older population will have been divorced and remarried during their lifetimes, so that their adult children may have responsibility for a greater number of parents, including stepparents and parents-in-law. Divorce among this generation of adult children has also resulted in more single-parent households, leaving more adult children without a spouse's assistance upon which to draw to care for an elderly relative (Subcommittee on Human Services, 1987).

Moreover, increasing numbers of women are entering and remaining in the paid labor force, and they are entering more diverse occupations across a range of statuses. According to the Bureau of National Affairs (1988, p. 23), an examination of findings from the Bureau of Labor Statistics population surveys for 1950, 1970, and 1987 revealed that "the number of women who work is 2.5 times the number of women who worked in 1950, and is half again the number who worked in 1970. In late 1987, 56.6% of women over age 20 were working." According to the U.S. Bureau of Labor Statistics (1988), most of these women (72%) worked full time. By the year 2000, it is estimated that 75% of all women between the ages of 45 and 60 will be employed (Gibeau, Anastas, & Larson, 1987).

It is this group of middle-aged females (e.g., adult daughters and daughters-in-law) that is most likely to assume primary responsibility for the care of a disabled husband or parent (Subcommittee on Human Services, 1987). Because women are the traditional caregivers (Subcommittee on Human Services, 1987), this trend has serious implications for the availability of caregivers and for the impact of caregiving on women. As noted by the U.S. Department of Labor, Women's Bureau (1986):

> With over 55% of all working age women either employed or looking for work, there is less time available for the services traditionally provided by wives, mothers, and daughters. This situation will not improve without new approaches to the provision of informal care services. (p. 1)

This report proceeds to suggest that the demographic trends toward increased longevity and delayed childbearing will result in rising median ages for both the population and the labor force and in even greater conflict among obligations to work, family, and caregiving.

In the 20 years from 1970 to 1990, the percentage of all U.S. children under age 18 with mothers in the labor force increased from 39% to 62% (U.S. Bureau of Labor Statistics, 1990), a change reflected in a similar rise in the percentage of the children of employed mothers cared for in centers, family day care, or other nonrelative care (Hofferth, Brayfield, Deich, & Holcomb, 1991). One consequence of the increased rate of maternal participation in the labor force is that the increasing demand for child care chases a decreasing supply of home-based care. Both relatives and nonrelatives, who are the resources for family day care, become less available because they too are employed outside the home (Emlen, 1991; Presser, 1989).

Still another reason for the declining availability of caregivers is that real wages have not risen in nearly 20 years. The U.S. economy is moving away from being manufacturing-driven toward being service-driven, but service jobs typically pay less than manufacturing jobs. As Akabas (1990) observed, lower wages create a need for more families to have two wage earners instead of one. She pointed out that wages, when adjusted for inflation, have not increased since 1973. There are also fewer jobs paying salaries high enough to support a middle-class life-style; because of the "widening gap between low- and high-income families and the fact that young families are almost inevitably poor (the income of families younger than 25 years of age with children dropped 43% from 1970 to 1986), more families need two earners" (Akabas, 1990, p. 368).

Smaller Work Force

The changing composition of the population is due to the declining birth rate (births per 1,000), decreasing fertility rates (number of children per woman), and the consequent increasing proportion of elderly. These changes are reflected in the labor force and the workplace. As the population growth rate declines, so does the number of new entrants into the labor force (Ontario Women's Directorate, 1990). As observed by Johnston and Packer (1987), the declining number of white males in the labor force will lead to an increasing dependence on women, minority males, and immigrants as labor sources.

DEPENDENT CARE AS A CORPORATE CONCERN

Most surveys of employees and their dependent-care responsibilities have revealed that about one quarter of those who responded were currently involved in providing care to an older person (Wagner, Creedon, Sasala, & Neal, 1989), and 45% were parents of children under the age of 18 living in their household (Emlen & Koren, 1984). Estimates regarding the prevalence of employees' providing elder care or child care are likely to vary based on the characteristics of the work force, such as average age, as well as the response rate to the survey. We know of no estimates for the proportion of employees caring for adults (between the ages of 18 and 59) who have physical or mental disabilities.

Reasons for Employers' Concern
About Work and Family Issues

Increasingly, employers are considering implementing "family-friendly" work-time and workplace policies, benefits, and programs. The question is why. What is the impetus? What, from the employer's perspective, are the advantages of these initiatives?

Galinsky and Stein (1990) asserted that the primary factors behind the growing salience of work and family issues to corporations are related to two of the demographic trends already described: The increasingly diverse nature of the work force and labor shortages. Interviews conducted with human resource vice presidents and directors of 71 Fortune 500 corporations (Galinsky, Friedman, & Hernandez, 1991) revealed the following major reasons for those companies' commitment to work-and-family issues: to improve recruitment and retention (mentioned by 41% of those interviewed); to improve morale (mentioned by 21%); to reduce stress that might lower productivity and service quality (mentioned by 18%); and to keep up with their competition (mentioned by 15%). Additional factors have been noted by Friedman (1987). Companies are also concerned about their image in the community, and some have a benevolent sense of corporate social responsibility and a belief in the need to invest in the future. Still other organizations may desire to increase their productivity through lowering the observed high rates of absenteeism and tardiness caused by instability in the child-care arrangements of employees who are parents. As John Hayes, Jr., President and Chief Executive Officer of Southwestern Bell Telephone Company, noted in his remarks at the first national conference that specifically addressed issues of elder care and the workplace:

> Telecommunications is a constantly changing industry that is entirely dependent on experienced and adaptable employees. We simply can't afford to give up valuable employees. Caregiving, then, has a direct and deepening influence on business, and business must respond. (Hayes, 1988, p. 5)

In its report, *Work and Family: The Crucial Balance,* the Ontario Women's Directorate (1990) asserted that the focus on technology of the 1980s would switch in the 1990s to a focus on people, in part because "in the workplace of the '90s, companies will be hard pressed to find any employee who does not share at least some responsibility for the care of one or more dependents" (p. 4).

The report noted that:

> Companies that put issues like child care and elder care at the forefront of human resource policies, and those companies which help to strengthen the relationship between family and work, will be leaders in their industry. That commitment will give them an edge in attracting, retaining and motivating the best people for their jobs. . . . Adjusting to the new realities of the workforce is not an altruistic approach to management. It is a practical means of achieving bottom-line results. It makes good business sense. (p. 4)

Recent attention has turned, in particular, to employees who have caregiving responsibilities for elderly family members. An early article addressing the role of employers in helping families to fulfill their elder-care responsibilities referred to corporate elder-care programs and policies as "the employee benefit of the 1990s" (Friedman, 1986). A 1987 article in *Dun's Business Month* heralded elder care as a "new company headache," and a survey by the American Express Company of its employees' off-work burdens found that elder care ranked higher than alcoholism, drugs, and divorce as a primary concern (Perham, 1987, p. 64). In describing his company's rationale for implementing a national information and referral network for employees with elder-care concerns, Mike Shore, spokesperson for IBM, said, "We're not doing this for altruistic reasons; we're doing it for good business reasons. If we can help our employees handle their various concerns, that directly translates into their productivity and morale on the job" (Martin, 1988, p. 11).

Negative Impacts of Dependent-Care Responsibilities on Work Force Participation and Productivity

There is a small but growing body of research connecting "employees' concerns for the care of children or elderly relatives with productivity losses from increased absences, tardiness, and stress on the job—and such time-wasters as excessive use of the phone" (Ehrlich, 1988, p. 113). The following paragraphs briefly summarize the research findings to date on the negative impacts of caring for children, adults with disabilities, and/or elders on employees' work and stress.

Studies on the negative impact of having children on employees' work and stress have found that compared with employees without children, employees with children miss more days of work (Emlen, 1987; Emlen & Koren, 1984; Scharlach & Boyd, 1989), have more conflict between work and family (Scharlach & Boyd, 1989; Voydanoff, 1988), and take more time off during the workday (Scharlach & Boyd, 1989). Married female employees with children experience more depression than do those without children (Cleary & Mechanic, 1983). There can be adverse effects on physical health as well. Karasek, Gardell, and Lindell (1987) found that employees with very young children experienced more physical ailments and fatigue than other employees. Kessler and McRae (1982) found that employed women with children had poorer physical health than did employed women without children. Haynes and Feinleib (1980) found that having a greater number of children increased the incidence of coronary heart disease among working women, especially for those in blue-collar occupations.

With respect to employees caring for elders, Scharlach and Boyd (1989) found that these employees had more conflict between work and family, missed more days of work, and took more time off during the workday than did their noncaregiving co-workers. A 1989 survey of the executives of Fortune 1000 companies regarding elder care (*Fortune Magazine* and John Hancock Financial Services, 1989) revealed that the work-related problems these executives associated with employees' having elder-care responsibilities included employee stress, unscheduled days off, absenteeism, lateness for work or early departure from work, and personal telephone usage on the job. The New York Business Group on Health survey of managers (Warshaw, Barr, Rayman, Schachter, & Lucas, 1986) found that a high percentage of respondents perceived that employees who were caring for older relatives experienced numerous work productivity problems; 75% perceived unscheduled days off the job as a problem, while 73% noted tardiness, 67% cited absenteeism, 64% mentioned excessive use of the telephone while at work, and 58% noted emergency hours off.

Caregiving for elders or adults with disabilities has a number of other costs for employees as well. A national survey of preretirees conducted by Retirement Advisors Inc. found that 28% of the respondents were currently caring for older relatives. These employees were themselves aware that caregiving was affecting their performance at work, and several indicated that caregiving-related costs were forcing them to postpone their own retirement plans and restricting their choices of lifestyle (Creedon, 1987). Caregiving also forces many employees to leave work in order to provide care. Among wives of patients with heart attacks, one quarter stopped work temporarily (Skelton & Dominian, 1973); an equal proportion of family members of persons with chronic mental illness reduced or stopped work temporarily (Sainsbury & Grad, 1962). Stone, Cafferata, and Sangl (1987) reported that between 5% and 14% of male and female adult children and spouse caregivers quit work to become full-time caregivers. Another potential negative impact of caregiving on employees' work was revealed in a study by the University of Bridgeport (Wagner, 1987). That study found several adverse health indicators that were experienced more by employees involved in elder care than by other employees; the indicators included frequent anxiety or depression, difficulty in sleeping, frequent headaches, or a weight gain or loss.

DEPENDENT CARE AS A FAMILY CONCERN

The preceding section of this chapter discussed the combination of work and family as a concern for employers. But we can also think of this combination of roles as a social concern—as a concern for the family and for the community.

Kanter (1977) considered the "myth of separate worlds"—the myth that has been dominant both in the literature and in the minds of most Americans that work and family are (or should be) separate spheres of life: "The myth goes like this: In a modern industrial society work life and family life constitute two separate and non-overlapping worlds, with their own functions, territories, and behavioral rules. Each operates by its own laws and can be studied independently" (Kanter, 1977, p. 8). This notion of separation was fostered by Parsons and Bales (1955) within the field of sociology. They distinguished between the instrumental orientation of the workplace and the affective orientation of the family, arguing that the norms of the two were incompatible; for either to work effectively, the two must be separated. More recent writers, however, including Kanter (1977) and Piotrkowski (1978), have recognized that both work and family involve tasks to be performed and interpersonal relations to be maintained. That is, both worlds require both instrumental and affective skills.

Although we may take for granted the role of the family as the primary provider of care to children, it is also the primary provider of support to the elderly and probably to adults with disabilities as well. Horowitz (1986) reviewed the evidence and found that family and friends covered more of the costs of home care for the elderly than did public sources (U.S. General Accounting Office, 1977); according to the National Center for Health Statistics (1975), families provided 80% of all home health care for older people. Brody (1990) reported on the 1985 Long-Term Care Survey, which revealed that 74% of the assistance needed by disabled elders was provided by nonpaid helpers only, 21% was provided by both paid and nonpaid helpers, and just 5% was provided by paid helpers only. Of the nonpaid helpers, the majority were family members. The role of the family as caregiver involves the provision of direct care but also the arrangement and management of care provided by others. Both direct and indirect care may be made more difficult when combined with employment.

The effect of work on the family and, specifically, on the ability of the family to provide care for dependents, can take the form of spillover onto the distribution and performance of household tasks among family members, as well as onto the emotional health of family members and interpersonal relationships within the family. In reviewing the impact of combining work and caregiving on the family, we will focus on both instrumental and emotional impacts on the employee, the employee's family relations, and the dependent or recipient of the care. By *family relations* we mean the quality of the relationships among the employee, his or her spouse or partner, and other members of the household. Table 1.1 illustrates some of these impacts.

Instrumental Impact of Combining Work and Dependent Care

The effect of combining work and family on instrumental tasks must be considered in terms of the influence on both the division of labor within the family and the quality of care for recipients of care.

Effects on the Division of Labor Within the Family. In the traditional American family, men have typically combined work and family roles, but they have done so by allocating many of the family concerns to their spouses. Based on this pattern, the literature on work and family has historically identified employed mothers as "the problem" and made that group the target of research. As a consequence, much of the literature reviewed in this section has focused on the effects of the employment of mothers on the family. The parallel literature for the effects of fathers' employment on the family is sparse.

TABLE 1.1   Impact on the Family of Combining Work and Family

	Type of Impact	
Effect on:	Instrumental	Emotional
Employee	Division of Labor	Employee Well-Being
Family Relations	Division of Labor	Family Well-Being
Care Recipient	Quality of Care	Recipient Well-Being

The central research question is, "When both spouses work, how are family responsibilities shared?" When paid and unpaid labor are combined, research has shown that employed women all over the world work more hours than employed men: an average of 80 hours a week for employed women and 50 for employed men (Scarr, Phillips, & McCartney, 1989). Thus the effect of combining work and family roles weighs on average much more heavily on women than on men. The extra burden of care for the house and family is not reallocated among family members when women join the paid work force. Hochschild (1989) referred to employed women's work at home after their paid work as the "second shift"—a shift that consists of an additional full month of 24-hour days each year that employed women devote to caring for home and family, compared with employed men. Michelson (1985), for example, in his detailed time budget study of the daily activities of Canadian husbands and wives, found that wives employed full time spent fewer minutes per day on housework, child care, and passive leisure than did those wives who were employed part time or not employed. At the same time, the husbands of women employed full time spent only 14 minutes a day more on the combination of housework and child care than did husbands whose wives were not employed (57 minutes versus 43 minutes). Although employment reduced the time that women devoted to household tasks, they still spent about 3 times as much time as their husbands did on housework and child care. Hochschild (1989) argued that society is now engaged in a "stalled revolution," in which there has been a rapid change in the experience of women moving into the work force, but little adjustment by men, the workplace, and the rest of society to adapt to that change. As one of our respondents commented,

When I first came to work here I had three children at home, they were 13-14-15, one girl, two boys. It was pretty hard because I had two jobs, one at home. Even though my kids had their duties to perform, I still had to see to it that they were done. And my husband acted like those jobs were mine because that's what wives did, besides cleaning and gardening and laundry, etc. It put a lot of stress and strain on me. One day I set him down and told him if I had to work I expected him to help do everything around the house and I told him we should take turns and he did for a while but he keeps slipping back to his old habits until I tell him about it. There are a lot of young people today that both work and the husbands don't share the work at all. I know it puts the wife under a lot of stress.

Effects on the Quality of Care. To what extent does combining work and caregiving have an effect on the quality of care for the dependent? Research attempting to answer this question has tended to focus on the well-being of dependents whose caregivers are or are not employed. Hoffman (1989) reviewed research on the effects of maternal employment on parent-child interaction. Data indicate that employed mothers tend to spend less time per week with their preschool children, but they may interact with them more when they are together. Employed mothers also place more emphasis on training their children to be independent. Bronfenbrenner and Crouter's (1982) review of the literature both before 1960 and between 1960 and 1980 revealed no evidence of uniform effects of maternal employment on children. They did find evidence that maternal employment might have beneficial effects for girls but disruptive effects for boys from middle-income families, and they reported four studies that showed a salutary effect of part-time maternal employment on both teenagers and school-age children.

Within the literature on caregiving to the elderly, and to adults with disabilities, little attention has been paid to the effect of combining work and elder care on the quality of the care received by the older person. There is a small literature comparing the effect of employment on the amount of care provided to the elder, but the results of this literature are inconsistent. Some researchers (Cicirelli, 1981; Stoller, 1983) found that employment did not significantly reduce the hours of care that daughters provided to parents, but others (Brody & Schoonover, 1986) found that employed daughters provided significantly less help to their impaired parents than did nonemployed daughters (25 hours per week vs. 42 hours per week). These hours were replaced by care from other members of the informal network and from paid help. Stoller (1983) also found that employment significantly decreased the amount of assistance provided to elders by sons but not by daughters. The impact of employment on caregiving may be more complex, depending on the numbers of hours worked, the distance lived from the care recipient, and the type and severity of the disability of the care recipient. Stueve and O'Donnell (1989), for example, found that employment is particularly likely to limit caregiving if a daughter is employed full time and lives within an hour's drive of the parent. Thomas (1988) explored the effect of adult children's competing responsibilities (including work) on the elderly parents' satisfaction with the help they received from these children. Surprisingly, having employed adult children reduced the satisfaction with help received for younger (age 60 to 74) but not older parents. The only clue the author presents for this finding emerges from indications from pilot interviews that the older parents, raised during the Great Depression, expressed strong reservations about depending on their children. Because they expect less help, they may be more satisfied with the help received.

Emotional Impact of Combining Work and Dependent Care

The emotional impact of combining work and family can be considered with respect to its impact on the employee, on family relationships, and on the care recipient.

Emotional Impact on Employees. The implicit assumption in most investigations of people occupying multiple roles, such as employee and caregiver, is that multiple roles are likely to have negative effects. These effects include role overload, caused by the excessive time or physical demands of the roles, and role conflict, caused by conflicting expectations or demands. Role conflict may be exacerbated by cultural ambiguity about which role or roles should have precedence when conflict occurs. Do family or work roles take precedence when there is conflict? Does the pattern differ for men and women? What happens when care for disabled or frail relatives interferes with the social and emotional well-being of the nuclear family?

Recent literature has pointed out that multiple roles may have positive as well as negative effects, due to an expansion of energy to accommodate roles to which the individual is positively committed (Marks, 1977) or to the provision of multiple sources of identity and meaning for the self (Thoits, 1986). Thus Crosby (1987) reported that working women do not necessarily report more stress than nonworking women. In their study of 2,000 adult men and women, Gove and Zeiss (1987) found that, in general, those with more roles (marriage, work, parenthood, children at home or away) were happier. For both men and women, marriage was most closely tied to happiness, followed by employment, and then by parental status.

Baruch and Barnett (1986) pointed out that the *quality* of the experience within each role may be as important as the *number* of roles occupied. Multiple roles may thus have positive effects to the extent that they yield a net gain of benefits over costs. Baruch and Barnett (1986) interviewed 238 mid-life women about the quality of the roles they occupied, as indicated by their ratings of rewards and concerns involved in their roles as workers, wives, and mothers. They found that the more roles the women occupied, the happier they tended to feel with each particular role. In addition, their psychological well-being (self-esteem, depression, and pleasure) was more closely associated with role quality than with the number of roles. Role quality was also found to be the major predictor of role overload, role conflict, and anxiety (Barnett & Baruch, 1985).

The stress of combining multiple roles is likely to be as much a consequence of the preferences of the participants as of the actual roles occupied (Menaghan & Parcel, 1990). Thus, Thoits (1987) found that if both partners were happy with their own and their partner's employment status, whether employed or not, they were likely to experience low stress. Husbands experienced the most stress when their wives were working reluctantly and still had primary responsibility for the house and for child care. Wives were most distressed when they had chosen to work but their husbands did not share responsibility at home.

Pleck (1977) suggested that the nature of the spillover between work and family is different for men and women. He argued that for men, work intrudes into the family, while the reverse is true for women. Voydanoff (1988) tested this hypothesis and found some evidence that work role characteristics had a slightly greater impact on work/family conflict for men, while family demands were marginally more important for women. More striking in the data, however, was evidence of similarities between men and women in the level of work/family conflict and in its predictors.

Barnett and Baruch (1987) cited evidence to contradict the hypothesis that closer ties exist between women and family or between men and work. Marriage and motherhood do not necessarily improve well-being for women. Indeed, Barnett and Baruch found that the role of mother, but not the roles of employee or wife, was associated with role strain and overload among women. They also found that men's family roles had a more significant effect on their well-being than did their paid work roles, while work roles were central to women's well-being. The emphasis on women in much of the research on the impact of multiple roles should not conceal the efforts of men in caregiving roles. Brody (1985) commented on the important roles played by sons as secondary caregivers to their parents (often carrying out gender-defined tasks) and as primary caregivers for parents with absent or distant daughters. She noted that some sons-in-law are the "unsung heroes" of caregiving.

To summarize, the emotional impact of combining multiple roles on employed caregivers has more often been found to be positive than negative. The important determinants of emotional response appear to include the quality of the experience within each role and whether or not the roles are chosen. Although it has been theorized that men's emotional well-being is more determined by work and women's by the family, the evidence indicates more similarities than differences between men and women, and at times has found precisely the opposite.

Emotional Impact on Family Relationships. Piotrkowski (1978) identified three predominant patterns of interplay between work and family in her qualitative study of 13 families, only 4 of which were dual-earner families: positive carryover, negative carryover, and energy deficit. In those families experiencing positive carryover, the energy and positive emotional state that the employee derived from a satisfying work setting was reflected in more energy devoted to the family and more positive exchanges with family members.

Negative carryover was characterized by a stressful work situation that was reflected in tension in the home. The employee's anger, hostility, and tension were carried into home life, with family energy being expended to create a buffer between the employee and other family members. In this case, Piotrkowski argued, "both workers and work organizations are dependent upon families to 'replenish' the family member who must go out to work" (p. 47).

The third pattern found by Piotrkowski was energy deficit, which she characterized in terms of workers who were so depleted by work that they withdrew from family life. The personal depletion or energy drain might derive from physically demanding work, but also from work that was monotonous or emotionally draining. Another perspective on energy drain is reflected by a couple from our survey who chose to work

nonoverlapping shifts in order to handle their work and family responsibilities. The husband noted:

> Our child-care problems are a big burden for my wife and I to carry. Having
> three young children we find it almost impossible to pay the $350 a month
> plus for child care. This almost eliminates one of my wife's paychecks which
> is 2 weeks' work. It would almost not pay to ever have her work. We solve
> this by working separate work shifts. This makes communication between
> my wife and I during the week very bad. Problems occur, stress levels rise,
> and by the time Saturday rolls around all hell breaks out. I'm not saying
> every weekend is like this, but when problems do occur, working separate
> shifts makes it worse because we can't communicate with each other and
> the stress builds and so do our tempers and patience. This adversely affects
> myself, my wife and our relationship which flows downhill to our children
> and last but not least to my attitude and job performance at work.

Interestingly, although most of the families that Piotrkowski interviewed described carryover from work to family, they stated their *belief*
that there should be separation between the worlds. Aldous (1969) identified another potential effect of work on family, which she has labeled
"compensatory." She argued that blue-collar men "look to their homes
as havens from job monotonies and as sources of satisfaction lacking
in the occupational sphere" (p. 172).

Scarr, Phillips, and McCartney (1989) reviewed research showing
that "maternal employment per se is not the major issue in marital
relationships. Rather, the circumstances of the family, the attitudes and
expectations of fathers and mothers, and the distribution of time available have important effects" (p. 1402). Spitze (1988) reported that the
effect of women's employment on marital satisfaction has "changed from
a negative to a null or perhaps even a positive one, and any negative
effects are now likely to be due to specific aspects of her employment,
such as long hours or dissatisfaction with her job" (p. 599). Gilbert (1985,
cited in Scarr, Phillips, & McCartney, 1989) classified men in dual-earner
families with children into three types: traditional, participant (helps
with child care but not with household chores), and role-sharing. The
marital satisfaction reported by couples depended on their socialization
experiences and current attitudes about male and female roles, rather
than on their classification into one of these types.

Through in-depth interviews and home visits, Hochschild (1989) explored the adaptations that couples made to combining work and family.

In her sample, she found that 18% to 20% of the husbands shared housework and child care; 80% of the husbands did not feel that they should help out, although 30% of their wives were trying to change the division of labor. Despite the relative imbalance in the workload, she reported that most wives seemed more grateful to their husbands than their husbands felt toward them. "Women's lower wages, the high rate of divorce, and the cultural legacy of female subordination together created a climate that made most women feel lucky if their husbands shared 'some' " (Hochschild, 1989, p. 203). According to the U.S. Bureau of the Census (1989b), 60% of separated and divorced mothers had court orders to receive child support; of these, 50% received full payments and 23% partial payments. With single parenthood and minimal child support as an alternative, perhaps it is not surprising that psychological accommodations are made to keep marriages intact.

In his interviews with men in managerial and administrative occupations, Weiss (1987) corroborated aspects of Hochschild's work. He found that men's traditional understandings of marriage were not altered by having a working wife. The wife's work was viewed as different in meaning from his own (wives worked to "help out" or for their own well-being). Although the men might have "helped out" at home, their understanding of "who is genuinely responsible for tasks" tended not to change.

In summary, the literature has identified a number of patterns of interplay between work and family. These include evidence that work has a positive or negative impact on family life, depending on the worker's satisfaction with his or her work life, and that work can create an energy deficit that depletes family life. As with emotional impacts on the individual, the emotional impacts of dual roles on the family often depend on family expectations and preferences regarding both employment and sharing of tasks.

Emotional Impact on the Care Recipient. The literature on child care has historically placed its emphasis on the impact of combining work and family on the child. In contrast, the literature on the care of elders and adults with disabilities has focused almost entirely on the impact of caregiving on the caregiver, not the care recipient. There are a few clues in the literature, however, about potential sources of emotional strain for the adult or elder recipient of care. For example, in some cases, quality of care received may be less an issue than is mutual negotiation of appropriate roles between caregiver and care recipient. Thus, Brody

(1985, p. 23) commented that, "If successful adaptation is to be made, not only must the adult child have the capacity to permit the parent to be dependent, but the parent must have the capacity to be *appropriately dependent* so as to permit the adult child to be dependable." Another source of emotional strain for the care recipient may be a perception that either too much help is being offered or too little. Walker, Pratt, Shin, and Jones (1989) studied mothers' and daughters' perceptions of the motives of the caregiver. They found that daughters classified their own helping motives as about equally split between discretionary (e.g., love) and obligatory (e.g., duty to parent), while mothers were more likely to perceive that their daughter's help derived from discretionary motives. Mothers who believe the help they receive is freely given are surely less distressed about their own dependency.

With regard to child care, Bronfenbrenner and Crouter's (1982) review concluded that daughters in families where women worked were more independent and had a more positive conception of the female role. The impact of infant day care was reviewed by Clarke-Stewart (1989), with the conclusion that while there is some evidence among such infants of insecure attachment, less compliance with parental wishes, and more aggression toward peers, there is also advanced sociability, social competence, and self-confidence. Examining longitudinal studies of the effects of maternal employment, Hoffman (1989) concluded:

> The overwhelming impression of these studies is the reconfirmation of the previous observation that maternal employment is not so robust a variable that it can be related to child outcomes. It operates through its effects on the family environment and the child care arrangements, and these are moderated by parental attitudes, family structure, and other variables. (p. 289)

DEPENDENT CARE AS A COMMUNITY CONCERN

Acceptance of the positive function of separating the worlds of work and family has decreased, replaced by a recognition of work and family as open systems in constant interplay. If we think of the worlds of work and family as interacting open systems, a third system must also be included to complete our understanding of the employed caregiver. This third system is the formal caregiving system. It includes various services that substitute for and supplement the care provided by informal caregivers (that is, family and friends) for dependent groups of all ages. For children, the services include center and family day care for preschool children and forms of after-school care. For adults with disabilities, services include paid assistants, home-care services, sheltered workshops, and supportive living environments. For the elderly, services range from homemaking services to adult day care and various levels of residential care. The ability of employed caregivers to combine work and family comfortably depends on the availability, affordability, accessibility, and quality of these services in their community, as well as on accommodations of the workplace and in the family (Emlen, 1991).

Therefore it is not just the family as a private institution but the community as a whole that is currently struggling to address the conflict between work and caregiving. The formal sector (public and private) provides a relatively small proportion of dependent care now, and the private and public resources to increase the role of the formal sector are limited. Brody and Schoonover (1986) found that employment of a female caregiver did increase the amount of formal care received by their elderly mothers, but that care was largely paid for by the family rather than subsidized by the state. Similarly, Archbold (1983) identified two parent-caring roles: care provision and care management. Women who were care-managers, locating and managing the care provided by others, were more likely to be higher in economic status and employed full time in socially valued career positions. Soldo and Sharma (1980, cited in Stueve & O'Donnell, 1989) found that employed female caregivers were less likely to share a home with an elderly relative and more likely to pay for care in an institution. Additional evidence that employed caregivers are more likely than nonemployed caregivers to institutionalize care recipients with Alzheimer's disease was presented by Colerick and George (1986) and Nardone (1980). Indeed, Brody (1990) noted that a number of the women in her survey who had quit working had done so because they could not afford to purchase substitute services from the formal sector. At the same time, the movement of women into the work force has reduced the volunteer energy available in the community to support schools, churches, hospitals, and other institutions that provide alternative sources of care for dependents.

Changes in the earning capacity of workers have made it more difficult for a one-earner household to support a family. The number of single parents is increasing, but such parents are often unable to afford quality care for their dependents. These and similar societal changes move the issue of care for dependent family members from a private family concern to a public concern. Zigler (1990) noted that the political feasibility of public response to social issues depends on the context within which the issues are viewed. Thus political support for child care varies in part according to whether child care is defined as a welfare issue, a women's issue, or a societal issue. Once defined as a societal or community issue, all segments of the society have a stake in developing solutions. In discussing the stalled revolution associated with women's work roles, Hochschild (1989) described the need for such solutions:

> The exodus of women into the economy has not been accompanied by a cultural understanding of marriage and work that would make this transition smooth. The work force has changed. Women have changed. But most workplaces have remained inflexible in the face of the family demands of their workers and at home, most men have yet to really adapt to the changes in women. (p. 12)

The decade of the 1970s ended with an erosion of political support for an active governmental role in service delivery. The Reagan era ushered in a movement to redefine the burden of responsibility for dependent care, placing more of the responsibility under the purview of the family rather than the state. A questioning of public entitlements was coupled with an exhortation to rely on private responsibility. The metaphoric "safety net" was held far below the high-wire act performed by working families. Private responsibility rested with individuals, families, businesses, and voluntary community effort. Funds for community child-care systems dried up, and the White House promoted "public-private initiatives" in its campaign to elicit corporate support for family needs. Through a number of surveys of employees, the business community became aware that their employees' struggle in coping with dependent-care responsibilities was having an impact on the workplace (Emlen & Koren, 1984; Fernandez, 1986; Galinsky & Hughes, 1987; Vartuli & Stubbs, 1986). According to Brody (1985), such moves toward private responsibility reflected a belief in the myth that "adult children nowadays do not take care of their elderly parents as they did in the good old days" (p. 19). Although 15 years of research has consistently rejected that myth, it lives on in the minds of many policymakers.

The changing demographic, social, and economic trends reviewed in this chapter point to the need to broaden the focus of the field of work and family. In particular, integrated conceptual models that include all types of dependent care—care for children, adults with disabilities, and elders—must be developed. Solutions must be sought in the family, the workplace, and the formal institutions in the community. All sectors of society that have a stake in how care is provided should be included in the dialogue that seeks solutions to balancing work and family responsibilities. The division of labor within the family, within the community, and within the nation in providing care must be reassessed.

PLAN OF THIS BOOK

In this book, we explore the problem of balancing work and family responsibilities. Our focus is on individuals who are employed and who also have unpaid responsibilities for the care of family members and friends of various ages, including children, adults with disabilities, and elders. In writing this book, our goals have been to:

1. broaden understanding of the effects of caregiving on absenteeism and stress among employees;
2. explore how these effects are influenced by employees' personal characteristics, the demands placed on them by their work and their family responsibilities, and the resources they derive from their work, family, and community to help them balance their jobs and their caregiving;
3. explore the similarities and differences in the effects on employees of caring for children, adults with disabilities, and elders;
4. assess the effects of simultaneously providing care for more than one of these groups; and
5. describe and evaluate the informal and formal programs and policies that may be implemented by employers and by the community at large to support individuals who both are employed and are caregivers to family members and friends.

The book is organized into four sections. The first, containing two chapters, introduces the central concerns. In Chapter 1, we have presented the rationale for attending to work and family issues. Chapter 2 describes the conceptual framework guiding the book's second section as well as the methodology for the survey that provided the primary data analyzed in that section.

In the second section, "Research," we review the research literature concerning each of three groups of employees—those caring for children, for adults with disabilities, and for elders—with respect to the employees' personal characteristics, the demands of their caregiving situations, the resources available to them, and the effects of these variables on time lost from work and levels of stress experienced. In the second half of each chapter in this section we present the results from our large-scale survey of employees and their dependent-care responsibilities. Chapters 3, 4, and 5 are thus devoted to each of the three caregiver groups (i.e., caregivers of children, of adults with disabilities, and of elders). Chapter 6 compares employees with and without caregiving responsibilities, addressing the question of whether employees with one or more caregiving roles do, in fact, experience more absenteeism and/ or stress than employees without such roles; we also consider the consequences of multiple caregiving roles (i.e., caring for more than one type of dependent) on absenteeism and stress. The final chapter in this research section compares the caregiver groups, synthesizing and discussing the findings presented in the previous four chapters.

In the third section of the book, "Policies, Benefits, and Services in the Workplace," we describe various formal and informal workplace-related approaches that have been developed for, or may be used by, the different caregiver groups in an effort to reduce the negative effects of combining work and family and to enable individuals to continue both their employee and caregiver roles. Where they are available, we present research findings concerning the effectiveness of these approaches. Specifically, Chapter 8 describes the range of workplace policies and employee benefits that have relevance for employees with dependent-care responsibilities, as well as pertinent national and state tax-related legislation. Chapter 9 details the various types of programs and direct services that have been implemented by employers for employed caregivers of children, adults with disabilities, and/or elders. Chapter 10 focuses on methods for conducting needs assessments in the workplace to identify and plan for employees' caregiving-related needs.

In the fourth and final section of the book, Chapter 11, we discuss the implications of the findings reported in the previous sections and make recommendations about the needed range of supports. We highlight workplace-based programs, leave policies, and benefit packages that appear to hold particular promise. In addition, we offer recommendations for national and state legislation concerning private and public employers (e.g., mandated benefits, such as parental leave) and for increasing the availability and accessibility of community services to assist employees who have informal caregiving responsibilities. Suggestions concerning attitudinal and behavioral changes within employed caregivers' families are also made. Finally, we delineate issues that require exploration through further research.

REFERENCES

Akabas, S. H. (1990). Reconciling the demands of work with the needs of families. *Families in Society, 71,* 366-371.

Aldous, J. (1969). Occupational characteristics and males' role performance in the family. *Journal of Marriage and the Family, 31,* 707-712.

Archbold, P. (1983). Impact of parent-caring on women. *Family Relations, 32,* 39-45.

Barnett, R. C., & Baruch, G. K. (1985). Women's involvement in multiple roles and psychological distress. *Journal of Personality and Social Psychology, 49,* 135-145.

Barnett, R. C., & Baruch, G. K. (1987). Social roles, gender, and psychological distress. In R. C. Barnett, L. Biener, & G. K. Baruch (Eds.), *Gender and stress* (pp. 122-143). New York: Free Press.

Baruch, G. K., & Barnett, R. (1986). Role quality, multiple role involvement, and psychological well-being in midlife women. *Journal of Personality and Social Psychology, 51,* 578-585.

Brody, E. M. (1985). Parent care as a normative family stress. *The Gerontologist, 25,* 19-29.

Brody, E. M. (1990). *Women in the middle: Their parent-care years.* New York: Springer.

Brody, E. M., & Schoonover, C. B. (1986). Patterns of parent-care when adult daughters work and when they do not. *The Gerontologist, 26,* 372-381.

Bronfenbrenner, U., & Crouter, A. C. (1982). Work and family through time and space. In S. B. Kamerman & C. D. Hayes (Eds.), *Families that work: Children in a changing world* (pp. 39-82). Washington, DC: National Academy Press.

Bureau of National Affairs. (1988). *33 ways to ease work/family tensions—An employer's checklist* (Special Report No. 2). Rockville, MD: Buraff Publications. (Product Code BSP-84)

Carter, J. D., & Piktialis, D. (1988, Autumn). IBM's program for elder care. *Compensation & Benefits Management, 5*(1), 53-56.

Cicirelli, V. G. (1981). *Helping elderly parents: The role of adult children.* Boston: Auburn House.

Clarke-Stewart, K. A. (1989). Infant day care: Maligned or malignant? *American Psychologist, 44,* 266-273.

Cleary, P. D., & Mechanic, D. (1983). Sex differences in psychological distress among married people. *Journal of Health and Social Behavior, 24,* 111-121.

Colerick, E. J., & George, L. K. (1986). Predictors of institutionalization among caregivers of patients with Alzheimer's disease. *Journal of the American Geriatrics Society, 34,* 493-498.

Creedon, M. A. (1987). Introduction: Employment and eldercare. In M. Creedon (Ed.), *Issues for an aging America: Employees & eldercare: A briefing book* (pp. 2-4). Bridgeport, CT: University of Bridgeport, Center for the Study of Aging.

Crosby, F. J. (Ed.). (1987). *Spouse, parent, worker: On gender and multiple roles.* New Haven, CT: Yale University Press.

Crouter, A. C. (1984). Spillover from family to work: The neglected side of the work-family interface. *Human Relations, 37,* 425-442.

Ehrlich, E. (1988, September 19). For American business, a new world of workers. *Business Week,* pp. 112-114, 118, 120.

Emlen, A. C. (1987, August). *Child care, work, and family.* Panel presentation at the annual convention of the American Psychological Association, New York.

Emlen, A. C. (1991, May). *Rural child care policy: Does Oregon have one? 1991 Legislative Discussion Paper.* Legislative Discussion Series. Rural Policy Research Group (Oregon State University, University of Oregon, Oregon Economic Development Department). Obtain by writing to author at Regional Research Institute for Human Services, Portland State University, P.O. Box 751, Portland, OR 97207-0741.

Emlen, A. C., & Koren, P. E. (1984). *Hard to find and difficult to manage: The effects of child care on the workplace.* Portland, OR: Portland State University, Regional Research Institute for Human Services.

Fernandez, J. P. (1986). *Child care and corporate productivity: Resolving family/work conflicts.* Lexington, MA: Lexington Books.

Fortune Magazine and John Hancock Financial Services. (1989). *Corporate and employee response to caring for the elderly: A national survey of U.S. companies and the workforce.* New York: Time Magazine Company & John Hancock Financial Services.

Friedman, D. E. (1986). Eldercare: The employee benefit of the 1990s? *Across the Board, 23*(6), 45-51.

Friedman, D. E. (1987). *Family-supportive policies: The corporate decision-making process* (Report No. 897). New York: The Conference Board.

Galinsky, E., Friedman, D., & Hernandez, C. A., with Axel, H. (1991). *Corporate reference guide to work-family programs.* New York: Families and Work Institute.

Galinsky, E., & Hughes, D. (1987). *The Fortune Magazine child care study.* New York: Bank Street College.

Galinsky, E., & Stein, P. J. (1990). The impact of human resource policies on employees: Balancing work/family life. *Journal of Family Issues, 11,* 368-383.

Gibeau, J. L., Anastas, J. W., & Larson, P. J. (1987). Breadwinners, caregivers and employers: New alliances in an aging America. *Employee Benefits Journal, 12*(3), 6-10.

Gilbert, L. A. (1985). *Men in dual-career families: Current realities and future prospects.* Hillsdale, NJ: Lawrence Erlbaum.

Gove, W. R., & Zeiss, C. (1987). Multiple roles and happiness. In F. J. Crosby (Ed.), *Spouse, parent, worker: On gender and multiple roles* (pp. 125-137). New Haven, CT: Yale University Press.

Hayes, J. E., Jr. (1988). The challenge to business, government, and society: Corporate leadership. In D. E. Friedman (Ed.), *Issues for an aging America: Elder care: Highlights of a conference* (pp. 5-6). New York: The Conference Board.

Haynes, S. G., & Feinleib, M. (1980). Women, work and coronary heart disease: Prospective findings from the Framingham Heart Study. *American Journal of Public Health, 70,* 133-141.

Hochschild, A. R. (1989). *The second shift: Working parents and the revolution at home.* New York: Viking.

Hofferth, S. L., Brayfield, A., Deich, S., & Holcomb, P. (1991). *The national child care survey 1991.* Washington, DC: The Urban Institute.

Hoffman, L. W. (1989). Effects of maternal employment in the two-parent family. *American Psychologist, 44,* 283-292.

Horowitz, A. (1986). Family caregiving to the frail elderly. In M. P. Lawton & C. Maddox (Eds.), *Annual review of gerontology and geriatrics* (pp. 194-246). New York: Springer.

Johnston, W. B., & Packer, A. E. (1987). *Workforce 2000: Work and workers for the twenty-first century.* Indianapolis: Hudson Institute.

Kanter, R. M. (1977). *Work and family in the United States: A critical review and agenda for research and policy.* New York: Russell Sage Foundation.

Karasek, R., Gardell, B., & Lindell, J. (1987). Work and non-work correlates of illness and behaviour in male and female Swedish white collar workers. *Journal of Occupational Behaviour, 8,* 187-207.

Kessler, R. C., & McRae, J. A., Jr. (1982). The effect of wives' employment on the mental health of married men and women. *American Sociological Review, 47,* 216-227.

Kraus, L. E., & Stoddard, S. (1989). *Chartbook on disability in the United States.* Washington, DC: U.S. National Institute on Disability and Rehabilitation Research.

Kraus, L. E., & Stoddard, S. (1991). *Chartbook on work disability in the United States.* Washington, DC: U.S. National Institute on Disability and Rehabilitation Research.

Marks, S. R. (1977). Multiple roles and role strain: Some notes on human energy, time and commitment. *American Sociological Review, 42,* 921-936.

Martin, E. (1988). "Eldercare" is good business for workers and employees. *AARP News Bulletin, 29*(4), 11.

Menaghan, E. G., & Parcel, T. L. (1990). Parental employment and family life: Research in the 1980s. *Journal of Marriage and the Family, 52,* 1079-1098.

Michelson, W. (1985). *From sun to sun: Daily obligations and community structure in the lives of employed women and their families.* Totowa, NJ: Rowman & Allanheld.

Nardone, M. (1980). Characteristics predicting community care for mentally impaired older persons. *The Gerontologist, 20,* 661-668.

National Center for Health Statistics. (1975). *Vital statistics of the United States, 1973 life tables.* Rockville, MD: Government Printing Office.

National Center for Health Statistics. (1990). *Advance report of final natality statistics, 1988. Monthly vital statistics report* (Vol. 9, No. 4, Suppl.). Hyattsville, MD: Public Health Service.

Neal, M. B., Chapman, N. J., Ingersoll-Dayton, B., Emlen, A. C., & Boise, L. (1990). Absenteeism and stress among employed caregivers of the elderly, disabled adults, and children. In D. E. Biegel & A. Blum (Eds.), *Aging and caregiving: Theory, research, and policy* (pp. 160-183). Newbury Park, CA: Sage.

Ontario Women's Directorate. (1990). *Work and family: The crucial balance.* Toronto: Author. (Available from Consultative Services Branch, Suite 200, 480 University Avenue, Toronto, Ontario, M5G1V2; ph. 416-597-4570)

Parsons, T., & Bales, R. F. (1955). *Family, socialization and interaction process.* Glencoe, IL: Free Press.

Perham, J. (1987). Eldercare: New company headache. *Dun's Business Month, 129*(1), 64-65.

Piotrkowski, C. S. (1978). *Work and the family system: A naturalistic study of working-class and lower-middle class families.* New York: Free Press.

Pleck, J. H. (1977). The work-family role system. *Social Problems, 24,* 417-427.

Presser, H. B. (1989). Can we make time for children? The economy, work schedules, and child care. *Demography, 26,* 523-543.

Sainsbury, P., & Grad, J. (1962). Evaluation of treatment and services. In *The burden on the community: The epidemiology of mental illness: A symposium* (pp. 69-116). London: Oxford University Press.

Scarr, S., Phillips, D., & McCartney, K. (1989). Working mothers and their families. *American Psychologist, 44,* 1402-1409.

Scharlach, A. E., & Boyd, S. L. (1989). Caregiving and employment: Results of an employee survey. *The Gerontologist, 29,* 382-387.

Skelton, M., & Dominian, J. (1973). Psychological stress in wives of patients with myocardial infarction. *British Medical Journal, 2,* 101-103.

Spitze, G. (1988). Women's employment and family relations: A review. *Journal of Marriage and the Family, 50,* 595-618.

Stoller, E. P. (1983). Parental caregiving by adult children. *Journal of Marriage and the Family, 45,* 851-858.

Stone, R., Cafferata, G. L., & Sangl, J. (1987). Caregivers of the frail elderly: A national profile. *The Gerontologist, 27,* 616-626.

Stueve, A., & O'Donnell, L. (1989). Interactions between women and their elderly parents: Constraints of daughters' employment. *Research in Aging, 11,* 331-353.

Subcommittee on Human Services of the Select Committee on Aging, U.S. House of Representatives. (1987). *Exploding the myths: Caregiving in America* (Committee Publication No. 99-611). Washington, DC: Government Printing Office.

Thoits, P. A. (1986). Multiple identities: Examining gender and marital status differences in distress. *American Sociological Review, 51,* 259-272.

Thoits, P. A. (1987). Negotiating roles. In F. J. Crosby (Ed.), *Spouse, parent, worker: On gender and multiple roles* (pp. 11-22). New Haven, CT: Yale University Press.

Thomas, J. L. (1988). Predictors of satisfaction with children's help for younger and older elderly parents. *Journal of Gerontology: Social Sciences, 43,* S9-S14.

Trieschmann, R. B. (1980). *Spinal cord injuries: Psychological, social and vocational adjustment.* Elmsford, NY: Pergamon.

U.S. Bureau of Labor Statistics. (1988). *Labor force statistics derived from the Current Population Survey, 1948-87* (Bulletin 2307). Washington, DC: Government Printing Office.

U.S. Bureau of Labor Statistics. (1990). *Marital and family characteristics of the labor force from the March 1990 Current Population Survey.* Washington, DC: Government Printing Office.

U.S. Bureau of the Census. (1983, December). *1980 Census of the population: Characteristics of the population: General social and economic characteristics* (Vol. 1) (PC80-1-C1). Washington, DC: Government Printing Office.

U.S. Bureau of the Census. (1989a). *Current population reports: Fertility of American women: June 1988* (Series P-20, No. 436). Washington, DC: Government Printing Office.

U.S. Bureau of the Census. (1989b). *Current population reports: Child support and alimony: 1985* (Series P-23, No. 154, Supplemental Report). Washington, DC: Government Printing Office.

U.S. Department of Labor, Women's Bureau. (1986, October). *Facts on U.S. working women: Caring for elderly family members* (Fact Sheet No. 86-4). Washington, DC: Author.

U.S. General Accounting Office. (1977). *The well-being of older people in Cleveland, Ohio.* Washington, DC: General Accounting Office.

Vartuli, S., & Stubbs, S. (1986). *Metropolitan child care project: Final report.* Kansas City: Missouri University, School of Education. (ERIC Document Reproduction Service No. ED 277 450)

Voydanoff, P. (1988). Work role characteristics, family structure demands, and work/family conflict. *Journal of Marriage and the Family, 50,* 749-761.

Wagner, D. L. (1987). Corporate eldercare project: Findings. In M. A. Creedon (Ed.), *Issues for an aging America: Employees and eldercare—A briefing book* (pp. 25-29). Bridgeport, CT: University of Bridgeport, Center for the Study of Aging.

Wagner, D. L., Creedon, M. A., Sasala, J. M., & Neal, M. B. (1989). *Employees and eldercare: Designing effective responses for the workplace.* Bridgeport, CT: University of Bridgeport, Center for the Study of Aging.

Walker, A. J., Pratt, C. C., Shin, H.-Y., & Jones, L. L. (1989). Why daughters care: Perspectives of mothers and daughters in a caregiving situation. In J. A. Mancini (Ed.), *Aging parents and adult children* (pp. 199-213). Lexington, MA: Lexington Books.

Warshaw, L. J., Barr, J. K., Rayman, I., Schachter, M., & Lucas, T. G. (1986). *Employer support of employee caregivers.* New York: New York Business Group on Health.

Weiss, R. S. (1987). Men and their wives' work. In F. J. Crosby (Ed.), *Spouse, parent, worker: On gender and multiple roles* (pp. 109-121). New Haven, CT: Yale University Press.

Zigler, E. (1990). Shaping child care policies and programs in America. *American Journal of Community Psychology, 18,* 183-216.

2

Conceptual Framework and Methodology

Until recently, I was a financially poor, single parent and, for long periods of time, cared for an elderly parent. Stress before the word became vogue. I just thought I was going crazy.

CONCEPTUAL FRAMEWORK

This chapter introduces the theories underlying the conceptual framework that has shaped both the literature review on work and caregiving roles and the analyses of the data set that form the core of this book. This conceptual framework relies on the concepts of stress, roles, and spillover among roles. Monat and Lazarus (1977) referred to stress as an area of research rather than as a specific theory or concept. They defined *stress* as "any event in which environmental demands, internal demands, or both, *tax* or *exceed* the adaptive resources of an individual, social system, or tissue system" (p. 3, emphasis in original). According to them, a potential stressor or demand does not produce a stress response unless the individual or group lacks the necessary resources to cope effectively with that stressor. From the perspective of the individual, resources are those personal (e.g., personality traits, coping styles), social (e.g., social support), and environmental (e.g., money) characteristics that may be available to aid the individual's efforts to cope with the stressor or demand.

Role theory provides several concepts that are useful in thinking about the demands of combining caregiving and employment. Within the caregiving literature, Morycz (1980) associated the subjective burden from caregiving with role strain (cognitive, affective, and physiological changes induced by the stress associated with a role). Objective burden, however, was associated with role conflict (competing roles, conflicting demands) and role overload (too many roles). A major source of role conflict is the competition between time spent at work versus time spent in caregiving. In terms of multiple roles, this line of thought within role theory has been summarized as the scarcity hypothesis (Baruch, Biener, & Barnett, 1987; Goode, 1960). This hypothesis assumes that the sum of human energy is fixed, so that more roles create a greater likelihood of overload, conflict, and strain. In contrast, the enhancement hypothesis (Marks, 1977; Sieber, 1974; Thoits, 1983) argues that multiple roles may augment our energy by increasing our sources of identity, self-esteem, and privileges. In addition, Kessler and McRae (1984) pointed out a third alternative, the hypothesis of self-selection. This hypothesis states that any association between multiple roles and emotional functioning may be a consequence of individuals self-selecting into and out of multiple roles, based on their emotional well-being and their ability to cope with the demands involved.

A number of researchers have used the concept of "spillover," rather than stress, to describe the consequences of performing multiple roles. The concept has sometimes been defined narrowly to mean the spillover of emotion from one setting to another (Voydanoff, 1988; Zedeck & Mosier, 1990) or a carryover of the structure of one setting (such as its hierarchical nature) to another setting (Champoux, 1978; Staines, 1980; Zedeck & Mosier, 1990). A broader definition, such as that of Eckenrode and Gore (1990), construes the concept of spillover as including stress and coping processes in which the effects flow from one individual to another, as well as from one social role to another.

Spillover between work and family may be positive or negative (Crouter, 1984). Examples of positive spillover in Crouter's qualitative work include applying skills and attitudes learned in one setting (often the family) to the other setting; negative spillover involves the negative impact of one setting (work or family) on the other. Small and Riley (1990) hypothesized at least three dimensions of negative spillover of work into family life: the time demands of work, the psychological absorption of the worker, and the fatigue from the physical and psychological challenges of work. Crouter (1984) found that patterns of spillover varied by gender and age, such that mothers with children under age 12 reported both more total spillover (positive and negative) from family to work and more negative spillover than did fathers. Mothers and fathers of adolescent children showed no difference in spillover.

Several other possible models of the relationships between work and family have been summarized by Zedeck and Mosier (1990). Two of these will be described here. The *compensation model* is the reverse of the spillover model, positing an inverse relationship between work and family (Staines, 1980). This model states that people tend to make differential investments of themselves in the two settings and to make up in one for what is missing in the other. Thus, if the paying job is physically demanding, the employee might be less likely to be involved in physical work in the home. The *segmentation model* argues that the environments are distinct and need not influence each other. The roles may be separated in time, space, and function. Some qualitative research with employed caregivers has provided evidence that might be considered a combination of the two models. For example, Brody (1990) found that a number of caregivers for the elderly reported that their paid work offered relief from the demands of caregiving. It allowed the caregiver time away, physically and psychologically, from the caregiving situation.

These theories, hypotheses, and models form the background for the conceptual framework to be used here, which is illustrated in Figure 2.1. The framework hypothesizes that employees' rates of absenteeism and levels of stress are influenced by the caregiving roles they perform, by their own personal characteristics, by the demands placed on them at work and in the family, and by the resources available to them, at work and in the family, that assist them in coping with those demands. Demands are shown as having both a direct and an indirect effect on absenteeism and stress outcomes. By indirect effects, we mean to indicate the possibility that the effect of demands may be buffered by the resources available to the employee. Thus resources may serve as "buffers" between demands and outcomes; their effect on stress and absenteeism may be heightened in the presence of a high level of work and family demand.

Of course, life is more complex and causally multidirectional than the simple statement above. Thus the conceptual framework in Figure 2.1 contains additional arrows that represent feedback loops in the dynamic system. For example, the arrow from the absenteeism and stress outcomes back to work and family demands might represent the employee who chooses to work fewer hours as a result of the stress of caregiving, as well as the employee who chooses to rely on other sources of informal or formal care in order to reduce his or her own involvement in the caregiver role. The arrow from resources to demands represents the possibility that resources can be used to reduce demands. Thus the

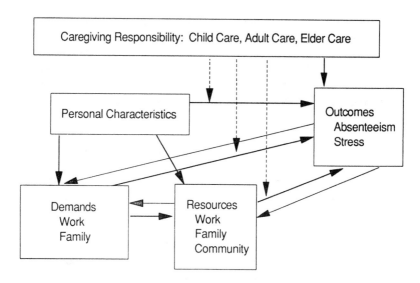

Figure 2.1. Conceptual Framework

presence of a nonworking partner who takes the major responsibility for caregiving reduces the need to make out-of-home care arrangements, with their attendant monetary and travel time costs. Although real life is indeed multidirectional and complex, our analytic strategy will be confined to a simpler unidirectional model that examines the effects of personal characteristics, resources, and demands on absenteeism and stress.

Finally, the effect of caregiving roles is implicit in the chapters that examine employees occupying each caregiving role. Their effects become explicit in the sixth chapter, in which the caregiving roles occupied are entered as variables into the equations. The solid arrows in Figure 2.1 represent the direct effects of caregiving roles on the outcomes experienced by employees. The dashed-line arrows represent interaction effects between caregiving roles and each of the predictor variables. Thus the relationship between the predictor variables and the outcome variables may be modified by caregiving responsibility. For example, it may be that it is the combination of gender (female) and caregiving roles that is likely to be associated with increased absenteeism. This aspect of the analysis will explore the degree to which the relationships discovered between the predictor and outcome variables are true for the entire population, or particularly characteristic of those who are caregivers.

The following sections describe how some of these demands, resources, and outcomes have been conceptualized in the work and family literature. The subsequent methodology section outlines how the concepts have been operationalized within our research and contains a simplified analytic framework (see Figure 2.3).

Demands

Within the context of our conceptual framework, demands derive from two sources: the workplace and the family. Workplace demands include time demands, which may be associated with a commitment to the job as a career (Marks, 1977), and shift assignments. We expect that demands associated with the shift worked may vary based on the family context and on the nature of the caregiving situation. For example, a parent with child-care responsibility may prefer an evening or weekend shift if his or her spouse is available to provide care on evenings and weekends. In addition, elder care may require contact with social service agencies and health care providers that can occur only during the day. Workers on evening, night, or weekend shifts without a partner available to provide care are likely to find it more difficult to combine work and family because alternate care arrangements for dependents are less available during these hours (Staines & Pleck, 1983; Voydanoff, 1987).

Family demands are those arising explicitly from caregiving roles, whether the care recipient is a child, an adult with disabilities, or an elderly person in need. The demands of caregiving are expected to increase with the level of dependency of the care recipient, the number of persons being cared for, and how far the employee must travel to provide care or arrange for care for the dependent.

Resources

The resources available for coping with these demands may arise from work and from the family but may also be provided by the community. Income, a resource derived from the workplace, may be spent on care arrangements to ease the burden of caregiving. Thoits (1987) has pointed out that money and education decrease the actual constraints on behavior and also decrease consensus about traditional role expectations. Both money and education allow people more room to negotiate their roles and to develop innovative solutions to instances of role conflict and overload. Other major work resources include flexible work schedules, personnel policies that allow employees to manage their work time and still be responsive to family demands, and programs in the workplace, such as on-site day care, that may ease the caregiving burden for employees.

The traditional family resource for caregiving, of course, is the wife who is not employed outside the home. The relationship between work and family has become a social problem largely because of the increasing scarcity of this resource as more women enter the work force and more families come to be headed by single parents. Thus the primary family resource is the presence of a partner, and particularly of a partner who is not employed outside the home. Additional family resources include relatives who can provide care for children and elders or adults with disabilities; for example, older siblings who can care for their younger brothers and sisters.

Other major resources are more properly considered community rather than family resources, although families remain the consumers who select and arrange these resources. These include care arrangements that can substitute for family resources, such as family and center day care for children, adult day care, in-home services for elders and adults with disabilities, and the presence of housing options for the elderly that provide various levels of care. Thus resources represent sources of support that can be provided by families, employers, and the community at large. In identifying the diverse sources of potential resources, we are also pointing to the arenas in which potential solutions to work-family conflict can be sought.

Spillover Outcomes

If the resources available to employees to help them cope with the combination of work and family demands are inadequate, a variety of negative outcomes can be expected. These outcomes can be conceptualized as the spillover of family problems into the workplace or the spillover of work problems into the family. Negative work outcomes may include decreases in productivity and increases in absenteeism. Negative personal and family outcomes may include perceived stress in the caregiving role, in family relationships (including marital relationships), and in physical and mental health. More likely, the task of balancing the demands of work and family has spillover in both directions simultaneously and may be perceived simply as difficulty in combining one's work and family roles.

RESEARCH METHODOLOGY

The purpose of our research to be presented in the following chapters was (a) to assess in detail the nature of employees' caregiving responsibilities for children, adults with disabilities, and elders; and (b) to explore the consequences of combining work and family responsibilities as those might be mediated by the personal characteristics of the employee, by the work and family demands on that employee, and by the resources available to her or him to cope with these demands. The study that we will present has a number of unique characteristics that make it particularly useful in addressing the questions raised in this book. Previous studies have focused on individuals caring for one group of individuals needing care, that is, elders, children, or, in a few cases, adults with disabilities. Our sample cuts across these caregiving groups and includes individuals who have caregiving responsibilities for more than one type of care recipient. Thus we are able to compare and contrast the effects of combining work with each of these three different caregiving roles, and also to examine the effects of occupying multiple caregiving roles.

Another strength is in the source of the sample for the study. Most studies on caregiving use samples derived from users of formal, often subsidized, services, and thus represent only those employees who make use of formal service as part of the "care package." This type of sample underrepresents those who rely entirely on informal sources of assistance, including family and friends. For caregivers of elders and adults with disabilities, samples composed of users of formal services underrepresent those caring for elders or adults who are less physically or mentally frail, but who nonetheless need some form of assistance. In contrast, our sample was derived from an employee population and thus represents the full range of types of caregiving situations and responses to those situations. This sampling approach better represents the needs of the population rather than the solutions adopted by a few.

The book combines a theoretical orientation with an emphasis on incorporating questions of interest to employers. Thus one criterion used in choosing outcome measures was their relevance and meaning to employers. As a result, instead of focusing just on stress outcomes, we also have included outcomes measuring time lost from work.

Sample

The research presented in the next section is based on a survey of employees concerning their informal caregiving responsibilities. Specifically, we surveyed employees of 33 businesses and agencies in the Portland, Oregon, metropolitan area. For 32 employers, the employee populations were surveyed; that is, surveys were administered to all employees. For one especially large company, a random sample of 500 employees was drawn. The employers chosen for participation in the study constituted a convenience sample selected to represent small, medium, and large employers and to represent employers within each of the seven major categories of the Standard Industrial Classification. Surveys were distributed through interoffice mail to 27,832 employees and returned by 9,573 employees of these 33 businesses and agencies, for an overall return rate of 34%. This rate varied dramatically by company, from a low of 10% to a high of 78%, and also by department within companies. Low return rates were associated with organizations having large numbers of part-time and short-term workers, as well as with those having poor interoffice mail distribution capability. Surveys were returned in sealed envelopes addressed to the research project at Portland State University in order to protect employee confidentiality.

Table 2.1 summarizes some general characteristics of the sample. This was a relatively affluent sample, with an average household income between $30,000 and $40,000 and a majority (64%) working as professionals, technical workers, managers, or administrators. Census data from 1980 identify 15% of the labor force in the Portland SMSA (Standard Metropolitan Statistical Area) in these occupational categories. Thus these categories are overrepresented in our sample. Full-time employment was reported by 90% of the respondents—that is, they worked at least 35 hours per week—and 87% worked a day shift. Only 7% of the sample represented a minority group, less than the 10% present in the metropolitan area as a whole. The sample also included more women (59%) than would be expected. This may be representative of the companies involved in the survey, although only 43% of the work force in the SMSA was female in 1980. Alternatively, it may be due to women being more likely to define themselves as caregivers and thus to respond to the survey, despite instructions asking all employees, regardless of their family responsibilities, to complete the first page of the questionnaire (see Appendix A: Model Cover Letter and Survey Instrument).

TABLE 2.1 Descriptive Statistics for Entire Sample, Caregiving Subgroups, and Noncaregiving Group: Means, Medians, and Percentages

Variable	Total Sample	Child Care	Adult Care	Elder Care	No Dependent Care
Number of employees	9,573	4,422	357	2,241	3,711
Age (mean)	39.7	37.7	40.8	43.5	39.8
Household income (median)[1]	6.4	6.6	5.9	6.5	6.1
Dependent Variables					
Days of work missed (annual rate)	8.0	8.4	9.4	8.5	7.5
Arrived late/left early (annual rate)	16.4	20.1	17.8	14.6	13.8
Interrupted at work (annual rate)	29.2	40.9	47.7	35.2	15.3
Personal health stress (mean)	2.22	2.22	2.45	2.33	2.18
Difficulty of combining work and family (mean)	2.69	3.02	3.03	2.85	2.28
Caregiving stress		2.02	2.13	2.11	
Percentages					
Gender (% female)	59	56	68	63	60
Ethnicity (%)					
White	93	92	90	93	94
Black	3	4	5	3	3
Hispanic	1	2	1	1	1
Asian	2	2	2	1	2
Other	1	1	2	2	1
Partner status (%)					
No partner	29	17	30	27	41
Employed partner	56	66	48	57	48
Nonemployed partner	15	17	21	16	11
Full-time employment (%)	90	90	92	92	93
Occupation (%)					
Professional/managerial	64	66	58	65	62
All other	36	34	42	35	38
Shift (%)					
Days	87	87	86	88	87
All other	13	13	14	12	13
Amount of work schedule flexibility (%)					
None/hardly any	19	19	28	22	18
Some/a lot	81	81	72	78	82

TABLE 2.1 Continued

Variable	Total Sample	Child Care	Adult Care	Elder Care	No Dependent Care
Care recipient lives (%)					
In employee's home		100	29	8	
In own home			49	76	
In nursing home			9	13	
Other			13	3	
Percentage of sample/ caregiver group with responsibility for:					
Children	46	100	41	42	0
Adult with disability	4	3	100	6	0
Elderly	23	21	34	100	0
Relation to care recipient (%)					
Spouse		0	13	2	
Child		100	22	0	
Parent		0	25	72	
Other relative		0	25	17	
Friend		0	12	7	

Note: 1. Scale for income is 1 = < $10,000; 2 = $10,000-$14,999; 3 = $15,000-$19,999; 4 = $20,000-$24,999; 5 = $25,000-$29,999; 6 = $30,000-$39,999; 7 = $40,000-$49,999; 8 = $50,000-$59,999; 9 = $60,000-$69,999; 10 = > $70,000.

To assess elder- or adult-care responsibility, employees were asked:

Do you have responsibilities for helping out adult relatives or friends who are elderly or disabled? This includes persons who live with you or who live somewhere else. By "helping out" we mean help with shopping, home maintenance or transportation, checking on them by phone, making arrangements for care, etc.

Respondents were identified as providing "elder care" if they were helping someone 60 or more years of age and as providing "adult care" if they were helping someone 18 through 59 years of age. This definition of care for elders and adults with disabilities is a relatively broad one compared with much of the caregiving literature. Our rationale for broadening the definition was our understanding that becoming a caregiver is often a gradual process and that employees are likely not to define themselves as caregivers even though they may provide a great deal of assistance.

Employees were identified as providing "child care" if they reported having children under the age of 18 living in their households. It is important to note that employees with children in the household did not report how much care they personally provided to the children in the household, whereas employees designated as "adult-care" or "elder-care" providers identified themselves specifically as providing assistance to an adult or elderly person. In addition, information about children under 18 who were not living in the household (often as a consequence of divorce) was not collected. Thus employees in this situation could not be included as potential child-care providers in this study.

Figure 2.2 and Table 2.1 show the numbers and percentages of individuals providing each of these types of care and the overlap for those providing more than one type of care. Child care was the most common caregiving responsibility, shared by 46% of the sample. Almost one-quarter (23%) provided elder care, and 4% provided care to adults with disabilities. Overlapping care was also common, with 21% of those with children also providing care to an elder and 42% of those providing elder care having children in the household. These caregivers have been referred as the "women in the middle" or the "sandwich generation" (Brody, 1981; Litwak, 1965; Miller, 1981). In addition, 25% provided care to multiple children and 16% to multiple adults with disabilities or elders. No caregiving responsibilities were reported by 39% of the sample.

Survey Design

The five-page survey (see Appendix A) included questions regarding demographic and social characteristics, work responsibilities, time lost from work, and types and amount of care provided to children, elders, and adults with disabilities. The survey was designed in part to serve as a needs assessment, to design worksite interventions for caregivers, and to inform employers about the nature and effects of employees' caregiving responsibilities. The major variables included in the analyses are named and briefly described in Table 2.2.

Independent Measures

Demographic and Personal Characteristics. Gender, age, ethnicity, relationship to care recipient, and occupation were used as control vari-

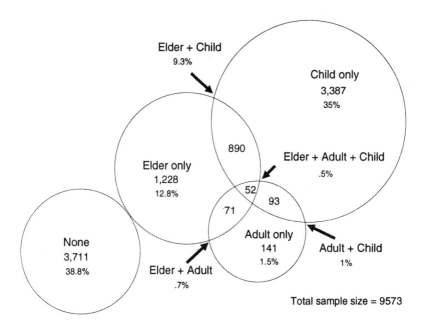

Figure 2.2. Overlapping Caregiving Responsibility: Number/Percentage With Responsibility for Each Group

ables in the major multivariate analyses included in this book. Ethnicity was measured by a dichotomous variable of white versus other. Although more differentiation among the ethnic groups would be desirable, the small minority proportion of the sample did not make that feasible for the major analyses. The relationship of the care provider to the care recipient varies from chapter to chapter. The major relationships of adults with disabilities to their caregiver were represented by the following dummy variables: spouse versus other, child versus other, and parent versus other. For elderly care recipients, the major relationships included parent, stepparent, or parent-in-law versus other, and spouse versus other. Occupation was measured by a dichotomous variable contrasting managerial, technical, and professional occupations with all others.

Demands. The demands placed on employees by their jobs were represented by two variables: the number of hours worked per week and the shift (day shift vs. evening, night, rotating, or other shifts). The demands

TABLE 2.2 Independent and Dependent Variables

Brief Name	Description	High Score	Scale Points
Personal Characteristics			
Gender	Gender of employee	Female	0-1
Age	Age of employee	Older	Continuous
Ethnicity	Ethnicity of employee	White	0-1
Occupation	Occupation of employee	Professional/manager	0-1
Caring for parent, AC/EC	Care recipient is parent	Yes	0-1
Caring for spouse, AC/EC	Care recipient is spouse	Yes	0-1
Caring for child, CC/AC	Care recipient is child	Yes	0-1
Demands			
Hours worked	Hours worked per week	More hours	Continuous
Shift	Day versus all other shifts	Day	0-1
⎡Number cared for, AC/EC	# elders/adults cared for	More	Continuous
⎣Number under age 9, CC	# children under age 9	More	Continuous
Caregiving roles	Care for child, adult, elder	More	0-3
⎡Distance from recipient, AC/EC	Distance from care recipient	Farther	0-6
⎣Travel time to child care, CC	Extra travel to child care	Farther	Continuous
⎡Hours of care provided, AC/EC	Hours of help provided	More hours	Continuous
⎣Age of youngest child, CC	Age of youngest child	Older	Continuous
⎡Special care needs, AC/EC	Elder difficult to care for	More difficult	Continuous
⎣Disabled child, CC	Care for a disabled child	Yes	0-1
Care cost as % of income, CC	Cost of child care as % income	High %	Continuous
Out-of-home care, CC	# hours in out-of-home care	Greater number	Continuous
Resources			
Household income	Household income	High	Continuous
Work schedule flexibility	Flexible work situation	Flexible	1-5
Working partner	Have employed partner	Yes	0-1

Variable	Description		Range
Nonworking partner	Have partner who is not employed	Yes	0-1
⌈Informal support, AC/EC	Help from family/friends	Yes	1-5
⌊Children 9-17, CC	# children aged 9-17	High	Continuous
⌈Self-care, CC	# children care for self	High	Continuous
⌊Kin care, CC	Kin provide child care	Yes	0-1
Formal support, AC/EC	Assistance from formal helpers	Yes	1-5
⌈Ease find/manage AC/EC	Ease of finding & managing care	Easy	1-6
⌊Ease find/continue CC	Ease of finding/continuing care	Easy	1-6
Satisfaction with care	Satisfaction with care arrange.	Satisfied	1-5
Dependent Variables			
Days missed	Days missed during past 4 weeks	More days	0-3
Arrived late/left early	Times left early, past 4 weeks	More times	0-3
Times interrupted	Times interrupted at work, 4 weeks	More times	0-3
Difficulty combining	Difficulty combining work and family	More difficult	1-6
Health stress	Stress from personal health	More stress	1-4
⌈Child-care stress, CC	Child care as source of stress	More stress	1-4
⌊Adult/elder stress, AC/EC	Adult elder care source of stress	More stress	1-4

Note: " [" indicates comparable variables used for the different caregiving groups; CC = child care, AC = adult care, EC = elder care.

placed on employees by their caregiving responsibilities included (a) number of dependents cared for (number of elders, adults with disabilities, or children under the age of 9); (b) number of different kinds of caregiving roles (child, adult with disabilities, or elder; ranging from 0-3); (c) distance from the caregiving situation (distance of the employee's home from the home of the adult or elder; the extra time that travel to child care added to the journey to work); (d) level of dependency (age of youngest child for caregivers of children; number of hours of care provided for caregivers of elders and disabled adults); and (e) special care needs, that is, how difficult it was to provide care. For caregivers of elders or adults, this latter demand, special care needs, was measured using a 4-item scale indicating the extent to which the care recipient could manage the activities of daily living, wandered, or was disruptive or aggressive; for caregivers of children, a dichotomous variable measured whether or not they had a disabled child. Finally, two additional demand variables were created for the child-care analyses: the cost of child care as a percentage of household income and the number of hours a week spent in child care outside the home (summed across children). These variables were scored so that a high score implied high demand. We hypothesized that demands would increase absenteeism and stress.

Resources. Resources associated with the workplace that were available to help employees cope with the demands of caregiving included household income and work schedule flexibility. The latter was measured by averaging responses to two questions: "How much flexibility do you have in your work schedule to handle family responsibilities?" and "To what extent do personnel practices in your department make it easy or difficult to [provide care for this person/deal with child-care problems during working hours]?"

The employee's family as a potential resource for assistance was measured first by two dichotomous variables reflecting the presence of a spouse or partner and the employment status of that partner. Specifically, the first variable, "employed partner," contrasted those employees who had an employed partner with those whose partner was not employed or who did not have a partner. The second variable, "nonemployed partner," contrasted those with a partner not in the work force with those who were either single or had an employed partner.

Formal or informal care arrangements constitute a resource to a family that may substitute for family care while the employee is at work. For caregivers of elders and adults with disabilities, two scales were created that sum and average the frequency with which the following types of care arrangements were used: care by other family members and by friends (for informal care) and care by a hired worker, a volunteer, an adult daycare center, and/or a nursing facility (for formal care). For caregivers of children, three measures were created: (a) the number of children in the household aged 9 to 17 who might be available to care for younger siblings; (b) a dichotomous indicator of reliance on at least one child caring for him- or herself at least part of the time; and (c) a dichotomous measure of whether kin provided child care, either in the employee's or the relative's home.

A measure of the ease of finding such care arrangements and managing them over time was developed. For elder and adult care, this measure was an average of responses to two questions: "In your experience, how easy or difficult has it been to find care arrangements for this elderly or disabled person?" and "In your experience, how easy or difficult has it been to manage or maintain these arrangements?" For child care, an average scale score was created from two parallel questions about the ease or difficulty of finding and then continuing child-care arrangements. Finally, a measure of the average level of satisfaction with the arrangements made to care for the dependent(s) while the respondent was working was also considered to be a caregiving resource.

These variables were scored so that a high score indicates that the caregiver has more resources. We hypothesized that resources would reduce absenteeism and stress.

Outcome Measures

Six outcome measures were chosen to assess the effects of combining work and family. The first three are measures of loss of time at work, or absenteeism. In addition to a traditional measure of absenteeism, that is, losing an entire day of work, we included types of time loss that we expected to be more likely to represent the choices employees make to balance their work and family demands. Specifically, the second absenteeism measure was arriving late to work or leaving work early. The measure was designed to capture behaviors that might be likely outcomes of the pressures of transporting the care recipient to a formal source of care or of the need to take some time off from work to handle contact with formal care institutions during their regular working hours (schools, doctors, social service agencies). The final absenteeism measure was number of interruptions at work to deal with family-related

TABLE 2.3 Correlations Among Dependent Variables
(sample size minimum = 9,109 except as noted)

Variables	Days Missed	Late or Left Early	Inter- ruptions	Personal Health Stress	Difficulty Combining Work and Family
Days missed	—	—	—	—	—
Late or left early	.17**	—	—	—	—
Interruptions	.07**	.34**	—	—	—
Personal health stress	.20**	.12**	.09**	—	—
Difficulty combining work and family	.09**	.14**	.20**	.22**	—
Child-care stress[a]	.09**	.18**	.15**	.16**	.40**
Dependent-care stress, elders[b]	.05*	.04	.12**	.12**	.22*
Dependent-care stress, adults[c]	.00	−.04	.18**	.22**	.22**

* $p < .01$; ** $p < .001$.
Notes: a. These correlations include only those employees caring for children; $n = 4,250$ minimum.
b. These correlations include only those employees caring for elders; $n = 2,149$ minimum.
c. These correlations include only those employees caring for adults; $n = 343$ minimum.

matters; this measure primarily reflects telephone calls from or about care recipients.

The second set of outcome measures we characterize as stress measures. The first of the three stress measures, employees' assessment of the difficulty they have combining work and family, was a direct measure of perceived stress resulting from multiple roles. The second stress measure was relevant only to those employees in caregiving roles: How much stress did caring for a child, adult with disabilities, or elder cause? Finally, personal health stress was chosen as an indirect measure of the probable consequences of overload caused by multiple roles. The research in the field of stress has consistently shown a wide variety of health consequences of perceived stress (e.g., Kasl & Cooper, 1987).

The correlations among the outcome measures are shown in Table 2.3. The highest correlations tend to be among the stress measures, and between interruptions at work and times that the employee left early or arrived late.

Absenteeism. Three measures were created to measure time lost from work or absenteeism. These were based on how many times in the preceding 4 weeks the respondent had missed a day from work, been interrupted at work (including telephone calls) to deal with family-related matters, and arrived at work late or left work early. Of the three measures, only the question about times interrupted asked directly about absenteeism resulting from the family role. In all cases, the scores of the individual items have been recoded from their original scales to a scale ranging from 0 to 3 in order to decrease the skewness of the distribution.

A problem with any indirect measure of absenteeism concerns the ability of the employee to recall instances of time loss. The 4-week period chosen was probably most appropriate for recalling missing days at work, but it may have been too long for employees to remember reliably how often they arrived late, left early, or were interrupted at work to deal with family-related matters.

Stress. The first stress measure was difficulty of combining work and family. This dependent variable was a single item: "Circumstances differ and some people find it easier than others to combine working with family responsibilities. In general, how easy or difficult is it for you?" The second stress measure was derived from one of two items, depending on the analysis. Respondents were asked to indicate to what extent child care and/or care for elderly or adult family members had been a source of stress to them during the preceding 4 weeks. The third stress measure was the extent to which the respondent's personal health had been a source of stress to him or her during the preceding 4 weeks.

Characteristics of the Sample

Table 2.1 summarizes some of the characteristics of the total employee sample, as well as the average characteristics for employees in each caregiving group and for employees with no dependent-care responsibilities. For the breakdowns by caregiving group, *all* employees with responsibility for a particular group are included in the subsample. Thus the total number of employees summed across caregiving groups is greater than the total sample size, due to employees with multiple caregiving roles who appear more than once. The table includes average age, household income, and average score on the dependent variables by group as well as percentages of each subgroup by gender, ethnicity, partner status, employment status, occupation, shift, and work schedule flexibility. Finally, percentages are shown for variables representing caregiving responsibility.

Gender. The sample as a whole includes more women (59%) than men. Women were particularly likely to identify themselves as caregivers of adults with disabilities (68%) and elders (63%).

Age. The total sample and its subgroups are, on the whole, quite similar in average age with the exception of employees caring for elders, whose average age was 43.5 as compared with the total sample mean age of 39.7.

Ethnicity. The entire sample was predominantly white (90% of those with adult-care duties, 92% of those with children, 93% of those caring for elders, and 94% of those with no dependent-care responsibilities), making it unrepresentative of the national minority population. The major minority groups in the sample were African American (3%), Hispanic (1%), and Asian/Pacific Islander (1.9%).

Partner Status. Compared with the total sample, employees with child-care responsibility were less likely to have no partner and more likely to have an employed partner. Employees with adult care were about as likely as the overall sample to have a partner, but that partner was less likely to be employed, perhaps because the partner and the disabled adult were in these cases the same person. Employees caring for elders were quite similar to the total sample, although they were somewhat less likely to lack a partner. Finally, employees without caregiving responsibilities were much more likely to lack a partner than the overall sample.

Household Income. The mean household income for the sample was high: between $30,000 and $39,999. Employees caring for adults and those with no dependent-care responsibility had a somewhat lower household income than those with children or those caring for elders, perhaps because they were more likely than these other two groups to have no partner or a nonemployed partner.

Work-Related Characteristics. Nearly all employees surveyed (90%) worked full time. Employees with adult-care responsibility, those caring for elders, and those with no dependent-care duties were somewhat more likely than the total sample to work full time. Employees caring for adults with disabilities were least likely to hold professional, management, or technical positions (58% compared with 66% of those with children, 65% of those caring for elders, and 62% of those with no dependent-care responsibilities). Most employees worked days (87%), and there was little difference between the three caregiving groups. Employees caring for adults were more likely to report having no or hardly any flexibility in their work schedules to deal with family-related matters (28% compared with 19% of employees with children in their households, 22% of employees caring for elders, and 18% of those caring for no dependents).

Caregiving-Related Characteristics. Most employees caring for elders were caring for a parent, stepparent, or parent-in-law (72%); 17% were caring for another relative, 7% for a friend, and 2% for a spouse. The relationships of employees caring for adults with disabilities to those adults were more broadly dispersed: 25% were caring for a parent, 13% were caring for a spouse, 25% were caring for another relative, 22% were caring for an adult child, and 12% were caring for a friend. Employees with children in their households were mostly the children's parents or stepparents, or in a few cases, grandparents.

While all surveyed employees with children in their households by definition resided with those children, only 8% of employees caring for elders lived in the same household with the elder; 76% of the elders lived in their own homes. Among those caring for adults with disabilities, 29% lived with the adult for whom they were providing care; 49% of the adult-care recipients lived in their own homes.

With regard to multiple caregiving roles, employees caring for adults with disabilities or for elders were more likely than those with children in the household to be caring for more than one type of dependent. Among employees caring for adults, 41% also had child-care responsibilities, and 34% had elder-care responsibilities. Among those caring for elders, 42% had children in their households, and 6% were caring for one or more adults with disabilities as well as an elder. Among employees with children, however, only 3% had adult-care duties, and 21% were caring for one or more elders.

Absenteeism. Employees caring for adults had missed the most days of work (annualized): 9.4 compared with 8.5 for those with elders, 8.4 for those with children, and 7.4 for those with no dependent-care duties. Employees caring for adults were also most likely to be interrupted at work to deal with family-related matters: 47.7 times (annualized rate) compared with 40.9 times for those with children, 35.2 times for those caring for elders, and 15.3 times for those with no dependent-care responsibilities. Employees with children, however, were more likely to arrive late or leave work early (annualized rate): 20.1 times compared with 17.8 times for those with adult-care duties, 14.6 times for those caring for elders, and 13.8 times for those with no dependent-care duties.

Stress. Employees caring for adults experienced the most personal health stress (mean of 2.45, compared to a mean of 2.33 for those caring for elders, 2.22 for those with children, and 2.18 for those caring for no dependents). Employees with adult-care duties also, as a group, experienced more caregiving stress (mean = 2.13) than those with elder-care (2.11) or child-care (2.02) responsibilities (caregiving stress was not measured for employees without dependent-care responsibilities). Employees caring for children or adults with disabilities reported the most difficulty combining work and family (mean = 3.02 and 3.03, respectively) compared to those caring for elders (2.85), and those with no dependent-care responsibilities (2.28).

Approach to Data Analysis

A technique called "hierarchical multiple regression" was used in the analyses. The purpose of hierarchical multiple regression is to discover those factors that account for differences among respondents in their scores on the outcomes of interest. In this study, we wished to account for differences among employees in the amounts of absenteeism and stress they experienced as a result of their caregiving responsibilities. Specifically, the outcome measures include the three outcomes assessing time lost from work and the three assessing stress. Figure 2.3 shows the analytic framework that guided our data analysis.

This analytic technique has two central features: (a) it looks at the simultaneous effects of a number of independent predictor variables on each of the outcome variables, and (b) it enters these variables into each of the equations in groups or blocks. In our model, the variables representing the personal characteristics of the employee were entered first, then the variables representing the work and caregiving demands placed on the employee, and finally the variables representing the resources available to the employee. In the discussion to follow, the term *equation*

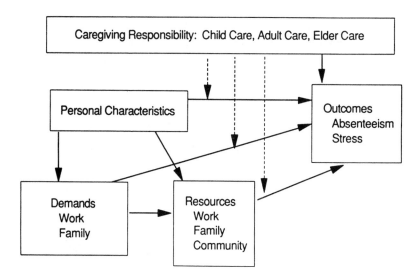

Figure 2.3. Analytical Framework

will be used to refer to the final regression equation after all of the blocks of variables have been entered.

Why is the first feature of hierarchical multiple regression important; that is, why is it important to enter all of the predictor variables into the equation at the same time rather than look simply at the individual relationships between each predictor variable and each outcome variable? We do this because the predictor variables are often related to each other as well as to the outcome variable; by looking only at relationships between two variables at a time, this complexity will be missed and the findings will be misleading. For example, if women are found to have more difficulty combining work and family, it may be because they lack certain resources (such as income or having a nonworking partner) that are more available to men. Using a multivariate analytic approach allows us to examine whether there are still gender differences after comparing men and women who are similar in their demands and resources.

The second characteristic of the analytic technique we used is that variables are entered into the equation for each outcome variable in blocks, and those blocks of variables are entered in a specific sequence. We chose the order in which the blocks were to be entered based on the causal priority we assumed each block to have as specified in our conceptual framework. In the set of analyses reported here, the rationale for ordering the three blocks was to understand how much each of the variables in each block accounted for variations in the stress and absenteeism of employees after controlling for the effects of the variables entered in previous blocks. In our analyses, the first step of the analysis contained only the first block of predictors, that is, those that represented the personal characteristics of the employees. This step allowed us to separate out the effects of the demographic differences among the employees providing child care, adult care, and elder care, respectively, from the effects of the demands and resources involved in the work and caregiving situation when predicting the outcomes. The second step added the second block of variables, that is, the demands of work and caregiving, to the personal characteristics of the employees included in the first equation. This step allowed us to test the extent to which the demands of the work and caregiving situation, after controlling for personal characteristics, accounted for variation in the outcome variables. The final step in the analysis added the resource predictors as a block. By entering this set last, we could test whether resources were able to reduce or eliminate the stress and absenteeism that we expected to be associated with work and family demands.

The tables in Chapters 3 through 7 report the statistically significant relationships between each independent measure and the outcome measures. The pluses indicate a direct relationship between the independent and outcome measures (as one increases in size, so does the other), while the minuses indicate an inverse relationship. These tables summarize the expanded tables included in the appendices. The expanded tables report the standardized regression coefficients (betas) associated with each variable. These coefficients represent the relative size of the relationship between each independent, or predictor, variable and the dependent, or outcome, variable at the final step of each analysis. Both sets of tables (i.e., the summary tables in the text and the detailed tables in the appendices) show, after each step of the analysis, the effect each block of variables had on the outcome variable. This information is labeled "change in R^2," which refers to the ability of that block of variables to account for differences among employees in stress and absenteeism. At the end of each table are rows labeled "total R^2/R^2 adjusted" and "overall F." The total R^2 tells us how much of the variation in the employees' scores on the outcome measures is explained by their scores on the independent measures. A significant overall F tells us whether we have explained more of this variation than might be expected by chance with a sample this size.

About Significant Predictors. In the chapters that follow, we sometimes point out that a variable that was a significant predictor of an outcome at an early step of the analysis was not a significant predictor at a later step, and vice versa. What does this mean? One would expect to find the former if the relationship between the predictor and the outcome was in fact accounted for by a variable added to the equation later. Thus in the earlier example regarding the relationship between gender and resources, we might expect that women would show more negative impacts of caregiving in the first and second step of an analysis, but that when the resources available to men and women are held constant in the third step, there would no longer be a significant relationship between gender and stress or absenteeism. The second case, in which a variable becomes significant at a later stage of the analysis, is more difficult to explain and is labeled a "suppressor" effect in multivariate analysis. This occurs when two predictor variables are associated with each other (for example, a personal characteristic and a demand, or a demand and a resource), but are associated with the outcome variable in opposite directions (one positive and one negative). Until both predictor variables (i.e., the blocks they are a part of) are included in the equation at the same time, their relationships with the outcome variable are "suppressed" and not visible.

About Interaction Terms. Chapter 6, which reports on noncaregivers versus those with at least one and sometimes multiple caregiving roles, includes interaction terms in a final step of the analyses (shown as dotted arrows in Figure 2.3). The interaction terms were created by developing a variable representing whether or not the employee was a caregiver and multiplying that variable by each of the personal characteristics and by the demand and resource variables. One purpose of the interaction terms is to provide a test of the stress-buffering hypothesis (Gore, 1981; Thoits, 1982). This hypothesis states that resources and supports may be important only to the extent that the individual is under stress and thus may be significant predictors of outcomes only for those under stress. An approach to test this hypothesis is to include interaction terms that represent the combination of stress level and presence of resources. Because we assumed that providing care for dependents was in most cases a stress-creating role, the interaction terms that multiply caregiving roles by resources allowed us to begin to test the stress-buffering hypothesis (Thoits, 1987). Interaction terms for personal characteristics indicated whether being a caregiver had a differential impact on employees who differed in gender, age, ethnicity, income, or occupation. Finally, interaction terms for demands showed whether the demands of the work role had a differential impact on employees who were caregivers in contrast to those who were not.

SUMMARY

This chapter has presented the conceptual framework and outlined the research methodology that will guide the analyses to be presented in Chapters 3 through 7. The central features of these are:

1. Stress, roles, and spillover among roles provide the theoretical basis for the research presented.
2. The conceptual framework includes caregiving responsibility; personal characteristics; work- and family-related demands on employees; and work-, family-, and community-based resources available to employees. We expect each of these to influence the stress levels and absenteeism rates of employees.
3. Our research is based on a survey of 27,832 employees (9,573 respondents) of 33 companies and agencies.
4. Hierarchical multiple regression is the data analytic technique that will be employed in the following chapters. This technique enters measures of the concepts included in the conceptual framework to predict the stress levels and absenteeism rates of employees with and without caregiving responsibility for children, adults, and/or elders.

This chapter has also provided the reader with guidance in understanding and interpreting the data analytic technique and the tables that will be presented in the following chapters.

In the upcoming section, "Research," Chapters 3 through 6 first review the research literature concerning the employee group of interest (i.e., those with children, those with adult-care responsibilities, those with elder-care duties, and those with multiple caregiving roles). Following each review of the literature, the relevant results from our survey of employees and their caregiving responsibilities are presented. The final chapter in this section, Chapter 7, synthesizes and discusses the previous four chapters.

REFERENCES

Baruch, G. K., Biener, L., & Barnett, R. C. (1987). Women and gender in research on work and family stress. *American Psychologist, 42,* 130-136.

Brody, E. M. (1981). "Women in the middle" and family help to older people. *The Gerontologist, 21,* 471-480.

Brody, E. M. (1990). *Women in the middle: Their parent-care years.* New York: Springer.

Champoux, J. E. (1978). Perceptions of work and nonwork: A reexamination of the compensatory and spillover models. *Sociology of Work and Occupations, 5,* 402-422.

Crouter, A. C. (1984). Spillover from family to work: The neglected side of the work-family interface. *Human Relations, 37,* 425-442.

Eckenrode, J., & Gore, S. (Eds.). (1990). *Stress between work and family.* New York: Plenum.

Goode, W. J. (1960). A theory of role strain. *American Sociological Review, 25,* 483-496.

Gore, S. (1981). Stress-buffering functions of social supports: An appraisal and clarification of research methods. In B. Dohrenwend & B. P. Dohrenwend (Eds.), *Stressful life events and their contexts* (pp. 202-222). New York: Prodist.

Kasl, S. V., & Cooper, C. L. (Eds.). (1987). *Stress and health: Issues in research methodology.* Chichester, England: John Wiley.

Kessler, R. C., & McRae, J. A., Jr. (1984). A note on the relationships of sex and marital status to psychological distress. In J. A. Greenley (Ed.), *Research in community and mental health* (Vol. 4, pp. 109-130). Greenwich, CT: JAI Press.

Litwak, E. (1965). Extended kin relations in an industrial society. In E. Shanas & G. Streib (Eds.), *Social structure and the family* (pp. 290-325). Englewood Cliffs, NJ: Prentice Hall.

Marks, S. R. (1977). Multiple roles and role strain: Some notes on human energy, time and commitment. *American Sociological Review, 42,* 921-936.

Miller, D. A. (1981). The "sandwich" generation: Adult children of the aging. *Social Work, 26,* 419-423.

Monat, A., & Lazarus, R. (Eds.). (1977). *Stress and coping: An anthology.* New York: Columbia University Press.

Morycz, R. K. (1980). An exploration of senile dementia and family burden. *Clinical Social Work Journal, 8,* 16-27.

Sieber, S. D. (1974). Toward a theory of role accumulation. *American Sociological Review, 39,* 467-478.

Small, S. A., & Riley, D. (1990). Toward a multidimensional assessment of work spillover into family life. *Journal of Marriage and the Family, 52,* 51-61.

Staines, G. L. (1980). Spillover versus compensation: A review of the literature on the relationship between work and nonwork. *Human Relations, 33,* 111-129.

Staines, G. L., & Pleck, J. H. (1983). *The impact of work schedules on the family.* Ann Arbor: University of Michigan Press.

56   INTRODUCTION

Thoits, P. A. (1982). Conceptual, methodological, and theoretical problems in studying social support as a buffer against life stress. *Journal of Health and Social Behavior, 23,* 145-159.

Thoits, P. A. (1983). Multiple identities and psychological well-being: A reformulation and test of the social isolation hypothesis. *American Sociological Review, 48,* 174-187.

Thoits, P. A. (1987). Negotiating roles. In F. Crosby (Ed.), *Spouse, parent, worker: On gender and multiple roles* (pp. 11-22). New Haven, CT: Yale University Press.

Voydanoff, P. (1987). *Work and family life.* Newbury Park, CA: Sage.

Voydanoff, P. (1988). Work role characteristics, family structure demands, and work/family conflict. *Journal of Marriage and the Family, 50,* 749-761.

Zedeck, S., & Mosier, K. (1990). Work in the family and employing organization. *American Psychologist, 45,* 240-251.

PART II

Research

3

Employees Who Have Children

I am divorced and share joint custody of my 8-year-old son. He is with me
half the week and with his mom half a week. I find it very difficult (as I
am not married or living with anyone) to juggle work, child rearing, day care,
housework, and personal time without feeling stress the majority of time.

Almost 50 years ago, at the height of World War II, women were called
to the work force, and the work week consisted of six 8-hour days. A
study of absenteeism was conducted at a war plant in Elgin, Illinois
(Schenet, 1945). It found that the women had 3 times as much absenteeism as the men; there were also major site differences in absenteeism
rates among plants and departments. These two sources of absenteeism
—gender and job—were destined to become major issues to unravel in
the succeeding decades. In the Elgin study, no attempt was made to in-
terpret the gender differences, and no mention was made of the fact that
many of the wartime women workers were mothers for whom child care
might have been a problem. For decades, the association between gender
and absenteeism mystified researchers, who considered differences in
attitude, temperament, and health before a dawning awareness of the
practical realities of daily child-care responsibility helped to clarify the
issues.

Not until the 1980s did research on absenteeism expand far beyond
questions of job satisfaction and the psychology of attitudes toward
work, job, or employer. Variables such as age and number of dependents
were analyzed, but with little curiosity about the family demands being
faced. Likewise, not until relatively recently have workplace factors
been cast in terms of demands and resources that can affect how employees manage work and family life in combination.

This chapter examines the work and family demands that are made on employees who must arrange child care in order to be at work or who worry about these arrangements when they have not been made to their satisfaction. The chapter also examines the work and family resources that reduce the impact of combining working with family responsibilities. In the first part, the examination is done through a review of the research literature and in the second part through a parallel statistical analysis that tests the model of expected relationships.

Personal Characteristics

Among the personal characteristics shown in the research literature as factors influencing how employees balance work and responsibility for child care are gender, ethnicity, and occupation.

Gender. Among all of the personal characteristics, gender dominates the work-family scene, accounting for major differences in such outcomes as absenteeism, stress, and work-family conflict. Gender is a complex cultural variable that reflects a constellation of behaviors, attitudes, and cultural norms shaping how child-care and related family responsibilities are assigned and carried out within the family.

In a review by Porwoll (1980) of 431 studies of absenteeism reported between World War II and 1979, 43 were found to have addressed gender differences in absenteeism. Women's rates were higher in 32 studies, no significant difference was found in 7 studies, and men's rates were higher in 4 studies. Greater severity of absenteeism (i.e., more days per episode) was found among men, however, as distinguished from the greater incidence of brief episodes among women. Few studies reviewed by Porwoll considered that child-care responsibilities might be a gender-linked reason for absenteeism.

A focus on the responsibilities of employed parents emerged in the 1980s as an increasing number of surveys assessed the child-care needs of the work force. In a study of employees in Portland, Oregon, Emlen and Koren (1984) found child care to be a source of worry or stress reported by 47% of employed mothers and 28% of employed fathers of children under age 12. Further, in a study of AT&T employees, Fernandez (1986) reported that 57% of women versus 38% of men employees missed work at least once in the previous year. A national survey of employed parents in dual-earner families conducted for *Fortune Magazine* by Bank Street College and the Gallup Poll (Galinsky & Hughes,

1987) found that, of those who missed work, 44% of the fathers and 67% of the mothers of children under age 6 missed 1 to 5 days in 3 months because of family obligations. Similarly, at Merck Co., 68% of mothers and 51% of fathers with children under age 6 reported high work-family conflict (Galinsky, 1988).

Hedges (1973) showed that gender differences in absenteeism rates emerge among married employees and that it is necessary to take marital status into account to understand those differences. Klein (1986) found that the gender effects of marriage are that married men lose less time and married women lose more time from work than unmarried employees. This behavioral difference cannot be explained without examining gender roles in relation to specific family demands and resources.

Studies that examine the effect of coping with a sick child have illustrated a major source of gender differences and accounted for much of the gender differential in absenteeism. Galinsky (1988) and Burden and Googins (1987) reported that women missed twice as many days as men due to a child's illness. Scott and McClellan (1990) found that, among secondary schoolteachers in two-earner families, 85% of fathers and 12% of mothers reported that their spouse usually stayed at home when their child was ill and that the men were absent significantly fewer days per year on average: 4.8 days, compared to 6.9 for women. This gender difference may emanate from the workplace as well from the parents themselves. In the words of one of our respondents:

> I have found my company to be very intolerant of me as the husband and father to take time off to be with a sick child during working hours. They (managers) have even gone so far as to suggest that it is or should be the responsibility of my wife, who holds a management position in another firm, to assume the responsibility of staying home with a sick child. I personally find the personnel policies of my firm and their attitude toward this situation to border on stone-age mentality.

A particularly useful analysis of gender issues in work-family conflict was reported by Shinn (1988). The study involved two samples of full-time employed parents of children under age 16 at four companies and four state agencies, and at a national retail sales firm. She reported that gender and marital status explained 7% of the variance in the perceived stress of combining work and family life and that women reported more stress than men, even after controlling for instability of child-care arrangements. The independent contribution made by gender to perceived work-family stress was only 2%. That contribution was so minimal because the power of gender differences tends to be explained largely by the specific demands associated with child care, which fall more heavily on women. As Shinn (1988) concluded, "Women consistently experienced more work-family conflict than men. This was true even after accounting for women's additional child care burdens" (p. 4). She also noted that the importance of gender is reduced when the unequal division of labor is accounted for. As Burden and Googins (1987) pointed out, men tend to respond much in the same way as women when they face the same responsibilities.

In general, however, employed fathers and mothers do not bear the same responsibilities, and unraveling the route taken by gender traces a trail that winds through a thicket of demands and resources at home and at work. Gender is expressed in roles played in every aspect of life, not only in the domestic division of labor, as documented by Pleck (1985) in his study of the roles of working wives and working husbands, but also in important differences in attitude toward responsibility for family tasks, as Gunter and Gunter (1990) demonstrated. Whether related to caring for an ill child at home or to arranging child care in the community, gender is also modified by work and family resources associated with marital status and the employment status of one's spouse or partner. These resources are discussed in a later section of this chapter.

Ethnicity. Like gender, ethnicity is a complex cultural variable that is difficult to analyze because it taps differences in occupation, income, education, and neighborhood, as well as cultural traditions. Ethnicity tends to be intertwined with socioeconomic status and is associated with differential use of some types of child care; the impact of these variables on work-family conflict, however, has not been clarified well by the research literature.

A 1988 household survey by the National Center for Health Statistics (Dawson & Cain, 1990), for example, reported that 60% of children under age 6 in the United States receive some sort of supplemental child care, most frequently during maternal employment. This survey found that there were ethnic differences in the patterns of child-care arrangements used. For 43.5% of Hispanics, the main source of child care was family or relatives providing care within or outside the home, compared to 36.6% for non-Hispanics; similarly, 47.9% of African Americans relied on family care, compared to 35.3% of whites. African Americans, for example, were twice as likely as whites to use a grandparent as their main source of child care. Still, almost no difference between Hispanics and non-Hispanics or African Americans and whites was found in use of out-of-home care, although Hispanics and African Americans relied more heavily on relatives for this out-of-home care and all others relied more on child-care centers or nonrelatives. Hispanics and African Americans both used multiple child-care arrangements somewhat less frequently. They had also changed their main source of child care in the past year slightly less frequently than other employees. Both of these factors were favorable for balancing work and family.

In Las Cruces, New Mexico, Mexican-American and Anglo women working in clerical positions were compared by Marlow (1990), who found no significant difference in the two groups' ability to manage work and family responsibility. The two samples reported no difference in social support. The Mexican-American women, however, thought it would be helpful if they could work a different shift, if their spouse could work a different shift, or if they could have an improved maternity-leave policy. All of these options represent work scheduling alternatives that serve as resources for reducing difficulty in managing work and family.

Occupation. Occupation is a variable that is associated with the personal characteristics of employees, but in the context of work-family issues, personal characteristics tend to be overshadowed by the flexibility or inexorability of job requirements associated with different occupations. Bus drivers and nurses cannot be late, while lawyers have greater flexibility (although it is frequently eliminated by court deadlines and the pressure to bill hours). Occupational differences per se, independent of the confounding effects of income, have not received systematic attention from researchers. This issue is discussed below in relation to household income as a resource predictor.

In summary, the research literature pertaining to the personal characteristics of employees with children suggests that:

1. Personal characteristics such as gender, ethnicity, and occupation are accompanied by major differences in how child care, work, and family life are arranged.
2. Gender differences are reflected in a sharp division of labor for child-care responsibilities.
3. Ethnic cultures vary in reliance on relatives for child care, with whites most likely to purchase care from nonrelatives outside the home.

4. Occupational differences reflect complex differences in educational background and income, but also in the flexibility or rigidity of job requirements,
which critically affects employees' abilities to balance their work and family
responsibilities.

Demands

Demands that influence the ability to balance work and family can
be classified in terms of those emanating from the workplace and those
emanating from the family or the caregiving situation. Workplace demands include work shift and hours worked. Family demands include
the ages and number of children, having a child with a disability, cost
of child care, and the amount of out-of-home child care.

Work Shift and Hours Worked. A number of characteristics of employment, such as working conditions and job requirements, create demands that affect an employee's ability to work and perform family roles.
These characteristics include the number of hours worked per day and
per week, work shift, severity of job requirements, work products, and
the nature of work.

Working a shift other than the day shift has negative consequences for
employees who need to purchase child care in the community, since the
accessibility of existing child-care resources tends to be restricted to a
limited range of day-shift hours (Kisker, Hofferth, Phillips, & Farquhar,
1991). Staines and Pleck (1983) found non-day-shift child care to be
associated with increased family stress and decreased family satisfaction. And Emlen, Koren, and Yoakum (1990b) found that 27% of employed
mothers, including those working day and non-day shifts, said that they
would work a different shift if they could.

Most of the recent research on the effects of work shift, however, has
focused on alternative work schedules through which companies attempt to alleviate work-family demands. We treated policies affording
greater flexibility for employee patterns of work as a resource predictor
in our model. Our predictive model of work-family stress did not concentrate specifically on job stress or on the demands of the job itself
but primarily on the spillover of job onto family and vice versa, as reflected
in our measure, "difficulty of combining work and family." Nonetheless, it is worth noting that in employee surveys like the one reported
in this book, job stress has consistently been the most frequently
reported source of perceived difficulty, worry, or stress for both men

and women, and for parents and nonparents, varying with occupation, as noted above in the discussion of the effects of income (Emlen & Koren, 1984).

Age of Child and Number of Children. Age of child is a factor in family demands due to developmental differences in dependency needs. Finding appropriate supplemental child care, while problematic for children of all ages, is especially difficult for infants and young children. At AT&T, Fernandez (1986) found that parents of younger children missed more days of work in a year, while leaving work early was associated with having older children. Klein (1986) found that women with one child under age 6 missed an average of 12.8 days, as compared to 6.7 days for women with one child aged 6 to 17. Galinsky (1988) reported that several studies show that the number of children has an impact on absenteeism as well as on other work-family issues.

Thus the research literature supports a predictive model in which the number of children under age 9 and the age of the youngest child are considered as demands on employed parents, because young children have both the least independence and the most need for child care. Having one or more children aged 9 to 17 can be treated as a net resource for caregiving, even though children in this age group still create some demands on employed parents. This is an age that is associated with self- or sibling-care arrangements (i.e., arrangements in which an older brother or sister is with the child or the child cares for him- or herself). Such care may result in more dissatisfaction with the care arrangements and more interruptions of the parent's job (Emlen & Koren, 1984). At the same time, these "built-in" care resources within the family do provide an alternative source of care for younger children.

Children With Disabilities. Children with disabilities create a special demand on families. Despite their greater need for respite and supplemental care, these parents encounter more difficulty in finding child care in the community to accommodate the special needs of their child. In a survey of child-care supply in three cities (Camden, Newark, and South Chicago), Kisker, Maynard, Gordon, and Strain (1989) found that approximately 4 out of 10 family day-care providers would accept children with special needs. This finding suggests that such parents have a significantly reduced supply of care available to them when they attempt to find child care. As Deiner (1992) pointed out, children with disabilities are often less responsive to caregivers; they require more

care, time, and energy, while the caregivers require more training in how
to meet their needs. Also, these children may be a greater financial burden
to parents because of the safety and liability concerns of providers (Deiner,
1992).

Child-Care Cost as a Percentage of Household Income. In general,
as household incomes increase, families do not report increased spending for child care until household income reaches around $60,000. The
average percentage of household income spent on child care levels out
at between 5% to 7% for household incomes of $30,000, whereas lower
income families spend 10%, 15%, even 20% or more (Emlen, Koren, &
Yoakum, 1990b). Most employees who pay 10% or more of their household income for child care have only one personal income in the family;
many of them are single mothers. Thus an appropriate family-demand
variable is child-care expenditures as a percentage of household income.
This variable is a measure of a family's ability or inability to afford child
care.

The percentage of household income spent on child care is related to
the perceived unaffordability of child care reported by employed parents, which is associated in turn with a number of measures of work-
family conflict. In a study of West Coast hospitals, Emlen and Koren
(1988) found the perceived difficulty in paying for child care to be related to household income, as one might expect, but also, and equally
strongly, to the actual amount spent for child care. That is, those who paid
more for child care found it more difficult to pay for child care than did
those who spent less on child care. The family's values and standards
appeared to prompt them to spend more than average for their child
care, despite the difficulty of doing so. Furthermore, those who reported
difficulty in paying for child care were significantly more likely to
report difficulty in combining working with family responsibilities,
difficulty in finding child care, changing care arrangements in the past
year, higher absenteeism (days missed), and greater stress or worry about
child care.

Total Hours of Out-of-Home Care. When is child care a resource, as
opposed to a demand, for the employed parent? The answer to this question
depends on the type of child care, on the quality of care, and on how
well the care fits in with family life and work. One possible demand
variable is "total number of hours of out-of-home care." Emlen and
Koren (1984) pointed to the importance of the daily task of maintaining

child-care arrangements—a task that creates demands on employed parents for their time, effort, and concern. Some types of child care are more demanding than others, however. In a later section of this chapter, we will describe research related to parents' satisfaction with their child-care arrangements, which we used as a resource variable in our model. We will also describe research related to disruptions in child-care arrangements and evidence that child-care issues are associated with spending unproductive time at work (Fernandez, 1986; Strohmer, 1988). Kossek (1990), for example, reported that employees with child-care problems were significantly less positive about their ability to manage child-care and work responsibilities.

The question arises, though, as to whether some kinds of child care result in more problems than others. Emlen and Koren (1984) compared the absenteeism rates of 2,430 parents with children under age 12 by the type of child care used. They found that the impact on absenteeism of using "market care" outside the home, such as care in centers or family day care (i.e., care in the homes of nonrelatives or relatives), was significantly higher than for care at home by a spouse or other adult. Fathers with a spouse at home to provide child care had absenteeism rates (days missed) comparable to men with no children at all. An annualized report of the number of times mothers were late to work was 15.8 for those using care outside the home, compared to 9.6 times per year for mothers relying on care by an adult at home. Similar findings were reported by Kossek (1990), who found that users of nonfamilial care experienced significantly more child-care problems than families with a stay-at-home parent; users of a mixed combination of familial and nonfamilial care experienced fewer problems than those using total nonfamilial care but more than those using total familial care.

Child-care arrangements that are not supervised by an adult, that is, "self-care" arrangements in which children are with an older sibling or looking after themselves, have a greater absenteeism cost (Emlen & Koren, 1984). The fact remains, however, that there is also some absenteeism cost associated with the demands of maintaining child-care arrangements outside the home on a daily basis. These costs apply even to using center care (Costa, 1988), probably because centers that are not on-site at a particular company may not accommodate work schedules or ill children easily, requiring parents to make multiple arrangements. An alternative hypothesis, however, is that center users work in higher paid occupations and tend to have jobs that permit time off, thus increasing absenteeism rates among center users.

There is some evidence that high quality, family-responsive on-site centers may reduce absenteeism, although the results are mixed. Milkovich and Gomez (1976) found that turnover and absenteeism were significantly lower for users of such centers than for either a matched sample of mothers whose children were not enrolled or for a general sample of employees. Similarly, Youngblood and Chambers-Cook (1984) reported a significant reduction in both turnover and absenteeism after on-site care was introduced in a textile firm, as did Ransom, Aschbacher, and Burud (1989) after on-site center care was introduced at a bank. In a quasi-experimental study, Marquant (1988) found that 2 years after the introduction of on-site care, the absenteeism rates declined for the experimental group of on-site users and stayed the same for the nonusers, although the nonusers had lower rates than the users at the start. In contrast, in a field study of employed parents of children under age 6 at a large midwestern electronics and communications firm, Goff, Mount, and Jamison (1990) found no evidence that on-site child care reduced the absenteeism or work-family conflict of employed parents. Still, those employees who were more satisfied with the quality of their child's care, regardless of location, experienced less work-family conflict and had lower absenteeism. We will take up the issue of quality of care in the next section, in which satisfaction with care is treated as a resource.

In summary, the research literature concerning the family and workplace demands affecting employees who have children indicates that:

1. Child care is especially inaccessible at times other than the standard day shift.
2. The different child-care and developmental needs of young versus older children are associated with different patterns of absenteeism: Parents of young children miss more days, while parents of older children experience more interruptions on the job.
3. Families having children with disabilities encounter greater difficulty finding child care in the community to accommodate their children's special needs.
4. The affordability of child care, when measured by child-care expenditures as a percentage of household income, is associated with a number of work-family conflicts such as difficulty finding and sustaining child-care arrangements, absenteeism, and worry about child care.
5. Both the amount of out-of-home child care used by a family, and especially the amount of reliance on self-care by older siblings, are associated with higher absenteeism, but this absenteeism is modified by the adequacy of the arrangements.

Resources

Resources, like demands, originate both in the workplace and within the family. The resources most commonly discussed in the literature include household income, work schedule flexibility, having an employed or nonemployed partner, ease of finding and continuing child-care arrangements, and satisfaction with child-care arrangements.

Household Income. Although income is generally thought of as a resource, the relationships between household income and child-care or work-family outcomes are often weak or negative. In 21 Kansas City, Missouri, companies, Vartuli and Stubbs (1986) found that higher household income was associated with higher job stress, higher absenteeism, and more use of out-of-home care, but also with less difficulty in combining work and family. Although some lower paying jobs may be high-stress occupations, they found an association between job stress and the responsibility, career pressure, and hours associated with many high-paying jobs. The negative effects of some occupations may thus outweigh any positive effects of having more money. In addition, some of the differences that appear to be positively related to family income may be a function of having a spouse who contributes a second income and additional caregiving resources.

Household income is a resource associated with the somewhat more frequent purchase of nonrelative child care outside the home (Dawson & Cain, 1990). In a statewide study of bank employees (Emlen, 1991), those with incomes of $50,000 or more were twice as likely to use center care (44% as compared to 20% for those with incomes less than $50,000), while family day care was used equally by employees with high ($50,000 or more) and low incomes (less than $25,000) and slightly more by employees whose household incomes were between $25,000 and $49,999.

Dependent-care resources may depend on the wealth of the community as well as on the household income of individual families; a limitation of behavioral studies of employees and their families is that the effect of the community context may not be taken into account sufficiently. Patterns of income or poverty may be geographically concentrated. A North Carolina study by Glasser (1991) has shown that urban and rural areas can differ dramatically in socioeconomic conditions that are associated with patterns of child care and working conditions. In Oregon, however, Emlen (1991) found that although regional differences in household income ranged from 75% to 125% of the statewide average, the variation was not on a rural-urban continuum; nevertheless, center care was scarce in the most rural counties, while family day care was ubiquitous. The presence of care alternatives is thus not simply a function of the wealth of the community.

Work Schedule Flexibility. The flexibility that employees need to balance their work and their family lives must come from family resources (such as the division of labor in the household), from the dependent-care resources found in the community, or from the workplace in the form of flexible schedules, part-time work, leave, or the ability to take time off for family emergencies. Research that compares the effects of alternative work schedules is inconclusive. Golembiewski, Hilles, and Kagno (1974) reviewed 17 studies of flextime, of which 16 reported beneficial effects. In a careful analysis of the flextime literature, however, Christensen and Staines (1990) concluded, "that flextime is beneficial in resolving work/family conflicts, but not as beneficial as often hoped" (p. 475). Still, they remained sanguine that better research will find more compelling evidence. They noted that "the notion of flexibility, and not the singularity of the flextime arrangement, should bear the burden of responding to work/family needs of employees" (p. 475).

Harrick, Vanek, and Michlitsch (1986) showed that alternative work schedules had a significant positive effect on reducing employee use of annual leave and sick leave, which resulted in more hours worked; individual productivity was not affected, however, nor was employee satisfaction with pay, working conditions, or supervision. Similarly, Kim and Campagna (1981) found that flextime did reduce unpaid absences of a short-term nature (for 2 hours or less a day) more strongly than long-term absence; it thus can serve as a substitute for brief absences. Although flextime is designed primarily to reapportion time, not reduce it, Winett, Neale, and Williams (1982) discovered that minimal flextime opportunities of an hour or less were used to go to work and return earlier, resulting in reduced commuting time and an increase in "quality time" spent in family, recreational, social, and chore-related situations. McGuire and Liro (1987) found that flextime reduced stress between work and nonwork aspects of life, but it was choice among staggered fixed schedules rather than a standard flextime schedule that was important.

In studying employees before and after parental leave, Bond (1987) found that, in firms that were family-friendly and accommodating, pregnant women employees missed fewer days due to illness during pregnancy than did those in nonresponsive firms. Trost (1989) reported a positive effect of parental leave on turnover rates at Aetna Life and Casualty Company; prior to the implementation of a family leave policy in 1988, 23% of new mothers chose to leave the firm as compared to 12% after the new benefit.

Steers and Rhodes (1978) cited unintended negative consequences of rigid attempts to ensure perfect attendance. Emlen (1987) found that the low absenteeism rates of some hospital employees were associated with higher levels of stress, while for others, some absenteeism was associated with low levels of perceived stress; thus, absenteeism appeared to serve as a safety valve.

Marital Status and Employment of Spouse or Partner. Perhaps the most powerful family resource for employed parents is either shared responsibility for child-care matters or a division of labor between parents and others in the family that favors whoever works the most hours outside the home. Of course, such sharing is affected strongly by the marital status and employment status of spouse or partner, as well as by the culture of parental roles. In commenting on the extreme divisions of labor that appeared to be associated with the management of child care, Emlen and Koren (1984) concluded,

> Absenteeism for men was low because the women's was high. In the division of labor, absenteeism was revealed not to be a "women's problem" but a family solution. It reflected who was carrying the child care responsibilities which made it possible for the employee to be at work and, more than half the time, for a spouse to be at work as well. (p. 6)

This assumption was confirmed by a subsequent survey of employees at a large western regional bank (Emlen, Koren, & Yoakum, 1990a), in which respondents were asked, "In your family, who takes responsibility for child-care arrangements?" A total of 5% of fathers and 79% of mothers said that they did completely or mostly, while 32% of fathers and 19% of mothers said that they shared equally. The percentage of fathers reporting shared responsibility reached 54% when wives or partners were employed full time, 25% when wives worked only part time, and 11% when wives were not employed.

Ease of Finding and Continuing Child-Care Arrangements. The capacity to find and maintain stable and satisfactory child-care arrangements was conceived in our predictive model as a key resource for employed parents. The absence of this resource means disruption of child-care arrangements and difficulty in finding child care in the community, which results not only in discontinuity of care for the child, but also has consequences for absenteeism and stress. In reporting the findings of the 1987 *Fortune Magazine* survey, Galinsky and Hughes (1987) wrote:

> We found that child care breakdown was significantly associated with higher levels of stress and stress-related symptoms such as shortness of breath, pounding or racing heart, back and neck pains, overeating, drinking more alcohol, smoking more, or taking more tranquilizers. . . . Only 17% of parents with no problem with child care breakdown reported feeling nervous and stressed *often* or *very often* over the past three months, as compared to 33% of the people who experienced more frequent breakdowns. (p. 4)

In the previous 3 months, 40% of the parents had experienced a breakdown in their child-care arrangements (Galinsky & Hughes, 1987). Shinn (1988) connected the disruption of child care to work-family conflict, saying, "By far the most important of any job or family predictors of work-family conflict was instability in child-care arrangements" (p. 3), which explained 13% of the variance in perceived stressors of work-family conflict and 9% of family interference with the job. A composite measure that included problems of finding and arranging child care, affording it, getting to it, and frequency of breakdowns in arrangements accounted for 29% of the variance of the work-family stressors, 12% of the variance of family interference with the job, and 9% of job interference with the family, before controlling for other variables (Shinn, 1988).

The instability of child-care arrangements appears to be part of an involved causal chain that precipitates and results from the difficulty of finding child care in the community. One half to two thirds of all employed parents surveyed in companies across the United States have reported that finding child care is difficult (Emlen, 1987). Moreover, employed mothers with children under age 12 who report difficulty in finding child care are:

> twice as likely to make arrangements with which they will be dissatisfied. They are also twice as likely to report worry or stress about child care, twice as likely to say that combining work and family responsibilities is difficult, and much more likely to feel that child care is difficult to continue or maintain. These difficulties reach the workforce in the form of lost time and stress. (Friedman, 1991, p. 13, citing Emlen, 1991)

Similarly, in two-parent families with young children, Love, Galinsky, and Hughes (1987) found an association between difficulty in finding child care and being absent more, between the breakdown of child-care arrangements and arriving late or leaving early, and between child-care breakdown (and dissatisfaction) and high levels of stress with negative physiological symptoms for both parents. As one of our survey respondents noted, "I'm old at 34. I truly believe that we need to do something about readily accessible child care. There was no greater stress to me in my life than scrambling for a caretaker."

Satisfaction With Care: Type and Quality of Child Care. Child care is most clearly a positive resource for employed parents when they have succeeded in making arrangements with which they are satisfied. Parental judgments of satisfaction are complex, reflecting such diverse elements as an assessment of its convenience, feelings about its cost, judgments about family relationships with the caregiver, and perceptions of the quality of care, including the appropriateness of the situation for a particular child (Powell & Bollin, 1992). In surveys of the work force (Emlen, Koren, & Yoakum, 1990a, 1990b), one third to one half of employed parents typically reported some degree of dissatisfaction with their current child-care arrangements for most types of care and for most ages of children.

Much of the research literature on child care addresses the issue of quality of care, which enters into our study of work-family relationships primarily through the eyes of parents, that is, through parents' reports of the stress they experience related to child care and their satisfaction with the child care that they have been able to arrange. Nevertheless, the general quality of care that is available to families in the community may have a greater effect on the balance of work and family than we have been able to measure in our model.

There appears to be wide variation in the quality of care provided within each of the major types of child care, whether centers (Whitebrook, Howes, & Phillips, 1989), family day care (Pence & Goelman, 1991), relatives, care at home, or self-care by a child. Few work-family issues are more disturbing than those related to the quality of care, and few have attracted more interest from researchers and the public (Cooke, London, Edwards, & Rose-Lizee, 1986; Galinsky, 1986; Hayes, Palmer, & Zaslow, 1990; National Commission on Children, 1991; Phillips, 1987). Yet despite researchers' partial knowledge of what characterizes quality of care, questions that remain unanswered include how well care is provided by caregivers, how well consumers understand it and are willing to pay for it, or how well the community is able and willing to support it.

Among family day-care providers, Pence and Goelman (1991) found professional motivations, specific training, and licensing to be associated with quality of care, as measured by the best-documented scales. They lamented, however, the "increasing barrenness" of neighborhoods where isolation, loneliness, and skill deficiencies beset the remaining caregivers. The quality of care in child-care centers, as reflected in developmental gains for children, was found by Ruopp, Travers, Glantz, and Coelen (1979) to be associated with group size in classrooms, adult-child ratio, and quality of staff. Since these variables affect the cost as well as the quality of care, the prospects for quality of care have remained bleak. A more recent national study of centers (Whitebrook, Howes, & Phillips, 1989) found discontinuity in staffing to be associated with the low salaries that prevail in centers. Fuchs and Coleman (1991) provided a dismal view of the economics of achieving quality of care in their conclusion that "there is simply no way simultaneously to hold down the cost of care, reduce the child/worker ratio, and increase the pay and qualifications of child-care workers" (p. 79).

In a national study comparing child-care providers of the 1970s with those of 1990, both in centers and in family day care, Kisker et al. (1991) found that although the educational levels of preschool teachers had improved, other indicators of quality of care had declined, such as turnover rates and the average group size in both centers and regulated family day care.

Summarizing the effects of work and family resources for employees with child-care responsibilities, as revealed in the research literature:

1. Although higher household income is presumably a resource that facilitates managing work and family, its effects are mixed due to concomitant conditions associated with higher income. The price often paid by those in higher-paid occupations is high job stress, yet the perquisites enjoyed often include greater flexibility in work schedules.

2. Extensive experimentation with flextime work schedules points to the superiority of no particular alternative schedule, but rather to flexibilities associated with choice of schedule and the ability of employees to adapt work schedules to family needs. More clearly supported by research are the beneficial effects of having flexibility to respond to emergencies.

3. Among family resources, most powerful are the differential effects of division of labor, or shared responsibility, which depends in large part on marital status and the employment status of the spouse or partner.

4. The capacity to find and maintain stable and satisfactory child-care arrangements is a resource of well-documented importance, primarily due to negative effects of disrupted and unstable care on employees' work and family lives.

5. This capacity is heavily dependent on the child-care resources that exist in the community, as is satisfaction with the child-care arrangements that employees have been able to find.

The Relative Contribution of Alternative Forms of Child Care in the Balance of Work-Family Demands and Resources. As a final summary of the research literature, it may be useful to think about one question constantly asked by employers. That question concerns the extent of the effect of different types of child-care arrangements on workplace outcomes such as absenteeism. Emlen (1987) summarized this effect based on a comparison of the number of days missed by subgroups of employees:

In a workforce that overall misses about 9 days per year, on the average, men employees who have no children miss 7½ days. Add to that ½ day for being a father, 1 day for out-of-home care, or 5½ days if the kids are looking after themselves. The men are now up to 13½ days per year. Women employees, even without kids, start out at 9½ days, having lost a couple of days more than men per year probably because of a division of labor in which they assume more family responsibilities in general. Add 2 days if the kids are in care outside the home, or 3½ if they are looking after themselves. The mothers are at 13 days per year—nearly up to the fathers whose kids look after themselves. Add another 3 days if she is a single parent having no one with whom to share parental responsibilities. If she's management she'll miss a day or two less, but she'll be late to work more often, because her job will allow it. Having a family income of $30,000 or more, as compared to less, saves women in management and professional positions nearly two days, or ½ for women who are not. The income difference saves men 1 day at either occupational level. Take off several days if company policies clamp down on absenteeism, but add stress. (p. 3)

This review of the research literature highlights the problems, difficulties, conflicts, and stresses of balancing work and family for employees who have children under the age of 18 in their households. It should be noted, however, that most employees with children manage successfully most of the time. In the survey reported in this book, approximately three quarters of employed parents report that they do have the flexibility they need to respond to child-care emergencies and family matters; two-thirds say they do not have difficulty in balancing working with family responsibilities.

The averages, however, mask sharp differences in circumstances between those for whom balancing work and family is easy and those for whom it is difficult. Because these averages are based on samples of those who do currently manage to combine work, family, and dependent care in one way or another, they also omit those who have dropped out of the labor force, or have never entered it, in order to provide child care. The data also do not depict those who have postponed or passed up childbearing in order to pursue a career. Schwartz (1989), for example, reported that 65% of executive women and 10% of executive men did not have children by age 40.

The remainder of this chapter uses our survey data to help understand the conditions under which employed parents have difficulty managing both their work and child-care responsibilities.

ANALYSIS OF SURVEY RESULTS

Description of the Sample. The purpose of the analyses reported here was to explore how absenteeism and stress, including difficulty in combining work and family, were affected by the demands and resources arising from both work and family life for employees with children at home. The sample in these analyses included only those employees with children under the age of 18 in their households—a total of 4,422 employees.

Of the 4,422 employees, 56% had children under age 9 (i.e., the age for whom child-care arrangements are most likely to be made), and 60% had children aged 9 to 17. These are the children who are most likely to be in before- or after-school programs or to be looking after themselves and possibly a younger brother or sister. A total of 16% of the sample of employed parents had children in both age categories. About 29% of the families with children under age 9 also had a child aged 9 to 17. The average number of children under age 18 was 1.7. The percentage of families reporting having children with a disability was 2.3%.

Two thirds of all families with children under age 18 used some kind of out-of-home child-care arrangements or activity other than school. Table 3.1 shows the percentages of parents of children under age 18 using the different kinds of child care. These percentages total 154% because families make multiple child-care arrangements. The patterns of child care varied widely by age of child, of course. Among parents with children under age 9 who use either family day care or centers, half were using a total of 45 hours per week or more of out-of-home care, and 21% were spending 10% or more of their household income on it.

The typical employee with children in the household was only slightly more likely to be female than male (56% female) and was slightly younger than the total sample of employees (37.7 years of age). Of all employees with children in the household, 17% were single parents, and another 17% had a nonemployed partner available to provide child care. Most employees with children in the household (90%) were employed full time, although 81% reported that they had at least some flexibility in their schedules to handle child-care responsibilities. Most were caring only for children; nonetheless, one fifth (21%) were caring for one or more elders, and 3% were caring for adults with disabilities.

To explore the factors that influence absenteeism and stress for such employees, we analyzed the findings from our study using hierarchical multiple regression analysis. The independent variables in the analyses reported here parallel those around which the literature review was organized and include personal characteristics, work and family demands, and work and family resources. These three sets of independent variables were entered in three separate blocks. First, the personal characteristics of the employee (gender, age, ethnicity, and occupation) were entered into the equation. Next, the demand variables (hours worked, job shift, number of children under the age of 9, number of caregiving roles [child, adult, elder], extra travel time to child care, age of youngest child, having a child with a disability, child-care cost as a percentage of household income, and total hours of out-of-home child care) were entered. Finally, the resource variables (household income, work schedule flexibility, having an employed partner, having a nonemployed partner, number of children aged 9 to 17, having a child in self-care, informal child-care support from kin, ease in finding and continuing child care, and satisfaction with child care) were entered into the equation. As with the other caregiver groups examined in this book, there were six dependent measures: three forms of absenteeism and three forms of stress. This approach allowed us to test whether the resources were able

TABLE 3.1   Percentages of Parents of Children Under 18 Using Various Kinds
of Child Care

Child Care	Percentage
At home with a relative	25
At home with someone else who	
comes in (mostly nonrelatives)	6
At home in self-care or with a sibling	37
In someone else's home	27
In a child-care center	17
In other group activities	42

Note: Percentages total more than 100 because families make multiple child-care arrangments.

to reduce or eliminate the absenteeism and stress that we expected to
be associated with work and family demands.

The findings from the multiple regression analyses are shown in
Tables 3.2 and 3.3. Altogether, the predictors in the model accounted
for 3% of the days missed, 9% of instances of arriving late or leaving early,
8% of interruptions at work, 5% of personal health stress, 36% of caregiving stress, and 28% of difficulty in combining working with family
responsibilities.

The tables in Chapters 3 through 7 summarize the results of these analyses in a form that is relatively easy for the reader to review. Pluses
indicate a direct (positive) relationship between the predictor and the
outcome. Minuses indicate an inverse (negative) relationship between
the two variables. The full results are contained in the tables in Appendix B (Tables 3.2B and 3.3B), which report the standardized regression
coefficients (betas) associated with each variable.

Personal Characteristics

In terms of absenteeism, the personal characteristics of the employees, by themselves, accounted for only 2% of days missed, 3% of instances
of either arriving late or leaving early, and 1% of family-related interruptions on the job. The most consistent predictors of absenteeism were
gender, age, and occupation of the employee.

Gender made the strongest contribution to the three outcome variables
measuring absenteeism, with mothers having more work time loss of all
kinds than fathers; the effect of gender was later reduced by the introduction of work and family demands and resources. Specifically, the

TABLE 3.2 Effects of Personal Characteristics, Caregiving Demands, and Caregiving Resources on Absenteeism Among Employees With Child-Care Responsibilities

	Absenteeism Variables								
	Days Missed			Late or Left Early			Interruptions		
Step entered regression:	1	2	3	1	2	3	1	2	3
Predictors									
Personal Characteristics									
Gender (female)	+	+	+	+	+	+	+	+	
Age of employee				−	−	−			−
Ethnicity (white)									+
Occupation (professional)			+	+	+				
Change in R^2 at Step 1	.02			.03			.01		
Demands									
Hours worked	−						+	+	
Shift (days)				+	+		+	+	
Number of children under age 9									
Number of caregiving roles					+		+	+	
Extra travel time for child care				+	+		+	+	
Age of youngest child									
Child with disability	+	+							
Child care cost as % of household income									
Total hours of out-of-home care	+	+					−		
Change in R^2 at Step 2	.01			.03			.03		
Resources									
Household income			−			+			+
Work schedule flexibility						+			+
Working partner			+			−			−
Nonworking partner						−			
Number of children aged 9 to 17									+
Child has self-care arrangement									+
Informal support from kin									
Ease finding/continuing child care						−			−
Satisfaction with care						−			−
Change in R^2 at Step 3	.01			.04			.04		
Total R^2/R^2 Adjusted	.04/.03			.10/.09			.09/.08		
Overall F	6.04**			16.35**			13.73**		
Df (reg./res.) 22,3179									

Note: Based on standardized betas; "+" indicates a significant positive relationship; "−" indicates a significant inverse relationship.
* $p \le .05$; ** $p \le .01$.

TABLE 3.3 Effects of Personal Characteristics, Caregiving Demands, and Caregiving Resources on Stress Variables Among Employees With Child-Care Responsibilities

	Stress Variables								
	Personal Health Stress			Caregiving Stress			Difficulty Combining Work and Family		
Step entered regression:	1	2	3	1	2	3	1	2	3
Predictors									
Personal Characteristics									
Gender (female)	+	+	+	+	+		+	+	+
Age of employee	+	+	+	−			−		
Ethnicity									
Occupation (professional)				+	+	+			
Change in R^2 at Step 1	.02			.07			.06		
Demands									
Hours worked								+	
Shift (days)					−				
Number of children under age 9					−				
Number of caregiving roles		+	+		+	+		+	+
Extra travel time for child care					+	+		+	+
Age of youngest child					−	−		−	
Child with disability								+	
Child-care cost as % of household income		+			+	+		+	
Total hours of out-of-home care									+
Change in R^2 at Step 2	.01			.10			.04		
Resources									
Household income									
Work schedule flexibility			−			−			−
Working partner									
Nonworking partner						−			
Number of children aged 9 to 17									
Child has self-care arrangement						−			−
Informal support from kin						+			
Ease finding/continuing care			−			−			−
Satisfaction with care			−			−			−
Change in R^2 at Step 3	.03			.19			.18		
Total R^2/R^2 Adjusted	.06/.05			.36/.36			.28/.28		
Overall F	8.86**			82.06**			58.25**		
Df (reg./res.) 22,3217									

Note: Based on standardized betas; "+" indicates a significant positive relationship; "−" indicates a significant inverse relationship.
* $p \le .05$; ** $p \le .01$

independent effect of gender on work interruptions disappeared at step 3, with the introduction of predictors related to child-care resources. Younger employees were more likely to arrive at work late or leave early, and they were also more likely to be interrupted at work. Professional and managerial employees were more likely than other workers to miss days of work (step 3 only) and to arrive late or leave early (steps 1 and 2 only). (For an explanation of why variables are significant predictors at some steps but not others, see end of Chapter 2, Approach to Data Analysis section.)

There was only one significant contribution of ethnicity to any of the outcomes. White employees had more work interruptions (after accounting for demands and resources), perhaps because they were more likely to have jobs permitting interruptions on the job.

Among the dependent variables measuring stress, personal characteristics of the employees accounted for 2% of the variance in personal health stress, 7% of caregiving stress, and 6% of the difficulty in combining work and family. The most consistent predictors of stress were gender and age, followed by occupation.

Female employees showed consistently more personal health stress, caregiving stress, and difficulty in combining work and family, although the size of the effect tended to decrease somewhat as work and family resources were entered into the equation at step 3. Indeed, gender was no longer a significant predictor of caregiving stress at the third step, after including resources such as ease in finding and maintaining child-care arrangements, satisfaction with child-care arrangements, and flexibility in the employee's administrative unit to deal with family-related problems. The effectiveness of these resources may reflect gender differences in the division of labor regarding the carrying out of child-care responsibilities. Although gender effects disappeared or were reduced in the analysis, this does not mean that gender was not important; rather, gender was correlated with resources and demands, which in turn influenced the outcomes.

The age of employed parents was related to their personal health stress; that is, employed parents experienced more health stress with age. Younger parents experienced more caregiving stress and difficulty in combining work and family, although these effects disappeared when demands and resources were entered into the analysis. One personal characteristic found to be predictive only of higher child-care stress was occupation, with employees who were in professional, technical, management, or administrative positions reporting more stress than other employees.

Demands

Work and family demands were entered into the analyses at step 2. These demands accounted for 1% of days missed, 3% of instances of arriving late or leaving early, 3% of the number of interruptions at work, 1% of personal health stress, 10% of caregiving stress, and 4% of the difficulty in combining work and family.

The most consistent demand predictors of absenteeism were job shift and extra travel time for child care. Working days rather than other shifts was related to increased lateness, early leaving, and interruptions at work. The extra travel time required for child-care arrangements over and beyond the time it took to get to work also predicted being late or leaving work early and interruptions on the job.

Employees with more than one caregiving role were significantly more likely to be interrupted at work (steps 2 and 3 only) and to arrive late or leave early (step 3 only). The number of hours worked per week predicted more job interruptions but fewer days missed from work, although the latter relationship disappeared when resources entered the analysis (i.e., at step 3). Another caregiving demand that influenced absenteeism was having a child with a disability, which increased the days of work missed. Similarly, the total number of hours of child care arranged outside the home in centers or family day-care homes added to the demands on parents to arrange care. This variable predicted missing more days from work, but fewer job interruptions; the latter effect disappeared after accounting for resources. Two demand variables did not influence any form of absenteeism: age of the youngest child and child-care cost as a percentage of household income.

Among the demands that predicted the stress outcomes, the number of caregiving roles was clearly the most consistent. Our data indicated that those parents who had other caregiving responsibilities in addition to their children (i.e., child care plus elder care or care for an adult with a disability) experienced more stress regarding their own health, more caregiving stress regarding their child-care arrangements, and more difficulty in combining working with their family responsibilities. All of these relationships remained significant even after the resource predictors were considered.

The next most consistent demand predictor of stress was the extra travel time required for child-care arrangements, which was associated with increased child-care stress and difficulty in combining working with family responsibilities. Child-care cost to the family as a percentage of household income was also a relatively consistent predictor of stress. Although this measure of child-care affordability was not predictive of any of the absenteeism outcomes, it was predictive of all of the stress outcomes. The relationship between percentage of household income spent on child care and child-care stress remained significant after including the resource predictors at step 3. At the same time, although percentage of income used for child care was predictive of both health stress and difficulty in combining work and family, these effects disappeared at step 3 when resources were taken into account.

The younger the youngest child, the more likely the employee was to experience both caregiving stress and difficulty in combining work and family, although the latter effect was not significant at step 3. The other demand variables had quite scattered relationships with stress. Employees using more hours of out-of-home care experienced more difficulty in combining work and family (step 3 only). In addition, four variables were significantly associated with one of the stress variables, but the effect disappeared when resources were entered. Specifically, the number of hours worked was related to increased difficulty combining work and family; working a day shift and having more children under the age of 9 was associated with decreased caregiving stress; and having a child with a disability was related to increased difficulty in combining work and family.

In summary, two demand variables stood out in predicting both stress and absenteeism. These variables were having multiple caregiving roles and traveling greater distances to deliver children to child care.

Resources

Including the resource predictors for employees with children (i.e., step 3 of the analyses) added substantially to the percentage of variance accounted for in the outcome measures, depending on the outcome variable: 1% of the variance of days missed, 4% of arriving late or leaving early, 4% of job interruptions, 3% of personal health stress, 19% of child-care stress, and 18% of difficulty in combining work and family.

Perhaps the most interesting finding, theoretically as well as practically, was the way that resources, which were entered last after controlling for personal characteristics and demands, removed a number of the significant contributions by demand predictors at step 2. For at least one of the outcome variables, these demands included the number of hours worked, job shift worked, number of children under the age of 9, age of youngest child, cost of child care as a percentage of household income, having a child with a disability, and number of hours of out-of-home care. Only two demands—specifically, number of caregiving roles and extra travel time for child care—remained consistently significant after resources were entered.

In terms of absenteeism, the resources that were most consistently associated with the absenteeism outcomes were household income and having a partner who was also employed. Having a working spouse or partner was related to more days missed, but to fewer late arrivals, early departures, or job interruptions. Fewer late arrivals and early departures were also associated with having a nonworking spouse or partner. It would thus appear that shared responsibility reduced at least minor types of time loss. Household income had similar contradictory effects. High income was related to fewer days missed but also to more frequent lateness, early leaving, and job interruptions, presumably because such income was associated with jobs that tolerated minor episodes of time loss.

Resource variables that significantly predicted two of the three absenteeism measures included work schedule flexibility, ease in finding and continuing child care, and satisfaction with child care. Having flexible work schedules, personnel policies, and management practices for dealing with child-care problems in one's department or unit—a work resource—did not predict the number of days missed but was related to increased time loss in the form of lateness, early leaving, and job interruptions. The rates of time loss reflected tolerance of and support for dealing with child-care emergencies. Ease of finding and continuing child care and satisfaction with that care were both associated with fewer instances of arriving late, leaving early, and being interrupted at work.

Some resources predicted only one type of absenteeism; these included having a nonworking partner, the number of children between the ages of 9 and 17, and having a child with a self-care arrangement. Fewer instances of arriving late or leaving early were related to having a nonemployed spouse, as mentioned earlier. The number of children between ages 9 and 17 made no contribution to the absenteeism outcomes except to increase work interruptions. The use of self-care was also a predictor of work interruptions.

In terms of stress, three resources were consistently related to the stress outcomes for employees caring for children: work schedule flexibility, ease of finding and continuing child care, and satisfaction with child-care arrangements. All three of these variables functioned as predicted, reducing all three kinds of stress. In other words, the variables most consistently associated with reduced stress were likely to be influenced more heavily by the resources available at work and in the community than by family resources.

The variable of being able to rely on older children to care for themselves was related to both reduced child-care stress and the difficulty that employees experienced in combining work and family. Two additional variables were significantly associated with one form of stress each. Specifically, having a nonworking partner was related to reduced child-care stress, wheras receiving informal support from kin was associated with increased caregiving stress.

Finally, three resource variables were not significant predictors of any of the three stress variables: household income, having a working partner, and the number of children aged 9 to 17. Although household income had a significant impact on absenteeism, it made no contribution to parents' health stress, child-care stress, or difficulty in combining work and family. This might seem perplexing, but it should be noted that the predictive model already included, as a demand predictor at step 2, the cost of child care as a percentage of household income. Those percentages increased sharply for employed parents when household incomes dropped below around $30,000, because expenditures for child care did not drop as quickly as income dropped (Emlen et al., 1990b).

The fact that children between the ages of 9 and 17, who were expected to be a resource in caring for younger children, did not function as such might also appear puzzling. A number of the respondents to our survey pointed out, however, that child-care stress does not necessarily end when children are able to stay by themselves. One said:

> We went through many problems due to poor choices by the boys and lack of supervision before I got home. Those were the most stressful years—so far—of my life. I feel strongly that teenagers today require equally as much supervision as toddlers do.

DISCUSSION

These analyses demonstrate the power of resources from both work and family spheres of activity to make a critical difference in assisting employed parents to cope with the stress of dealing with child care while pursuing employment and career. Demands such as the number of hours worked, the shift worked, the number of caregiving roles, the age of the employee's youngest child, the cost of care as a percentage of household income, and having a child with a disability all registered negative effects on stress before taking family and work resources into account. However, with respect to the stress outcomes, many of these effects disappeared when also measuring the effects of major caregiving and workplace resources, including ease in finding and continuing child care, satisfaction with child-care arrangements, and work schedule flexibility. Only the number of caregiving roles an employed parent was trying to carry and the extra travel time required for child care were demands whose effects on personal health stress and/or difficulty combining work and family were not decreased or neutralized by family and work resources. Having work and family resources did not, however, decrease or neutralize the negative effects on absenteeism of the above-listed demands.

Having flexible work schedules, personnel policies, and management practices for dealing with child-care problems in one's department or unit—a work resource—did not predict the number of days missed but was related to increased time loss in the form of lateness, early leaving, and job interruptions. This finding supports research showing that flextime reduces short-term absence (Kim & Campagna, 1981); it reveals that some absenteeism, especially minor, short-term episodes of time loss, may also be viewed as a positive outcome, reflecting an informal policy that allows for time off to deal with child-care problems and other family emergencies. Ease in finding, continuing, or managing child care appeared to prevent the subtler forms of time loss from absenteeism, as did having found a child-care arrangement with which the parent was satisfied.

The findings from these analyses are largely consistent with existing research literature on the impact of having children on employees' work and on employees' ability to combine working with family responsibilities. Of special interest, however, is evidence of the moderating effects of resources from within the family and from the workplace. In particular, the presence of a partner with whom to share child-care responsibility and having a flexible work schedule made their mark in the reduction of stress and work-family conflict, and absenteeism itself appeared to be an informal form of work-schedule flexibility used by employees in some occupations.

REFERENCES

Bond, J. T. (1987). *Accommodating pregnancy in the workplace* (Report No. 1-4). New York: National Council of Jewish Women, Center for the Child.

Burden, D. S., & Googins, B. K. (1987). *Boston University balancing job and homelife study.* Paper presented at a symposium of the Conference Board on Workplace Research on the Family, Boston University School of Social Work, Boston.

Christensen, K. E., & Staines, G. L. (1990). Flextime: A viable turnover: A methodological critique and an empirical study. *Journal of Applied Psychology, 68*(1), 88-101.

Cooke, K., London, J., Edwards, R., & Rose-Lizee, R. (1986). *Report of the task force on child care.* Ottawa: Canada Government Publishing Centre.

Costa, N. D. (1988, March). *Work and family life studies: Highlights of work in progress.* A paper presented at a symposium of the Conference Board on Workplace Research on the Family, Arden House, New York.

Dawson, D. A., & Cain, V. S. (1990). *Child care arrangements: Health of our nation's children, United States, 1988* (DHHS Publication No. PHS 90-1250). Hyattsville, MD: National Center for Health Statistics.

Deiner, P. L. (1992). Family day care and children with disabilities. In D. L. Peters & A. R. Pence (Eds.), *Family day care: Current research for informed public policy.* New York: Teachers College Press.

Emlen, A. C. (1987, August). *Child care, work, and family.* Panel presentation at the annual convention of the American Psychological Association, New York.

Emlen, A. C. (1991, May). *Rural child care policy: Does Oregon have one? 1991 legislative discussion paper.* Legislative Discussion Series. Rural Policy Research Group (Oregon State University, University of Oregon, Oregon Economic Development Department). Obtain by writing to author at Regional Research Institute for Human Services, Portland State University, P.O. Box 751, Portland, OR 97207-0741.

Emlen, A. C., & Koren, P. E. (1984). *Hard to find and difficult to manage: The effects of child care on the workplace.* Portland, OR: Portland State University, Regional Research Institute for Human Services.

Emlen, A. C., & Koren, P. E. (1988, March). *New findings on the affordability issue.* Paper presented at a symposium of the Conference Board on Workplace Research on the Family, Boston University School of Social Work, Boston.

Emlen, A. C., Koren, P. E., & Yoakum, K. S. (1990a). *1989 dependent care survey: U.S. Bancorp.* Portland, OR: Arthur Emlen & Associates, Inc., and Portland State University, Regional Research Institute for Human Services.

Emlen, A. C., Koren, P. E., & Yoakum, K. S. (1990b). *1990 dependent care survey: 15 employers of Lane County, Oregon.* Portland, OR: Arthur Emlen & Associates, Inc., and Portland State University, Regional Research Institute for Human Services.

Fernandez, J. (1986). *Child care and corporate productivity: Resolving family/work conflicts.* Lexington, MA: Lexington Books.

Friedman, D. E. (1991). *Linking work-family issues to the bottom line* (Report No. 962). New York: The Conference Board.

Fuchs, V. R., & Coleman, M. (1991, Winter). Small children, small pay: Why child care pays so little. *The American Prospect,* pp. 74-79.

Galinsky, E. (1986). *Investing in quality child care: A report for AT&T.* Short Hills, NJ: AT&T Human Resources Organization.

Galinsky, E. (1988, March). *Child care and productivity.* Paper presented at the Child Care Action Campaign Conference on Child Care and the Bottom Line, New York.

Galinsky, E., & Hughes, D. (1987). *The Fortune Magazine child care study.* New York: Bank Street College.

Glasser, F. (1991). Rural child care. *Popular Government, 56*(3), 10-18.

Goff, S. J., Mount, M. K., & Jamison, R. L. (1990). Employer supported child care, work/family conflict, and absenteeism: A field study. *Personnel Psychology, 43,* 793-809.

Golembiewski, R. T., Hilles, R., & Kagno, M. S. (1974). A longitudinal study of flex-time effects: Some consequences of an OD structural intervention. *Journal of Applied Behavioral Science, 10,* 503-532.

Gunter, N. C., & Gunter, B. G. (1990). Domestic division of labor among working couples: Does androgyny make a difference? *Psychology of Women Quarterly, 14,* 355-370.

Harrick, E. J., Vanek, G. R., & Michlitsch, J. F. (1986). Alternate work schedules, productivity, leave usage, and employee attitudes: A field study. *Public Personnel Management, 15*(2), 159-169.

Hayes, C. D., Palmer, J. L., & Zaslow, M. J. (1990). *Who cares for America's children: Child care policy for the 1990's.* Washington, DC: National Academy Press.

Hedges, J. N. (1973). Absence from work—A look at some national data. *Monthly Labor Review, 96,* 24-30.

Kim, J. S., & Campagna, A. F. (1981). Effects of flexitime on employee attendance and performance: A field experiment. *Academy of Management Journal, 24,* 729-741.

Kisker, E. E., Hofferth, S. L., Phillips, D. A., & Farquhar, E. (1991). *A profile of child care settings: Early education and care in 1990* (Vol. 1). Princeton, NJ: Mathematica Policy Research.

Kisker, E. E., Maynard, R., Gordon, A., & Strain, M. (1989). *The child care challenge: What parents need and what is available in three metropolitan areas.* Princeton, NJ: Mathematica Policy Research.

Klein, B. W. (1986). Missed work and lost hours, May 1985. *Monthly Labor Review, 109*(10), 26-30.

Kossek, E. E. (1990). Diversity in child care assistance needs: Employee problems, preferences, and work-related outcomes. *Personnel Psychology, 43,* 769-791.

Love, M., Galinsky, E., & Hughes, D. (1987). Work and family: Research findings and models for change. *ILR Report, 25*(1), 10-12.

Marlow, C. (1990). Management of family and employment responsibilities by Mexican American and Anglo American women. *Social Work, 35*(3), 259-265.

Marquant, J. M. (1988). *A pattern-matching approach to link program theory and evaluation data: The case of employer-sponsored child care.* Unpublished doctoral dissertation, Cornell University, Ithaca, NY.

McGuire, J. B., & Liro, J. R. (1987). Absenteeism and flexible work schedules. *Public Personnel Management, 16*(1), 47-59.

Milkovich, G. T., & Gomez, L. R. (1976). Day care and selected employee work behaviors. *Academy of Management Journal, 19,* 111-115.

National Commission on Children. (1991). *Beyond rhetoric: A new American agenda for children and families.* Washington, DC: National Commission on Children.

Pence, A. R., & Goelman, H. (1991). The relationship of regulation, training, and motivation to quality of care in family day care. *Child & Youth Care Forum, 20*(2), 83-101.

Phillips, D. A. (Ed.). (1987). *Quality in child care: What does research tell us?* Washington, DC: National Association for the Education of Young Children.

Pleck, J. H. (1985). *Working wives/working husbands.* Beverly Hills, CA: Sage.

Porwoll, P. J. (1980). *Employee absenteeism: A summary of research.* Arlington, VA: Educational Research Service.

Powell, D. R., & Bollin, G. (1992). Dimensions of parent-provider relationships in family day care. In D. L. Peters & A. R. Pence (Eds.), *Family day care: Current research for informed public policy.* New York: Teachers College Press.

Ransom, C., Aschbacher, P., & Burud, S. (1989). The return in the child-care investment. *Personnel Administrator, 34*(10), 54-58.

Ruopp, R., Travers, J., Glantz, F., & Coelen, C. (1979). *Children at the center: Summary findings and their implications* (Vol. 1). Cambridge, MA: Abt.

Schenet, N. G. (1945). An analysis of absenteeism in one war plant. *Journal of Applied Psychology, 29,* 27-39.

Schwartz, F. N. (1989). Management women and the new facts of life. *Harvard Business Review, 89,* 65-76.

Scott, K. D., & McClellan, E. L. (1990). Gender differences in absenteeism. *Public Personnel Management, 19*(2), 229-253.

Shinn, M. (1988, March). *Predicting work-family conflict for working parents.* Paper presented at a symposium of the Conference Board on Workplace Research on the Family.

Staines, G. L., & Pleck, J. H. (1983). *The impact of work schedules on the family.* Ann Arbor: University of Michigan Press.

Steers, R. M., & Rhodes, S. R. (1978). Major influences on employee attendance: A process model. *Journal of Applied Psychology, 63*(4), 391-407.

Strohmer, A. (1988). *Returns on investment for corporations investing in child care.* New York: Child Care Action Campaign.

Trost, C. (1989, December 19). Labor letter: A special news report on people and their jobs in offices, fields and factories. *Wall Street Journal,* p. A1.

Vartuli, S., & Stubbs, S. (1986). *Metropolitan child care project: Final Report.* Kansas City: Missouri University, School of Education. (ERIC Document Reproduction Service No. ED 277 450)

Whitebrook, M. C., Howes, C., & Phillips, D. A. (1989). *Who cares? Child care teachers and the quality of care in America* (Final Report). Oakland, CA: Child Care Employee Project.

Winett, R. A., Neale, M. S., & Williams, K. R. (1982). The effects of flexible work schedules on urban families with young children: Quasi-experimental, ecological studies. *American Journal of Community Psychology, 10*(1), 49-64.

Youngblood, S. A., & Chambers-Cook, K. (1984). Child care assistance can improve employee attitudes and behavior. *Personnel Administrator, 29*(2), 45-46, 93-95.

4

Employees Who Care for Adults With Disabilities

> When dealing with an ill or disabled adult over 21 who is young and does not qualify for Medicare or related services from the elderly there seems to be NO HELP. This is not a big enough group to have recognized needs, and over and over again it seemed to fall between the cracks. The [employer] doesn't have support services or even counseling available about what the process is when dealing with disability. My husband returned to work too early after his first round with cancer—we know it now but at the time we felt we had no choice. He was not working and struggled terribly—I think it is why he never got well, eventually ended up with a life threatening recurrence. No one came forward to explain disability—use of sick leave—what happened IF you couldn't work or you shouldn't. It took him almost dying and being totally disabled for us to find things out and then when it first happened, no one helped until the transition. He is getting close to wellness now, but probably will not be able to work a full day ever again, and the transition to work is equally vague and no one seems to have answers about partial disabled work obligation. . . . The future is muddy.

The situation of those who provide care to adults with disabilities can be particularly difficult, since such caregivers often comprise an over-looked group. The woman in the above illustration was caring for her spouse, but other caregivers of adults with disabilities care for an adult child or a sibling. These individuals may have been disabled from birth or have become disabled later in life through accident or disease.

Several aspects of caring for adults with disabilities differ from other caregiving situations. First, caregivers of adult children may be aging and experiencing their own frailty even while they are wondering who will care for their offspring (Cohler, Pickett, & Cook, 1991). Second, if the care recipient is a spouse, the disability may prohibit him or her from maintaining a job (Carpenter, 1974); thus, in addition to increased responsibilities, the caregiver may lose an accustomed source of financial support. Third, providing care to an adult is a nonnormative experience. Although caring for young children and perhaps even older relatives is anticipated, caring for an adult with disabilities is not an expected occurrence. This kind of off-time caregiving does not fit with our "social clock" (Neugarten, 1968, p. 143). It may feel particularly burdensome to be caring for an adult while peers are enjoying freedom and flexibility.

In this chapter, we focus on the factors involved in caring for an adult with disabilities. In the first part, we provide an overview of findings concerning the caregivers of adults with disabilities in general, followed by a summary of the small literature that considers such caring within the context of employment. Three populations of adults with disabilities are considered: those with chronic physical disabilities, those with developmental disabilities, and those with chronic mental illness. In the second part, we turn to the results from our survey to explore predictors of stress and absenteeism among employed caregivers of adults with disabilities.

LITERATURE ON CAREGIVERS OF ADULTS WITH DISABILITIES

There has thus far been minimal empirical work regarding employed caregivers of adults with disabilities. In fact, this body of literature has lagged significantly behind the work on the employed caregivers of children and of elderly persons. Using our conceptual model, the following section discusses the variables that predict caregiver absenteeism and stress within the context of personal characteristics, demands, and resources.

Personal Characteristics

The bulk of the research on caregivers of adults with disabilities falls within the category of personal characteristics. According to Biegel, Sales, and Schulz (1991), who conducted an extensive literature review on caregivers of those with chronic illnesses, demographic factors are the workhorse variables of social science. Because they are easily measured and predictive of many other outcomes, they tend to be included in most research studies. Therefore, it is no surprise that health researchers have examined a variety of caregiver background factors expected to predict distress. (pp. 204-205)

Gender. A fairly consistent finding among caregivers of adults with disabilities is that women report greater distress than do men. For example, in a study of patients undergoing chemotherapy and their spouses (Leiber, Plumb, Gerstenzang, & Holland, 1976), patients' wives reported more depressive symptoms than did patients' husbands. In addition, among spouses of chronically ill middle-aged persons, wives experienced poorer psychological adjustment than did husbands (Foxall, Ekberg, & Griffith, 1985). Similar findings have emerged from research on caring for a mentally ill adult child. In research conducted on parents who lived with their mentally ill children, most of whom were in their twenties, mothers experienced considerable distress: They felt more anxious, depressed, fearful, and emotionally drained than fathers (Cook, 1988). Fathers tended to be highly critical of their offspring with disabilities, but they experienced low levels of burden (Cook & Pickett, 1987-1988).

Such gender differences may be attributed in part to the differences in the kinds of care provided by men and women. A study by Stetz (1987) of adults with cancer suggested that men and women are attuned to different spheres of caregiving. Although both male and female caregivers were concerned about day-to-day financial and household management, wives were also concerned about trying to improve their husbands' condition. Perhaps the spheres of caregiving to which women attend exact "higher psychosocial costs" than do those attended to by men (Biegel et al., 1991, p. 97).

Alternative interpretations for gender differences in levels of stress have been proposed. Biegel et al. (1991) noted that on measures of psychological stress, women generally score higher than men, regardless of whether or not they are caregivers. It may be that women generally experience more stress and depression than men or that women are more comfortable expressing such feelings. Alternatively, Rustad (1984) suggested that the nurturant orientation that men often develop in later life contributes toward gratification with the role of caregiver. Similarly, Biegel et al. (1991, citing Williamson & Schulz, 1990) proposed that older men may be more sustained by their caregiving activities because they are repaying for care that they had received in the past.

Age. Findings pertaining to the effect of the caregiver's age on stress are less consistent. In their literature review, Biegel et al. (1991) concluded that among caregivers of patients with cancer, younger spouses had more emotional difficulties, whereas older spouses had more problems with the physical demands of the caregiving tasks. For the caregivers of adults disabled by stroke, adjustment by age was related to the phase of the disability. That is, in the period immediately following the stroke, age was not related to depression. Eight months after the stroke, however, older caregivers were less depressed than younger caregivers (Schulz, Tompkins, & Rau, 1988).

The literature on caregivers of persons with developmental disabilities is similarly ambiguous. Engelhardt, Brubaker, and Lutzer (1988) determined that among caregivers ranging in age from 40 to 87, having the physical ability and the time to care for a mentally retarded child was not related to the caregiver's age. By contrast, another study of the parents of those with developmental disabilities has indicated that older parents were more likely than younger parents to report difficulty in leaving their caregiving responsibilities. The primary factors that contributed to this difficulty were the inability to afford alternative care and to locate a caregiver who was qualified (Engelhardt, Lutzer, & Brubaker, 1987).

Age appears to have similarly mixed effects on the caregivers to those with chronic mental illness. Stevens (1972) interviewed relatives (aged 50 and over) of persons with chronic schizophrenia. On the one hand, she noted that some of the persons with schizophrenia actually helped their infirm caregiving relatives. On the other hand, relatives who were advanced in age were more concerned than younger relatives about the future of the person with schizophrenia.

For caregivers of those with chronic mental illness, their own aging may have both negative and positive effects. With age, such caregivers may become more socially isolated, due to the deaths of their friends and family, and more fearful of their own death and its effect on the surviving mentally ill child (Cohler et al., 1991). At the same time, aging caregivers may be more likely to "experience a cohort effect," in that some of their peers are also caring for adult children, although for different reasons (e.g., failed jobs or marriages), thus making their caregiving responsibilities less unusual (Cohler et al., 1991, p. 95).

Relationship. The caregiver's relationship to the adult with disabilities also has a complex effect on their psychological adjustment (Biegel et al., 1991). For example, among spouses of persons with spinal cord injuries, those who had married after the injury appeared happier and more satisfied than those who married before the injury (Crewe, Athelstan, & Krumberger, 1979). Such findings may be understood by considering people's expectations. That is, a spouse who chooses to marry a person with disabilities does so anticipating the caregiving that will follow (Biegel et al., 1991).

Research on caregivers of those with chronic mental illness has produced somewhat contradictory findings with respect to the relative difficulty of providing care to offspring as compared to spouses. Hoenig and Hamilton (1969) found that when caregivers of the mentally ill were asked how much their households had experienced a sense of burden due to the illness, spouses reported less subjective burden than did parents. Hoenig and Hamilton suggested that "the parental home is more intolerant and reacts more severely to the sick person than do the other types of households" (p. 106).

There is some evidence, however, that parents have an easier time of coping with the illness of their offspring. In the study described above, Hoenig and Hamilton (1969) discovered that parents, as compared to spouses, were less objectively burdened in terms of the extent to which the person with the mental illness interfered in the life of his or her caregiver. Others have offered interpretations that help explain this finding. One is that the parents of persons with mental illness may have become accustomed to their caregiving role over time, whereas younger spouses may not have anticipated providing care at this stage of their marriage and may not yet have developed the necessary coping skills (Biegel et al., 1991). Another interpretation is that the dependence of adult children with chronic mental illness may be gratifying to some aged parents who feel fulfilled by maintaining their parental role (Stevens, 1972).

In their research on caregivers of adults with mental retardation, Seltzer, Begun, Seltzer, and Krauss (1991) focused on mothers and siblings. They found that mothers tended to provide most of the instrumental support needed, but that siblings often provided considerable emotional support. Further, positive interaction between adult children with mental retardation and their siblings was strongly predictive of the mother's well-being.

Ethnicity. In the literature on caring for adults with disabilities, only a few studies have examined the influence of ethnicity. On the one hand, findings indicate that white caregivers of patients with cancer were somewhat more distressed than their black counterparts (Cassileth, Lusk, Brown, & Cross, 1985). Similarly, nonminority caregivers of adult children with mental illness were more burdened and more critical of their child than minority caregivers (Cook & Pickett, 1987-1988). On the other hand, Wellisch, Fawzy, Landsverk, Pasnau, and Wolcott (1983) determined that nonwhite families caring for a member with cancer experienced more problematic family relationships than white families. In addition, Vachon et al. (1982) found that widows who were Jewish or for whom English was not a primary language had more adjustment difficulties, suggesting that being from a particular ethnic background can be problematic for some bereaved caregivers.

Family Life Cycle. Depending upon the family life stage of the care-giver, different stresses emerge. Vess, Moreland, and Schwebel (1985) divided the caregivers of cancer patients into three life stages. Caregivers with school-aged and younger children experienced the most disagreement between spouses about the performance of roles and needed more help from outside the nuclear family. Those with school-aged children who were adolescents and younger showed the most conflicts among family members in general, whereas those with children who were adolescents and older experienced the least family disruption. The authors' interpretation is that caregivers with young children and with adolescents experience multiple demands, but that families with older children have more members capable of assuming household responsibilities and thus more resources upon which to draw.

Cohler et al. (1991) noted, however, that parent caregivers of adult offspring with mental illness experience major adjustments throughout later life. They contended that:

> Factors contributing to elderly parents' increased feelings of role strain appear to be related to particular points in the course of life and are a result of role exits and losses such as retirement, grandparenthood, and deaths of loved ones, exacerbated by the need to care for an adult offspring. (p. 93)

Similarly, among caregivers of those with developmental disabilities, there are unique stressors during later life stages that may even surpass those of earlier stages. Turnbull and Turnbull (1990, p. 123) suggested that the "stigma of exceptionality" increases with age. Certain stages within their children's development appear to make caregivers more aware of the limitations of their children. Suelzle and Keenan (1981) found that, rather than gradually accepting their child's disability, parents encounter developmental milestones (e.g., entrance to grade school and exit from high school) that arouse new concerns about their child's abilities and options. A study by Wikler, Wasow, and Hatfield (1981) asked parents of children with developmental disabilities to graph their feelings throughout 10 specific developmental stages. They discovered that parental sorrow and stress were periodic, from the time of first diagnosis through discussions of the parents' own death and the need for guardianship of their child with disabilities. These researchers concluded that deviance from normal behavior at each developmental stage could result in renewed family stress.

In summary, this review of the personal characteristics of caregivers for adults with disabilities indicates that:

1. Female caregivers are more stressed than male caregivers.
2. The relationship between the age of the caregiver and the amount of stress experienced is not clear.
3. Caregivers of adult children are burdened by their caregiving responsibilities, but caregivers of spouses may be even more burdened.
4. The relationship between the ethnicity of the caregiver and the amount of stress experienced is not clear.
5. There are unique stressors at each life stage for those providing care to an adult over the life span.

Demands

In the literature on caregivers of adults with disabilities, two demands have emerged as predictors of strain: severity of disability and the length of disability.

Severity of Disability. Based upon an extensive review of the literature, Biegel et al. (1991) concluded that severity of disability is the single most consistent predictor of stress. They noted that, in general, the increased severity of illness among adults with disabilities contributes to greater difficulty for their caregivers. For example, a study on the caregivers of persons with a stroke found a strong relationship between the severity of the stroke and caregiver depression (Schulz et al., 1988). Relatives of persons with cancer who were receiving palliative end-stage treatment had greater mood disturbance and anxiety than did those of persons with earlier stages of cancer (Cassileth, Lusk, Strouse, et al., 1985). Among caregivers of those with mental retardation, the same pattern emerged, such that, with increased levels of mental retardation, caregivers expressed decreasing abilities to provide care in the future (Engelhardt et al., 1988).

An interesting exception to the problems associated with severe disability emerges in a few studies in which the ambiguity of the disability appears to be an even greater problem than its severity. In an early study on physical disability among married women, Skipper, Fink, and Hallenbeck (1968) found that whether husbands felt that their needs were being met was not associated with their wives' level of physical mobility. They postulated that complete disability might actually be easier on a couple than partial disability, because the more severe disability would leave no ambiguity about what functions the adult with a disability could perform. Bishop and Epstein (1980) suggested a somewhat different relationship between functional ability and stress. They postulated that a curvilinear relationship exists between level of disability and role ambiguity, and they predicted that role relationships may become most problematic when disabilities are either mild or severe. As they noted,

> with mild disability and attendant expectation confusion, clear allocation and role functioning may be disrupted. With increasing disability and functional incapacity, the need to reallocate roles may be more evident and may therefore cause fewer problems. With the most severe disability and functional incapacity, the role demands made on the family increase in terms of functions (e.g., assistance in bathing) and time. The family may then become overburdened and develop problems in the role area. (Bishop & Epstein, 1980, p. 339)

Cohler et al. (1991) noted a similar problem for caregivers of those who are episodically troubled by schizophrenia. They contended that the extent to which "families are confused and bewildered by the unpredictable course of schizophrenia" may be seriously underreported (Cohler et al., 1991, p. 93). As evidence for the prevalence of role ambiguity, Cook and Pickett (1987-1988) noted that among parents of offspring who were chronically mentally ill, there was a moderate degree of confusion regarding how they felt about problems concerning their children (e.g., not completing household tasks, being manipulative, insufficient time for themselves). Cook and Pickett suggested that the uncertainty of the parents, as indicated by the fact that more than one-quarter responded with "not sure" to such questions, may have resulted from their role ambiguity. One of our survey respondents discussed some of the factors associated with such role ambiguity:

> The problem of care for two schizophrenics seems to be more difficult than it ever was to find child care, although I did not work for 12 years of child rearing. Doctors, hospitals, and extended care after hospital just is not there for mental patients. The individual is cut off from society by a disease that is not understood or even treated sympathetically. [There aren't] any funds for research or help and families are torn apart about their care or totally abandoned because of their character change. Blindness, paralysis, cancer would be easier to live with.

Length of Disability. The findings on the effect of length of time since the beginning of disability are inconsistent (Biegel et al., 1991). For example, among cancer patients, some research indicates that following the discharge of the patient from the hospital the caregiver's level of strain increases over time. Oberst and James (1985) found, for example, that caregivers' emotional distress increased steadily until 2 months postdischarge and then persisted for the next several months. Other research, however, has shown that caregivers evidence better adjustment over time. According to Northhouse and Swain (1987), the husbands of women who were hospitalized with mastectomies reported exhaustion; difficulty with juggling work, home, and hospital-visiting responsibilities; and low-affect states. Still, within a month of their wives' surgery, the husbands' mood levels improved dramatically.

Among caregivers of those with mental illness, Grad and Sainsbury (1963) found that longer illness contributed to greater caregiver burden. There is some indication that the length of mental illness may affect men and women differentially. In Cook's (1988) research on adults with mental illness, fathers and mothers were similarly drained in early stages of the illness. After 5 years, however, the mothers were more emotionally drained than the fathers.

In summary, our review of the demands among caregivers for adults with disabilities suggests that:

1. Severe disability on the part of care recipients and disabilities that are ambiguous predict higher stress for caregivers.
2. The relationship between the length of time the care recipient has been disabled and the level of stress experienced by the caregiver is not clear.

Resources

The characteristics that appear to serve as resources for caregivers of adults with disabilities are health, socioeconomic status, and informal support.

Health. Although our conceptual framework considers health of caregiver as a measure of outcome, some researchers have examined health as a resource or a demand. Good health can help caregivers cope with their responsibilities, but poor health among caregivers can be associated with increased stress. Vachon et al. (1982) found that wives in poor health during their husbands' terminal illnesses were less well adjusted after their husbands' deaths than were their healthy counterparts (Vachon et al., 1982). Similarly, Schulz et al. (1988) found poor health to be associated with increased depression among caregivers who had been assisting stroke patients for several months.

Among caregivers of those with developmental disabilities or chronic mental illness, their own health also emerges as an important concern. Engelhardt et al. (1988) found that healthy caregivers of persons with developmental disabilities reported more ability to provide care than did their unhealthy counterparts. Grad and Sainsbury (1963) also found that if the caregivers were healthy, their relatives with mental illness posed fewer problems. Cohler et al. (1991) pointed out that declining health is of significant concern for caregivers of those with mental illness because they have less patience and physical stamina to meet the demands of caregiving. In addition, caregivers with declining health cannot anticipate receiving help in the future from the adults for whom they have been caring.

Socioeconomic Status. In their review of the literature, Biegel et al. (1991) found different effects of socioeconomic status, depending upon the type of disability. They concluded that, among caregivers of patients with strokes, low socioeconomic status was associated with greater distress, whereas among caregivers of those with heart disease and mental illness, high socioeconomic status was associated with more distress. Biegel et al. (1991) interpreted these conflicting findings using a theory of differential expectations. They suggested that, on the one hand, caregivers with high socioeconomic status have greater expectations regarding control over their lives; they are therefore more devastated when they cannot control the course of the illness, as may be the case with mental illness and heart disease. On the other hand, such caregivers also have more financial resources with which to deal with the ongoing and more predictable demands of such disabilities as stroke.

Informal Support. The quality of the relationship between the caregiver and the adult with disabilities can play a crucial role in the caregiver's well-being. For example, Wellisch, Jamison, and Pasnau (1978) found that among husbands whose wives had undergone a mastectomy, a good marital relationship was associated with a less negative effect on their postoperative sexual relationship. Also, among couples in which one spouse had cancer, those who had the ability to reallocate responsibilities flexibly (e.g., child care, housekeeping) were more cohesive and competent to handle the new demands induced by illness (Vess et al., 1985). There does, however, appear to be a cost associated with close relationships for some caregivers. Vachon et al. (1982) discovered that wives with good marriages to husbands who had died within the past month were more likely to experience psychiatric disorders than those with poorer marriages. An interpretation of these findings might be that a good relationship between the caregiver and care recipient helps the caregiver cope with the disability but does not assist in coping with the loss of the recipient.

The amount of support provided by friends and family can also be an important factor in caregiver adjustment. In a study of a group of men who had had heart attacks, Finlayson and McEwen (1977) discovered that wives who received support from several sources during the initial aftermath of the heart attack had better psychosocial outcomes than did those with fewer sources of support. At the same time, Dhooper (1984) found that families particularly needed support one month after hospitalization, yet friends and family assumed that by this time the immediate families were again self-sufficient. Support after caregiving has ended can also contribute toward adjustment during bereavement. Vachon et al. (1982) discovered that a lack of social support was a key predictor of distress among widows a month after the death of their spouse.

Unfortunately, the disability itself sometimes drastically affects the amount of support available to the caregiver. For example, based on interviews with the families of aphasic adults, Malone (1969) found that the disability negatively affected social relationships on several dimensions. Due to feelings of embarrassment, caregivers often discouraged others from visiting and were therefore lonely and isolated. Thus, during a period when the family was in greatest need of support, assistance from others actually diminished.

In summary, the literature on resources for caregivers of adults with disabilities indicates that:

1. Good health among caregivers plays a vital role in their ability to cope with their responsibilities.
2. The relationship between the socioeconomic status of the caregiver and level of stress experienced is dependent upon the type of disability experienced by the care recipient.
3. Informal support serves as an important resource for assisting caregivers to cope with their responsibilities.

CAREGIVING WITHIN THE CONTEXT OF EMPLOYMENT

Although the literature on the extent and effects of employment among caregivers of adults with disabilities is limited, some interesting findings have emerged. These findings tend to cluster around three themes: the extent to which caregivers leave their jobs, the role changes associated with combining employment and caregiving, and the effects of employment on caregiver burden.

Caregivers' Departures From the Work Force

The impact of caregiving on employment is probably seriously underreported because, in fact, many caregivers have to leave their jobs to provide care. Using data from the National Hospice Study, Muurinen (1986) discovered that more than one quarter of the caregivers of persons with cancer stopped working to provide terminal care and that almost two thirds of those who remained employed were absent from work with subsequent salary loss. Caregivers who were female, who had low incomes, and who had less education were more likely to leave work to provide care to hospice patients. In a study of the wives of patients with heart attacks, Skelton and Dominian (1973) found that one quarter of those who were employed stopped work temporarily and that almost half took time off from work. Sainsbury and Grad (1962) had similar findings: In a quarter of the families of persons with chronic mental illness, someone's job had been affected. These figures demonstrate the

frequent need to leave the work force on a temporary or permanent basis
to provide care to an adult who has become disabled.

Role Changes Associated With Combining
Employment and Caregiving

In an early study of the effects of disability on work status, Klein,
Dean, and Bogdonoff (1967) found that a reduction in work activity on
the part of the ill partner was correlated with a reduction in work activity
on the part of the spouse. This finding is particularly interesting because, although spouses might be expected to increase their work activity
to compensate for lost income, this study provides evidence that caregiving instead forced them to cut back on work.

The hypothesis that disability leads to role changes was further elaborated in a study by Carpenter (1974). In examining differences between
the employed and unemployed wives of husbands who were disabled,
he found that the husbands of employed wives self-reported more performance of household chores and less independent decision making
(e.g., buying a car). This finding indicates that employment may result
in a reallocation of power between the caregiver wife and her disabled
husband.

The Effect of Employment on Caregiver Burden

The relationship between employment and various outcomes has
been explored among the chronically ill. For example, Rustad (1984)
pointed out that disability among husbands may force wives to seek
outside employment. Using interviews with the spouses of patients with
aphasia, Malone (1969) identified two distinct reactions to entering the
work force among wives: (a) resentment and fear or (b) enjoyment. Rustad
(1984) suggested that these different reactions may be related to the
developmental stage of the family. The first reaction may be experienced by younger wives with children or by those who are not interested
in a career. The second reaction may be more characteristic of wives
who have fulfilled their family responsibilities or of those who welcome
a change from domestic pursuits.

The effect of employment on caregivers has also been considered
among those who provide care to persons with chronic mental illness.
Cook and Pickett (1987-1988) found that employed parents tended to
be more critical of their offspring with mental illness than were parents

who were not employed, perhaps due to earlier expectations that their offspring would attain a high level of accomplishment. Cohler et al. (1991) also noted the potential benefits of work for caregivers of adults with mental illness. They pointed out that the workplace may serve as a refuge for caregivers and as an escape from their unremitting responsibilities.

In summary, our review of the small body of literature pertaining to employed caregivers of adults with disabilities suggests that:

1. Such employees may need to quit work to provide the care needed.
2. Combining work and caregiving can result in a reallocation of roles among men and women.
3. Employed caregivers may experience:

   resentment about entering the work force to support adults with disabilities; relief due to the respite that work provides from their caregiving responsibilities.

FINDINGS FROM THE SURVEY

To examine further some of the relationships discussed in the previous section, we turn to our survey data of employed caregivers. From these data, it is possible to portray a typical provider of adult care in our survey. She was a white 41-year-old who worked full time (92%) as a professional or manager (58%). Our employed caregiver was likely to be married to an employed spouse (48%), however there was also the possibility that the spouse was not employed (21%), or that the employee had no partner (30%). Our adult-care provider was more likely to be caring for a disabled parent (25%), other relative (25%), or child (22%) than for a spouse (13%). She had missed about a half-day of work during the preceding month and experienced some difficulty in combining work and family.

To explore the factors that influence absenteeism and stress for such employees, we analyzed the findings from our study using an analysis strategy parallel to that of the previous chapter on employed caregivers of children. Specifically, we used hierarchical multiple regression analysis and entered the independent variables in three blocks. First, the personal characteristics of the employee (gender, age, ethnicity, occupation, caring for parent, caring for spouse, and caring for child) were entered into the equation. Next, the demand variables (hours worked, shift, number of adults and elders cared for, number of caregiving roles, distance from recipient, hours of care provided, and special care needs) were entered. Finally, the resource variables (household income, work flexibility, working partner, nonworking partner, informal support, formal support, finding and managing care, and satisfaction with care) were entered into the equation. As with the other caregiver groups examined in this book, there were six dependent measures: three forms of absenteeism and three forms of stress.

The following discussion of the effects of background, demand, and resource variables among caregivers of adults with disabilities is presented in relation to these two sets of absenteeism and stress-related dependent measures. Due to the small size of this group of caregivers ($n = 357$) relative to that of the child-care group ($n = 4,422$) and the elder-care group ($n = 2,241$), any independent variable that was significantly associated with the outcome variables is discussed, even if the overall regression equation was not significant. Thus these findings must be considered to be preliminary and in need of testing further on larger samples of caregivers for adults with disabilities. Table 4.1 summarizes the results of the three steps of the regression analyses with respect to absenteeism; Table 4.2 provides a similar summary of the findings regarding stress.

Personal Characteristics

For the absenteeism variables, the personal characteristics explained from 5% to 11% of the variance. The best explained by personal characteristics were interruptions at work due to family-related matters. Being female, caring for a spouse, being younger, and being a nonprofessional or nonmanager were predictors of absenteeism. All but one of these predictors remained significant when demands and resources were entered into the equation. The exception was that being a nonprofessional or nonmanager no longer retained significance when resources were entered, suggesting that having resources decreases absenteeism among caregivers in these nonprofessional, nonmanagerial occupations.

With respect to the stress variables, the percentage of explained variance was small, ranging from 3% to 7%. The personal characteristics predictive of stress were being female, caring for a spouse or adult child, and being older. Two of these variables remained significant when demands and resources were added to the equation: being older and caring for a spouse. The variance explained by the other variables was exhausted,

TABLE 4.1 Effects of Personal Characteristics, Caregiving Demands, and Caregiving Resources on Absenteeism Variables Among Employees With Adult-Care Responsibilities

	Absenteeism Variables								
	Days Missed			Late or Left Early			Interruptions		
Step entered regression:	1	2	3	1	2	3	1	2	3
Predictors									
Personal Characteristics									
Gender (female)							+	+	+
Age of employee				−	−	−			
Ethnicity (white)									
Occupation (professional)	−	−							
Caring for parent									
Caring for spouse							+	+	+
Caring for child									
Change in R^2 at Step 1	.05			.07			.11		
Demands									
Hours worked									
Shift (day)		+	+		+			+	+
Number cared for									
Number of caregiving roles									
Distance from recipient									
Hours of care provided									
Special care needs									
Change in R^2 at Step 2	.04			.04			.06		
Resources									
Household income									
Work schedule flexibility									
Working partner									
Nonworking partner									
Informal support									
Formal support									
Ease finding/managing care									
Satisfaction with care									−
Change in R^2 at Step 3	.02			.01			.07		
Total R^2/R^2 Adjusted	.10/.01			.13/.04			.24/.16		
Overall F	1.14			1.43			3.04**		
Df (reg./res.) 22,213									

Note: Based on standardized betas; "+" indicates a significant positive relationship; "−" indicates a significant inverse relationship.
* $p \le .05$; ** $p \le .01$.

TABLE 4.2   Effects of Personal Characteristics, Caregiving Demands, and Caregiving Resources on Stress Variables Among Employees With Adult-Care Responsibilities

	Stress Variables								
	Personal Health Stress			Adult Care			Difficulty Combining Work and Family		
Step entered regression:	1	2	3	1	2	3	1	2	3
Predictors									
Personal Characteristics									
Gender (female)							+	+	
Age of employee	+	+	+						−
Ethnicity (white)									
Occupation (professional)									
Caring for parent						+			
Caring for spouse				+	+	+			
Caring for child				+					
Change in R^2 at Step 1	.03			.07			.05		
Demands									
Hours worked									
Shift (day)									
Number cared for					+	+			
Number of caregiving roles								+	
Distance from recipient						−			
Hours of care provided									
Special care needs		+	+		+	+			+
Change in R^2 at Step 2	.05			.16			.06		
Resources									
Household income									
Work schedule flexibility									−
Working partner									
Nonworking partner									+
Informal support									−
Formal support									
Ease finding/managing care									
Satisfaction with care						−			
Change in R^2 at Step 3	.05			.06			.25		
Total R^2/R^2 Adjusted	.13/.04			.30/.23			.37/.31		
Overall F	1.50			4.12**			5.82**		
Df (reg./res.) 22,213									

Note: Based on standardized betas; "+" indicates a significant positive relationship; "−" indicates a significant inverse relationship.
* $p \le .05$; **$p \le .01$.

however, by the inclusion of demands (for employees caring for a child) and by resources (for the female caregivers). Perhaps resources helped to compensate for the difficulties of women caregivers. When resources were entered, caring for a parent became significantly associated with stress and being younger became significantly associated with difficulty combining work and family.

In general, it appears that the personal characteristics were stronger predictors of absenteeism than of stress. Some personal characteristics predicted both absenteeism and stress (being female and caring for a spouse). Age had differential effects on the two types of outcome measures: being younger was related to increased absenteeism, whereas being older was related to increased personal health stress. Caring for a spouse was related both to increased absenteeism and increased stress, yet caring for an adult child was related only to increased stress. This latter finding supports the work of Hoenig and Hamilton (1969), who documented the subjective burden of parental caregivers whose children were mentally ill. Our findings also highlight another important point. Caring for a spouse contributed to absenteeism as well as to stress, perhaps because the employee had no other adult on whom to depend. Thus, when family emergencies arose, the employee had to handle the emergency by missing time from work.

Demands

Among the absenteeism variables, the demand variables accounted for an additional 4% to 6% of explained variance, after controlling for the personal variables. Interruptions at work due to family matters were the form of absenteeism best explained by the demands. Only one of the seven demands, being on day shift, significantly predicted absenteeism. This predictor retained its significance after the resources were entered into the equation.

After controlling for the personal variables, the demand variables accounted for an additional 5% to 16% of variance among the stress variables. What was best explained by the demands was the stress associated with caring for an adult dependent. Of the seven demand variables, three demands significantly increased stress, as predicted. Having recipients with special care needs, holding multiple caregiving roles, and caring for multiple disabled adults or elders predicted high stress.

With the exception of those with multiple caregiving roles, these variables retained their predictive value when resources were entered into the equation. Apparently, resources helped to overcome the difficulties associated with multiple caregiving roles. Another demand, distance from the caregiving situation, emerged as significantly related to stress when resources were entered. That is, caregivers who lived closer to the care recipient experienced more stress.

Once personal characteristics were controlled, the demand variables accounted for more explained variance in stress than absenteeism. In addition, several demands predicted stress, whereas only a single demand was associated with absenteeism. In general, these significant predictors of stress and absenteeism retained their explanatory power even after the inclusion of resources.

Resources

The resource variables accounted for 1% to 7% of the additional explained variance among the absenteeism variables, after controlling for personal and demand variables. Interruptions due to family-related matters was again the absenteeism variable best explained by resources. Of the eight resource measures, only satisfaction with care arrangements predicted decreased absenteeism.

In relation to the stress variables, resources accounted for an additional 5% to 25% of the variance, after controlling for personal and demand variables. Difficulty in combining work and family was the stress variable best predicted by resources. Three of the eight resources significantly reduced stress, as hypothesized. Specifically, having flexible work schedules and personnel policies, having informal support, and being satisfied with care arrangements were associated with decreased stress. In addition, having a nonworking partner predicted greater stress, perhaps because this partner was the individual with disabilities for whom the employee cared.

In general, resources were thus better predictors of stress than of absenteeism, after accounting for personal characteristics and demands. Satisfaction with care arrangements was a strong predictor of both lower absenteeism and stress. In addition, having flexibility within the workplace as well as having informal support (that is, the help of family and friends) further helped to decrease employees' stress.

DISCUSSION

The results from our survey help provide understanding for the research findings discussed in the first part of this chapter. Here, we will highlight some of the more important results, discuss their contribution to research on employment and caregiving, and suggest some implications for the workplace.

Our findings indicate that women who care for adults with disabilities are particularly vulnerable in terms of both greater absenteeism and higher stress, which is consistent with previous research (Cook, 1988; Foxall et al., 1985; Leiber et al., 1976). In our sample, women were more likely than men to be interrupted at work due to family-related matters and to perceive difficulty in combining work and family responsibilities. Significantly, their difficulty with combining the two roles was diminished when they had access to specific resources. We discovered two resources that helped employees to combine work and family responsibilities: having informal support and working at a job that allowed them a flexible work schedule and had family-supportive personnel policies. Although the benefits of informal support for women have been well documented (Finlayson & McEwen, 1977; Seltzer et al., 1991; Vachon et al., 1982), this is one of the first studies to demonstrate the beneficial effect of work policies on diminishing stress among caregivers of adults with disabilities.

Employees who were not professionals or managers were another group of caregivers likely to miss time from work. Jobs that are neither managerial nor professional may offer employees less flexibility to handle caregiving responsibilities (Archbold, 1983). Under the circumstances their only recourse is to lose time from work, unless they have other resources. Two particular resources (having informal support as well as flexible work schedules and supportive policies) were thus crucial to these employees. With these two resources, employees were less likely to miss work days; we expect these resources to be particularly helpful to nonmanagerial workers.

Our findings also address the controversy over what kinds of caregiving relationships are most difficult. Hoenig and Hamilton (1969) have found evidence for problems associated with being a caregiver to an adult child and being a spouse caregiver. We too found that caring for an adult child or a spouse was problematic, and both kinds of relationships contributed to caregiving stress. Caring for a spouse, however, also contributed to interruptions at work. Thus our data suggest that caring for a spouse is more likely to result in spillover between family and work than is caring for an adult child.

Further, our data address the question, also posed by previous researchers, of the effect of caregiver's age on his or her ability to cope (Cohler et al., 1991; Engelhardt et al., 1987, 1988). We found that the answer concerning whether older or younger caregivers coped better depended upon the outcome that we were addressing. Specifically, younger employed caregivers tended to miss more work and had more difficulty in combining work and family. Older employed caregivers, however, were more likely to experience personal health stress due to their caregiving, suggesting that the physical aspects of providing care were more difficult for them. It would thus seem that caregiving is strenuous for both the young and the old, but in different ways.

Another important finding is that working day shift represented a competing demand for caregivers. Day-shift employees handled this demand by missing more days at work and being interrupted on the job more frequently than their counterparts on other shifts. This missed time at work may have been due to a variety of factors. First, the adult(s) for whom they were caring were more likely to be awake and to need attention during the daytime. Secondly, the services utilized by the adult(s) (e.g., medical appointments) were more likely to be available during the day. This interpretation suggests the importance of extended hours among such services to accommodate the needs of employed caregivers.

Our study also explored the influence of multiple roles among employees with adult-care responsibilities. Although this area of research has been pursued with respect to caregivers of children and the elderly, there has been minimal attention paid to employees who are balancing adult care with other kinds of caregiving. We found that employees with multiple caregiving roles experienced more difficulty in combining work and family than did those with fewer caregiving roles. Significantly, caregivers who had resources such as informal support and flexible work schedules had less difficulty in combining work and family.

The above discussion highlights the importance of two major resources to help reduce absenteeism and stress for employees with adult-care responsibilities. The first resource, flexible work schedules and supportive personnel policies, allows employees to care for their dependent adult while remaining responsible employees. We discuss ways in which the workplace can allow for this kind of flexibility and provide such policies in Chapter 8. The second, informal support, provides employees with crucial assistance in caring for adults with disabilities. In Chapter 9, we describe ways in which employers can enhance this kind of support for employees by providing services in the workplace.

REFERENCES

Archbold, P. G. (1983). Impact of parent-caring on women. *Family Relations, 32,* 39-45.

Biegel, D. E., Sales, E., & Schulz, R. (1991). *Family caregiving in chronic illness.* Newbury Park, CA: Sage.

Bishop, D. S., & Epstein, N. B. (1980). Family problems and disability. In D. S. Bishop (Ed.), *Behavioral problems and the disabled: Assessment and management* (pp. 337-364). London: Williams & Wilkins.

Carpenter, J. O. (1974). Changing roles and disagreement in families with disabled husbands. *Archives of Physical Medicine Rehabilitation, 55,* 272-274.

Cassileth, B. R., Lusk, E. J., Brown, L. L., & Cross, P. A. (1985). Psychosocial status of cancer patients and next of kin: Normative data from the profile of mood states. *Journal of Psychosocial Oncology, 3,* 99-105.

Cassileth, B. R., Lusk, E. J., Strouse, T. B., Miller, D. S., Brown, L. L., & Cross, P. A. (1985). A psychological analysis of cancer patients and their next-of-kin. *Cancer: Diagnosis, Treatment, Research, 55,* 72-76.

Cohler, B., Pickett, S. A., & Cook, J. A. (1991). The psychiatric patient grows older: Issues in family care. In E. Light & B. D. Lebowitz (Eds.), *The elderly with chronic mental illness* (pp. 82-110). New York: Springer.

Cook, J. A. (1988). Who "mothers" the chronically mentally ill? *Family Relations, 37,* 42-49.

Cook, J. A., & Pickett, S. A. (1987-1988, Fall/Winter). Feelings of burden and criticalness among parents residing with chronically [mentally] ill offspring. (Insertion requested by Cook & Pickett). *The Journal of Applied Social Sciences, 12,* 79-107.

Crewe, N. M., Athelstan, G. T., & Krumberger, J. (1979). Spinal cord injury: A comparison of preinjury and postinjury marriages. *Archives of Physical Medicine Rehabilitation, 60,* 252-256.

Dhooper, S. S. (1984). Social networks and support during the crisis of heart attack. *Health and Social Work, 9,* 294-303.

Engelhardt, J. L., Brubaker, T. H., & Lutzer, V. D. (1988). Older caregivers of adults with mental retardation: Service utilization. *Mental Retardation, 26,* 191-195.

Engelhardt, J. L., Lutzer, V. D., & Brubaker, T. H. (1987). Parents of adults with developmental disabilities: Age and reasons for reluctance to use another caregiver. *Lifestyles: A Journal of Changing Patterns, 8,* 47-54.

Finlayson, A., & McEwen, J. (1977). *Coronary heart disease and patterns of living.* New York: Prodist.

Foxall, M. J., Ekberg, J. Y., & Griffith, N. (1985). Adjustment patterns of chronically ill middle-aged persons and spouses. *Western Journal of Nursing Research, 7,* 425-444.

Grad, J., & Sainsbury, P. (1963). Mental illness and the family. *The Lancet, 1,* 544-547.

Hoenig, J., & Hamilton, M. W. (1969). *The desegregation of the mentally ill.* New York: Humanities Press.

Klein, R. F., Dean, A., & Bogdonoff, M. D. (1967). The impact of illness upon the spouse. *Journal of Chronic Disease, 20,* 241-248.

Leiber, L., Plumb, M. M., Gerstenzang, M. L., & Holland, J. (1976). The communication of affection between cancer patients and their spouses. *Psychosomatic Medicine, 38,* 379-389.

Malone, R. L. (1969). Expressed attitudes of families of aphasics. *Journal of Speech and Hearing Disorders, 34,* 146-151.

Muurinen, J. (1986). The economics of informal care: Labor market effects in the national hospice study. *Medical Care, 24,* 1007-1017.

Neugarten, B. L. (1968). Adult personality: Toward a psychology of the life cycle. In B. L. Neugarten (Ed.), *Middle age and aging: A reader in social psychology* (pp. 137-147). Chicago: University of Chicago Press.

Northhouse, L. L., & Swain, M. A. (1987). Adjustment of patients and husbands to the initial impact of breast cancer. *Nursing Research, 36,* 221-225.

Oberst, M. T., & James, R. H. (1985). Going home: Patient and spouse adjustment following cancer surgery. *Topics in Clinical Nursing, 7,* 46-57.

Rustad, L. C. (1984). Family adjustment to chronic illness and disability in mid-life. In M. G. Eisenberg, L. C. Sutkin, & M. A. Jansen (Eds.), *Chronic illness and disability through the life span* (pp. 222-242). New York: Springer.

Sainsbury, P., & Grad, J. (1962). Evaluation of treatment services. In *The burden on the community: The epidemiology of mental illness: A symposium* (pp. 69-116). London: Oxford University Press.

Schulz, R., Tompkins, C. A., & Rau, M. T. (1988). A longitudinal study of the psychosocial impact of stroke on primary support persons. *Psychology and Aging, 3,* 131-141.

Seltzer, G. B., Begun, A., Seltzer, M. M., & Krauss, M. W. (1991). Adults with mental retardation and their aging mothers: Impacts of siblings. *Family Relations, 40,* 310-317.

Skelton, M., & Dominian, J. (1973). Psychological stress in wives of patients with myocardial infarction. *British Medical Journal, 2,* 101-103.

Skipper, J. K., Fink, S. L., & Hallenbeck, P. N. (1968). Physical disability among married women: Problems in the husband-wife relationship. *Journal of Rehabilitation, 34,* 16-19.

Stetz, K. M. (1987). Caregiving demands during advanced cancer: The spouse's needs. *Cancer Nursing, 10,* 260-268.

Stevens, B. C. (1972). Dependence of schizophrenic patients on elderly relatives. *Psychological Medicine, 2,* 17-32.

Suelzle, M., & Keenan, V. (1981). Changes in family support networks over the life cycle of mentally retarded persons. *American Journal of Mental Deficiency, 86,* 267-274.

Turnbull, A. P., & Turnbull, H. R. (1990). *Families, professionals, and exceptionality: A special partnership.* Columbus, OH: Charles E. Merrill.

Vachon, M. L. S., Rogers, J., Lyall, W. A., Lancee, W. J., Sheldon, A. R., & Freeman, S. J. J. (1982). Predictors and correlates of adaptation to conjugal bereavement. *American Journal of Psychiatry, 139,* 998-1002.

Vess, J. D., Jr., Moreland, J. R., & Schwebel, A. I. (1985). An empirical assessment of the effects of cancer on family role functioning. *Journal of Psychosocial Oncology, 3,* 1-16.

Wellisch, D. K., Fawzy, F. I., Landsverk, J., Pasnau, R. O., & Wolcott, D. L. (1983). Evaluation of psychosocial problems of the home-bound cancer patient: The relationship of disease and the sociodemographic variables of patients to family problems. *Journal of Psychosocial Oncology, 1,* 1-16.

Wellisch, D. K., Jamison, K. R., & Pasnau, R. O. (1978). Psychosocial aspects of mastectomy: II. The man's perspective. *American Journal of Psychiatry, 135,* 543-546.

Williamson, G. M., & Schulz, R. (1990). Relationship orientations, quality of prior relationship, and distress among caregivers of Alzheimer's patients. *Psychology and Aging, 5,* 502-509.

Wikler, L., Wasow, M., & Hatfield, E. (1981). Chronic sorrow revisited: Parent vs. professional depiction of the adjustment of parents of mentally retarded children. *American Journal of Orthopsychiatrics, 51,* 63-70.

5

Employees Who Care for Elderly Persons

My mother became more isolated and confused over the past 5 years, but refused any alternative to staying in her own home. I was fortunate to be able to live and work near her so that I could go by in the a.m.—fix breakfast, dress her leg (and sometimes her)—Meals on Wheels brought both lunch and another contact with the outside world. Then after work I would go by to see that she had dinner and was ready for bed. Frequently calls came at night or at work that required "talking down" or a visit. I luckily work with wonderfully caring, supportive people who helped both my mother and me through this very hard time. . . . Within our worksite several other caretakers shared their problems at coffee, etc., which was very valuable— misery does love company I guess. My mother broke her hip in February and died shortly after—I have been very lucky to be able to keep her cared for and work, but this has been the most difficult time of my life.

The provision of elder care involves a wide range of responsibilities, from anticipatory caregiving to full-time caregiving. Such responsibilities necessitate some special accommodations. Although some employees are not yet providing actual care for their older relatives or friends, simply anticipating such care can influence their choice of jobs, their readiness to take on more job responsibility, and their willingness to consider geographic transfers. Some have fairly light responsibilities, such as periodically calling on the telephone to check on their relative's safety and well-being. Others sometimes provide transportation, fix occasional meals, or perform some household chores. Still others, like the woman described above, manage a myriad of services and/or live with the elder to provide such services directly. When elder care reaches this level of intensity, employees must struggle to fulfill both their caregiving and their job responsibilities.

In this chapter, we consider the factors associated with absenteeism and stress for employed caregivers of the elderly. The first part of this chapter reviews literature pertaining to this topic. The second part describes findings from our own survey of employed caregivers.

LITERATURE ON EMPLOYED
CAREGIVERS OF THE ELDERLY

The literature on employed caregivers of older adults is more extensive than that dealing with caregivers of adults with disabilities but less than that on employees who have child-care responsibilities. During the past decade, awareness of and empirical research on individuals who are balancing the responsibilities of employment and elder care have increased. Estimates regarding the proportion of employees who provide care to an elderly person range from 23% to 32% (Wagner, Creedon, Sasala, & Neal, 1989), although the intensity of caregiving varies from providing emotional support to providing complete physical care. The findings from this literature are described within our conceptual framework that considers personal characteristics, demands, and resources as predictors of absenteeism and stress outcomes. This review examines the relationships among these variables for caregivers of elders in general and highlights literature pertaining to caregivers who are employed.

Personal Characteristics

Like the literature on caregivers to adults with disabilities, the research on caregivers of elders has devoted considerable attention to the personal characteristics of the caregiver.

Gender. The provision of informal care to frail elderly is predominantly a female role. A national study of caregivers found that the vast majority (72%) of caregivers were women (Stone, Cafferata, & Sangl, 1987). Even when employed, women assume a disproportionate share of caregiving responsibilities. Stoller (1983) found that employed men tended to reduce their amount of caregiving, whereas employed women did not.

Women also generally provide more overall assistance than do men (Horowitz, 1985; Stoller, 1983). The difference in level of assistance is more dramatic for some tasks than for others. For example, women tend to provide more domestic and personal care services, whereas tasks such as decision making, financial management, and providing linkages with outside resources are more evenly divided between male and female caregivers (Horowitz, 1985).

Similar findings have emerged from research on employed caregivers of the elderly. In a study conducted by The Travelers Companies in their home office, female caregivers averaged 16 hours of care per week, whereas their male counterparts averaged 5 hours of care (Wilson, 1988). Further, female caregivers have been more likely than male caregivers to change their work schedules (e.g., decrease work hours or take time off from work) to accommodate their caregiving responsibilities (Stone & Short, 1990). Such gender differences may decrease, however, among caregivers of severely impaired elderly. In a study of caregivers to brain-impaired adults who were predominantly over 65, male and female employees both spent similar amounts of time in caregiving (Enright, 1991).

Female caregivers also experience considerably higher stress than do male caregivers (Horowitz, 1985). A number of explanations have been offered to account for this difference. First, male caregivers, particularly if they are employed, receive more help from others than do female caregivers (Enright, 1991). Second, men and women tend to cope with and think about their responsibilities in different ways. In a qualitative study examining caregivers of cognitively impaired spouses, Miller (1987) identified several ways in which husbands conceived of their role differently from wives. Husbands were more comfortable with an authoritative, teaching role and more able to find personal time and space away from their impaired spouses; one technique included leaving the spouse alone. The caregiving wives, by contrast, were less likely to maintain such personal time. Instead, they remained very attentive to their husbands' needs and expended considerable energy attempting to remedy any of their complaints. Thus the way in which women think of their responsibilities may contribute toward their feelings of stress. The tendency on the part of female caregivers to conceive of caregiving as a reflection of their self-worth has been supported by research conducted by Abel (1990). She found that adult daughters felt that their mothers' continued requests for assistance indicated that they had failed as caregivers.

Finally, it appears that men and women who are employed tend to cope with their caregiving responsibilities in different ways. In her study of adult child caregivers, Stoller (1983) found that employed sons decreased their caregiving assistance by an average of 23 hours per month, but employed daughters did not reduce their amount of assistance. Further, working daughters were more likely than working sons to change their work schedules by reducing hours, rearranging their schedules, and taking time off without pay.

Age. Stone et al. (1987) provided a national profile of caregivers to the frail elderly: Their average age was 57 years, one quarter were 65 to 74 years old, and one tenth were 75 and older. Stone et al. (1987) noted that their figures support previous research indicating that much of caregiving involves the "young-old" assisting the "old-old."

Employed caregivers are probably somewhat younger than the general population of caregivers, as evidenced by a review of the literature conducted by Wagner, Neal, Gibeau, Anastas, and Scharlach (1989, cited in Wagner, Creedon, Sasala, & Neal, 1989). Using data from six studies of employees with informal elder-care responsibilities, they have categorized employees according to their ages. The modal age category for employed caregivers was between the ages of 41 and 50.

Evidence about the relationship between the age of the caregiver and stress is not consistent. On the one hand, Noelker and Poulshock (1982, cited in Horowitz, 1985) and Scharlach, Sobel, and Roberts (1991) found no relationship between age and stress. On the other hand, Cicirelli (1981) discovered that older caregivers experienced more stress than younger caregivers. Orodenker (1990) found that aged caregivers were more likely to experience poor health—a possible contributor to their increased difficulty with caregiving. However, Robinson (1983) and Montgomery, Gonyea, and Hooyman (1985) found evidence of greater stress among younger caregivers; further, Robinson (1983) found a relationship between being employed and greater stress. Taken together, these two studies could be interpreted as supporting the hypothesis that younger caregivers may experience greater stress because they are trying to balance work and caregiving responsibilities. Alternatively, it may be that a curvilinear relationship exists between age and caregiver stress. That is, both young adults and the frail elderly may be more susceptible to stress related to caregiving.

Relationship. According to national statistics (Stone et al., 1987), caregivers to the elderly are predominantly daughters (29%) and wives (23%), followed by husbands (13%) and sons (9%). Brody (1985) contended that husbands and wives have the greatest difficulty in providing care because they exert extreme effort but are limited by their own advanced age, increased physical problems, and reduced energy. The 1976 Survey of Income and Education (Soldo & Myllyluoma, 1983) found similar results in terms of spouse effort. This large-scale survey indicated that spouse caregivers provided more support to elderly recipients than did their nonspouse counterparts. A survey based on a national sample of caregivers (Stone et al., 1987) lent support to Brody's notion that spouse caregivers have physical problems; in this survey, almost half of the spouse caregivers had poor or fair health. However, Zarit, Reever, and Bach-Peterson (1980) found no difference in the burden experienced by daughters as compared to that experienced by spouses of older people with senile dementia.

Ethnicity. Ethnic differences among caregivers have received limited attention. In her review of this small body of research, Horowitz (1985) found little evidence of differences in caregiving between African-American and white families. Cantor's (1979) study revealed that Hispanic elderly showed the most marked differences from white and African-American elders with respect to care received from children. Hispanic elders had more interaction with their children and received more assistance from them than either of the other groups.

Research on ethnicity within the context of caregivers who are employed is even more limited. One notable exception is a study by Stone and Short (1990), which found that white caregivers were more likely to be working than were nonwhite caregivers. Further, white caregivers tended to alter their work patterns (e.g., rearranged or reduced hours) more than their nonwhite counterparts. Such differences at work may derive partially from differences in flexibility within the workplace. That is, nonwhites may be more likely to be employed in jobs that offer less flexibility to alter their work patterns than whites.

Occupation. Occupation can also influence the ways in which caregivers modify their work responsibilities to accommodate their caregiving responsibilities. For example, Stone (Select Committee on Aging, 1987) found that, among female primary caregivers, clerical and sales workers tended to reduce their work hours. These workers and, to some extent, professionals and managers were also likely to rearrange their work schedules. Blue-collar employees, however, often had to make another kind of work accommodation in taking time off without pay. Occupational differences in workplace policies may thus influence employees' options for work accommodations. As Mutschler (1989) concluded, employees in different occupations have differing opportunities available to them for adjusting their work and care demands.

In a qualitative study of female caregivers, Archbold (1983) differentiated between two groups of caregivers: those who provided direct care to their elderly parents (care providers) and those who identified resources and managed their parents' care (care managers). She found that, among those who were employed, the care managers tended to have higher status jobs and higher incomes than the care providers. The higher status jobs allowed the former group more flexibility to fulfill their caregiving responsibilities than did those of the latter group. Further, due to the importance of their more socially valued jobs, the care managers also experienced less conflict about continuing to work than did the care providers and more ease with delegating caregiving responsibilities. The care providers, whose jobs were less valued and provided them with less income, sometimes quit work to become full-time caregivers.

In summary, the literature on the personal characteristics of caregivers of the elderly suggests that:

1. Employed women are more likely to provide caregiving, are more likely to change their work schedules, and are more likely to experience stress than employed men.

2. The relationship between the age of caregivers and their level of stress is not clear.

3. Caregivers of spouses experience more difficulty providing care than do caregivers of nonspouses.

4. White caregivers are more likely to be employed and are more able to alter their work schedules than are nonwhite caregivers.

5. Caregivers with higher status jobs can more easily accommodate their work schedules to their caregiving responsibilities than can those with lower status jobs. They also experience less conflict about continuing to work.

Demands

Certain demands within the caregiving situation or the workplace can exacerbate the conflict between work and family. This section identifies several such demands: number of hours employed, distance from the care recipient, special care needs, number of caregiving roles, and number of persons for whom care is provided.

Number of Hours Employed. One question examined by researchers has been whether those who are employed provide less care than those who are not employed. Studies that explore this question have had inconsistent results. Brody and Schoonover (1986) studied employed and nonemployed daughters to determine which group was providing more help. In five out of seven categories of tasks, the two groups of daughters provided similar amounts of help. On only two tasks (personal care and meal preparation) did the nonemployed daughters provide more assistance than the employed. Enright's (1991) study of caregivers to brain-impaired adults revealed a somewhat different picture. Specifically, unemployed caregivers spent almost twice as much time (an average of 109 hours per week) providing assistance as did the employed caregivers (an average of 57 hours per week). At the same time, Enright (1991) noted that the amount of time provided by the employed caregiver is "the equivalent of more than one and a third full-time jobs" (p. 379).

A second more directly related issue is the extent to which increased hours of employment are associated with stress. Although it seems likely that working more hours per week would be associated with increased stress, there is some indication that working fewer hours per week is associated with greater stress. For example, the study of caregivers to brain-impaired adults found that those who worked the fewest hours (i.e., 20 hours per week or less) experienced the most burden (Enright & Friss, 1987). These caregivers, however, were also responsible for the more impaired care recipients, received less paid help, and spent more time providing care.

Distance From Recipient. National estimates indicate that shared living arrangements are normative when the elderly become functionally impaired. Stone et al. (1987) found that, in a national sample of disabled elderly, approximately three-quarters lived with their spouses and/or children. In their review of studies of employed caregivers, however, Wagner, Creedon et al. (1989, cited in Wagner, Neal, et al., 1989) found that the percentage who shared a household with their elder ranged from 8% to 33%.

Shared living arrangements can avoid the difficulty of managing two households but can be problematic in terms of maintaining control over time and space (Stoller & Pugliesi, 1989). Indeed, in examining the effects of living arrangements, Stoller and Pugliesi (1989) found that coresidence was significantly related to higher levels of psychological stress. Similar findings appeared in several studies reviewed by Horowitz (1985), who concluded that sharing a household was associated with higher levels of impairment on the part of the elderly care recipient, more demands on the caregiver's time, and more likelihood for conflict.

Special Care Needs. Certain kinds of dependencies on the part of the care recipient are particularly stressful for the caregiver. Providing care for cognitively impaired elders who are in the early stages of disease appears to be more anxiety-provoking than caring for those whose disease has progressed (Miller, 1987; Zarit, Todd, & Zarit, 1986). Further, the provision of personal care to the recipient has been related to psychological stress among caregivers (Stoller & Pugliesi, 1989). One of our survey respondents described caring for her mother who had Alzheimer's disease as "far and away the hardest thing I ever did."

In a study of employed female caregivers, Gibeau and Anastas (1989) found that these caregivers helped with an average of eight different tasks. The number of caregiving tasks performed was correlated with the caregivers' feelings of conflict between work and family but not with hours missed from work. According to Gibeau and Anastas, the latter finding indicates that workplace constraints or other norms prohibit women from taking time off from work, even when they experience considerable conflict because of their caregiving responsibilities.

Certain kinds of tasks may be more burdensome for caregivers than others. In a study of caregivers, most of whom were employed, Montgomery et al. (1985) examined the relative impact of seven categories of tasks on caregiver burden. Two categories of tasks emerged as most objectively burdensome; that is, they affected sensitive areas of caregivers' lives, such as time and privacy. One category involved nursing care, bathing, and dressing. The other category included assistance with walking, transportation, and errands. The burden associated with such tasks could be attributed not so much to hours of service as to lack of freedom; these tasks represented confinement in relation to geographical proximity and time scheduling. In sum, these kinds of tasks were particularly burdensome because they put "the caregiver on the care receiver's time schedule" (Montgomery et al., 1985, p. 23).

Among employed caregivers, some kinds of dependencies are more predictive than others of employees' making accommodations in their work schedules (Stone & Short, 1990). Specifically, the presence of problem behavior and the number of hours during which the elder could be left alone were significant predictors of caregiver work accommodation, whereas the number of impairments in activities of daily living was not. Stone and Short suggested that providing help with functional limitations was fairly predictable and could often be scheduled around the caregiver's work day. Gibeau and Anastas (1989) found that the elder's limitations in activities of daily living, memory impairment, poor judgment, and emotional health were all predictors of conflict between work and family for employed caregivers. Still, only memory impairment and poor emotional health were significantly associated with their work absenteeism.

The special difficulties of combining employment and care for a cognitively impaired elder have been highlighted by Scharlach (1989). Comparing employed caregivers of cognitively impaired versus physically impaired elders, he found that those who cared for the cognitively impaired reported more stress, more interference between work and caregiving, and more absenteeism from work. Further, caregivers of the cognitively impaired "were more than twice as likely to consider quitting because of the demands of caregiving" (Scharlach, 1989, p. 237).

Number of Caregiving Roles. Employees who have elder-care responsibilities often have caregiving responsibilities for other dependents as well. On the one hand, multiple caregiving demands can have negative effects; Gibeau and Anastas (1989) found that having children at home was related to greater conflict between work and family for women providing elder care. On the other hand, multiple roles can also be associated with positive effects; for example, Stoller and Pugliesi (1989) found that even though multiple responsibilities produced greater burden for caregivers, they also contributed positively to well-being. In particular, being employed was associated with less depression, and having a greater number of nonfamilial roles was associated with less stress. Taken together, these findings suggest that although multiple roles may place more demands on caregivers, they can also be a source of personal satisfaction.

Number of Persons Receiving Care. Caregivers may be helping more than one elder. For instance, in a study conducted by the American

Association of Retired Persons (1987) of employees at five worksites, 27% of caregivers provided help to two elderly people, and 3% provided assistance to three or more elderly.

Caregivers may also have several dependents who are not elderly. Stoller (1983) examined whether having multiple children affected sons' and daughters' abilities to provide assistance to an elder. She found that, regardless of their ages, the number of children in a household did not influence how many hours of care the adult daughters provided. For sons, however, having more children under the age of 6 was related to more hours of assistance to the elder. In fact, for each preschool child, the son provided an additional 5.2 hours of help per month to his parent. Stoller interpreted these findings to mean that sons assumed more responsibility for providing elder care when their wives were caring for small children, but they then transferred elder-care responsibilities to their wives when the children were older.

In summary, our review of demands experienced by caregivers of the elderly shows that:

1. The relationship between the number of hours employed per week and caregiver stress is not clear.
2. Sharing a home with an elderly care recipient eliminates the need for the caregiver to manage two households but increases caregiver stress nonetheless.
3. Among employed caregivers, providing care for elders with cognitive impairments is particularly stressful and is more likely to interfere with work than ongoing care for elders with physical impairments.
4. Multiple caregiving roles are a source of personal satisfaction as well as stress.
5. Having multiple dependents results in a redistribution of labor among men and women.

Resources

In the literature on caregiving to the elderly, several variables have emerged as potential resources. Among these are socioeconomic status, informal support, and ease of finding and managing care.

Socioeconomic Status. Based on national statistics, most providers of elder care fall into the middle-income bracket. Nevertheless, almost one third of caregivers are in the poor to near-poor bracket, and most of these are women (Select Committee on Aging, 1987). After all, the responsibilities associated with caregiving can affect the caregiver's ability to work. In a study of brain-damaged adults, Enright and Friss (1987) discovered that more than a quarter of their caregivers stated that they would be working if they were not providing care. These individuals estimated that their lost earnings averaged $20,400 per year. Enright and Friss noted that this lost income probably had a major impact on the families' ability to purchase care for their relatives as well as respite care and support for themselves.

According to a review of the literature on caregivers of the elderly conducted by Horowitz (1985), social class was a key predictor of the type of assistance provided to the elder. Horowitz found that lower-class caregivers tended to live with the elder and to provide direct services, whereas those with higher socioeconomic status were more likely to provide financial assistance to the elder and to purchase services.

With respect to the effects of social class on caregiver stress, Horowitz (1985) found that the conclusions from the literature were inconsistent. Specifically, some studies found no relationship between social class and stress, whereas others found evidence for greater stress among those with higher socioeconomic status. Horowitz hypothesized that one reason that higher-income caregivers experienced more stress was that they had greater expectations for leisure time opportunities during their retirement than lower-income caregivers; such expectations contrasted markedly with their actual experience once they became caregivers.

Partner Status. For married adult children, the presence of a spouse can be both a support and a conflicting demand on their time that interferes with caregiving responsibilities for their parents. Indeed, in a study of adult daughters and sons who were providing care, being married reduced the level of assistance to the parents by more than 20 hours per month (Stoller, 1983). These data suggest that marriage represents a competing demand on caregiving and that unmarried caregivers provide a disproportionate amount of care to their parents.

Informal Support. Family and friends can play a crucial role in supporting the caregiver. Enright (1991) found that caregivers received about 5 hours of help per week from family and friends. When the caregiver was employed, the amount of this support increased dramatically for men but not for women.

Some studies have shown that informal support for caregivers decreases as the elder's impairments increase (Miller, 1987). In a qualitative study of caregivers of spouses with cognitive impairments, Miller identified some reasons for the caregivers' reduced social lives: Caregivers' responsibilities allowed less time for social activities; the elders' problem behaviors resulted in embarrassment and in decreased desire to attend social functions; and the problem behaviors resulted in fewer invitations from friends. Further, some caregivers were upset that their friends treated them as if they were single rather than as part of a couple.

Most of the research indicates that caregiver stress is less when informal support is greater. For example, Montgomery et al. (1985) found that reduced burden among caregivers was related to having more family members to help provide assistance. Similarly, Zarit et al. (1980) discovered that family visits were associated with diminished caregiver burden. Stoller and Pugliesi (1989) found no evidence of a direct effect of emotional or instrumental support on caregiver burden but some indication of a buffering effect from these support functions. Specifically, social support diminished the burden for those caregivers with multiple caregiving demands (that is, those with children living at home). Finally, with regard to caregivers who were employed, there is some evidence that the existence of secondary caregivers allowed the primary caregivers to continue to work. Working caregivers who had help from others were less likely to change their work schedules (Stone & Short, 1990), an activity that was shown to be associated with stress by Orodenker (1990). Furthermore, Scharlach et al. (1991) found less interference between caregiving and work for employed caregivers who had more social support.

Ease of Finding and Managing Care. Caregiving involves not only providing direct services but also finding and managing the assistance of others (Archbold, 1983). Although Archbold concluded that providing personal care was more stressful than managing such care, others discovered that finding and managing formal services involve greater stress. Using data from the National Long-Term Care Survey, Orodenker (1990) found that caregivers who had assistance from formal service providers were more stressed than those without such paid assistance. She speculated that the process of locating and coordinating outside help may put additional pressure on caregivers who are already strained by their caregiving responsibilities.

The findings from another study of caregivers to the elderly are partially, but not entirely, consistent with those of Orodenker. Stoller and Pugliesi (1989) examined the relative effect of formal services on caregivers' psychological distress and caregivers' sense of burden. They discovered that the use of formal services was associated with reduced psychological distress, indicating that formal services can relieve the stress of providing direct care. At the same time, the use of formal care was also associated with increased caregiver burden. Stoller and Pugliesi suggested that this relationship may be explained by the elder's high level of dependency and by the caregiver's feelings of inadequacy and guilt that are generated by turning to outside help.

In summary, this review of resources for caregivers of the elderly indicates that:

1. The relationship between the social class of the caregiver and the level of stress experienced is not clear.
2. The caregiver's spouse can be a source of support but may also present a conflicting demand for time.
3. Having a greater amount of informal support tends to reduce stress among employed caregivers.
4. Finding and managing formal services may be as problematic as providing care directly.

Outcomes

Research has considered the effects of caregiving on employment as well as the influence of employment on caregiving. Many studies of employed caregivers have emphasized the negative effects of caregiving on employment and work productivity. As described below, these effects include time lost from work (scheduled and unscheduled), a lack of energy and experience of worry while at work due to caregiving responsibilities, the need to rearrange one's work schedule, the loss of career or job opportunities, and other productivity-related effects. In addition, also described below, are studies that demonstrate the beneficial influence of employment on caregiving.

Time Lost From Work. Enright and Friss (1987) found that 55% of caregivers who worked more than half time reported missing time at work. Among these employees, absenteeism averaged 9 hours per month (Enright & Friss, 1987). Scharlach and Boyd (1989) found that more than two thirds of caregivers reported making or receiving phone calls at work related to elder care. Another commonly reported source of work interruption was the need to take time off from work to accompany elders to medical appointments (Gibeau & Anastas, 1989). Scharlach and Boyd (1989) and Stephens and Christianson (1986) found that employed caregivers reported taking leave from their jobs because of their caregiving responsibilities.

Worry and Lack of Energy. Enright and Friss (1987) surveyed caregivers about the problems they experienced at work related to their caregiving and found that 58% stated that they sometimes worked more slowly because of worry or upset. Gibeau and Anastas (1989) found that 35% of employed female caregivers were concerned that their job performance was affected by their caregiving, often because of worry or time pressure.

A study by the University of Bridgeport (Wagner, 1987) discovered several adverse health indicators that were experienced more often by employees involved in elder care than by other employees, including frequent anxiety or depression, difficulty in sleeping, headaches, or weight gain or loss. Such symptoms resulted in not only lower productivity at work due to physical health stress but also increased use of health-care benefits.

Rearrangement of Work Schedule. In their analysis of data from the National Long-Term Care Survey of Caregivers, Stone et al. (1987) found that among caregivers who were employed, nearly 3 out of 10 had re-arranged their work schedules in order to accommodate their caregiving duties. Gibeau, Anastas, and Larson (1987) found that of the female employed caregivers whom they studied, 35% had made work adjustments for similar reasons. Orodenker (1990) found that altering work schedules to accommodate dependent-care needs was a significant predictor of stress among employed caregivers.

Lost Job or Career Opportunities. Perhaps the most dramatic impact of caregiving on employment is the need to quit work to provide care. Indeed, the need to quit work may be one of the most stressful repercussions of caregiving. Brody, Kleban, Johnsen, Hoffman, and Schoonover (1987) found that, among female caregivers, those who quit work had more problems than those who did not work or those who remained employed. National statistics have indicated that approximately 11% of caregivers left their jobs because of their caregiving demands (Stone et al., 1987). In their study of caregivers, Stephens and Christianson (1986) found that of recently unemployed caregivers, 35% quit their jobs to provide care, and 28% were prevented from looking for work due to their caregiving responsibilities. Between 20% and 30% of employed caregivers have reported anticipating the need to quit their jobs (Gibeau & Anastas, 1989; Scharlach & Boyd, 1989). Several researchers have also found that employed caregivers reported turning down training and new job opportunities because of their caregiving responsibilities (Gibeau & Anastas, 1989; Scharlach & Boyd, 1989; Stephens & Christianson, 1986).

Other Productivity-Related Effects. Some studies have reported that caregiving can also result in employees' taking fewer vacations or having to use their vacation and/or sick leave allocations in order to care for elders, having less time for themselves and to spend with family and friends, or delaying retirement to pay for care-related expenses (Health Action Forum of Greater Boston, 1989). All of these effects ultimately can negatively influence a caregiver's productivity at work.

Beneficial Effects of Employment on Caregiving. Although many of the studies discussed thus far have emphasized the negative conse- quences of combining work and caregiving, there is some indication that this combination can have positive effects. For example, Orodenker (1990) hypothesized that employment may buffer the negative conse- quences of elder care. Indeed, in comparing three groups of caregivers (i.e., currently employed, previously employed, and never employed), she confirmed that the currently employed group was significantly less stressed than the other groups of caregivers.

When employed caregivers are providing assistance to elders with particularly problematic behavior, employment may become an even more important buffer from caregiving responsibilities. Scharlach (1989) discovered that 15% of caregivers for cognitively impaired elders stated that employment made their caregiving responsibilities less stressful. Similarly, Stone and Short (1990) found that those who cared for an elder with behavior problems were more likely to work than those whose elder had no such problems. These findings emphasize the respite function of employment for some caregivers (Brody et al., 1987; Enright & Friss, 1987). In addition, the literature on multiple roles has suggested that combining roles (e.g., employment and caregiving) may bolster the caregiver's competence and offer more exposure to additional resources (Stoller & Pugliesi, 1989).

In summary, our review of the literature on the effects of combining caregiving for elders and employment suggests that:

1. Caregiving can interfere with work. In particular, employees with elder-care responsibilities have been found to:

   worry while at work,
   alter work schedules,
   have more interruptions at work,
   take time off,
   turn down job opportunities,
   experience health problems,
   quit work.

2. Work can have beneficial effects for caregivers by:

   providing a respite from caregiving responsibilities,
   offering exposure to new resources,
   enhancing the caregiver's sense of competence.

FINDINGS FROM OUR SURVEY

We now turn to the survey results to explore further some of the directions indicated by previous research relating to employees who provide elder care. First, it might be useful to portray a typical employee providing elder care in our sample. The caregiver was a 43-year-old white woman. She worked full time (92%) on the day shift (88%) as a professional or manager (64%). She was caring for her parents or in-laws (72%) who lived in their own home (76%). She had missed about half a day of work during the previous month and experienced some difficulty in combining work and family.

To understand what factors influenced stress and absenteeism among our employees who provided elder care, we used an analysis strategy parallel to that used in the previous two chapters on caregivers of children and adults. Data pertaining to employees with elder-care responsibilities were tested using hierarchical multiple regression. The six absenteeism and stress variables were regressed on the independent variables in three blocks. In the first block, variables representing personal characteristics (gender, age, ethnicity, occupation, caring for parent, and caring for spouse) were entered. The second block consisted of the demand variables (hours worked, shift, number cared for, number of caregiving roles, distance from recipient, hours of care provided, and special care needs). Finally, the resource variables (household income, work schedule flexibility, working partner, nonworking partner, informal support, formal support, finding and managing care, and satisfaction with care) were entered in the third block to determine their effects over and above the personal characteristics and the demands.

The findings are presented in relation to each of the three blocks. Within each block, the results are discussed in relation to, first, the absenteeism variables and, second, the stress variables. The three steps from the multiple regression analyses for the absenteeism variables are presented in Table 5.1. Likewise, the three steps for the stress variables are presented in Table 5.2.

Personal Characteristics

The personal characteristics predicted from 1% to 5% of the variance for the absenteeism variables. Leaving work early or arriving late was the variable best explained by the personal characteristics. Being female, younger, and caring for a parent or spouse was associated with high absenteeism. When the demand and resource variables were entered into the regression, the same predictors generally remained significant.

For the stress variables, the background characteristics predicted from 1% to 7% of the variance, with caregiving stress having the largest amount of its variance explained. Being female predicted high personal health stress, elder-care stress, and difficulty combining work and family. Both caring for a parent and caring for a spouse predicted increased caregiving stress and difficulty combining work and family. Age predicted the separate indicators of stress differentially. Specifically, employees who were younger had more difficulty combining work and family, whereas those who were older experienced more stress associated with caring for an elder.

With one exception, the predictors remained statistically significant when demands and resources were considered. The exception was that the relationship between being older and experiencing caregiving stress disappeared. This decrement in caregiver stress indicates that demands and resources exhausted the original variance explained by age. In general, the personal characteristics variables served as slightly better predictors of stress than of absenteeism, but a similar pattern of variables was associated both with high stress and high absenteeism.

TABLE 5.1 Effects of Personal Characteristics, Caregiving Demands, and Caregiving Resources on Absenteeism Variables Among Employees With Elder-Care Responsibilities

	Absenteeism Variables								
	Days Missed			Late or Left Early			Interruptions		
Step entered regression:	1	2	3	1	2	3	1	2	3
Predictors									
Personal Characteristics									
Gender (female)	+			+	+	+			
Age of employee	−			−	−	−	−	−	−
Ethnicity (white)									
Occupation (professional)									
Caring for parent	+		+				+		
Caring for spouse							+	+	+
Change in R^2 at Step 1	.01			.05			.02		
Demands									
Hours worked					+	+		+	+
Shift (day)									+
Number cared for					+	+		+	
Number of caregiving roles									+
Distance from recipient									
Hours of care provided									+
Special care needs									
Change in R^2 at Step 2		.01			.02			.07	
Resources									
Household income			−						+
Work schedule flexibility						+			
Working partner						−			
Nonworking partner						−			
Informal support									
Formal support									
Ease finding/managing care			−						
Satisfaction with care									−
Change in R^2 at Step 3			.01			.01			.02
Total R^2/R^2 Adjusted			.03/.02			.08/.07			.11/.10
Overall F			2.42**			6.83**			9.07**
Df (reg./res.) 21,1544									

Note: Based on significant betas; "+" indicates a significant positive relationship; "−" indicates a significant inverse relationship.
* $p \le .05$; ** $p \le .01$.

TABLE 5.2 Effects of Personal Characteristics, Caregiving Demands, and Caregiving Resources on Stress Variables Among Employees With Elder-Care Responsibilities

	Stress Variables								
	Personal Health Stress			Elder-Care Stress			Difficulty Combining Work and Family		
Step entered regression:	1	2	3	1	2	3	1	2	3
Predictors									
Personal Characteristics									
Gender (female)	+	+	+	+	+		+	+	+
Age of employee				+			−	−	−
Ethnicity (white)									
Occupation (professional)								−	
Caring for parent				+	+	+	+	+	+
Caring for spouse				+		+	+		+
Change in R^2 at Step 1	.01			.07			.04		
Demands									
Hours worked								+	+
Shift (day)									
Number cared for					+	+			
Number of caregiving roles					−	−		+	+
Distance from recipient					−	−			
Hours of care provided					+	+		+	+
Special care needs		+			+	+		+	
Change in R^2 at Step 2		.01			.12			.05	
Resources									
Household income			−						
Work schedule flexibility			−						−
Working partner									
Nonworking partner									
Informal support									
Formal support						+			
Ease finding/managing care						−			−
Satisfaction with care			−			−			−
Change in R^2 at Step 3			.03			.08			.13
Total R^2/R^2 Adjusted		.05/.04			.27/.26			.22/.21	
Overall F		4.16**			27.38**			20.97**	
Df (reg./res.) 21,1544									

Note: Based on significant betas; "+" indicates a significant positive relationship; "−" indicates a significant inverse relationship.
* $p \leq .05$; $p \leq .01$.

Demand Variables

Controlling for the personal characteristics, the demand variables accounted for an additional 1% to 7% of the variance for the absenteeism variables. Interruptions due to family-related matters were the form of absenteeism best predicted by the demand variables. Of the seven demand variables, three were significantly related to absenteeism and all were related in the expected direction. Specifically, working more hours per week, working the day shift, and having multiple caregiving roles were predictive of greater absenteeism. Each of these variables remained significantly related to absenteeism even after resource variables were entered. An additional variable, hours of care provided, also obtained significance at the final stage. The number of days missed was not predicted by any of the demand variables.

Among the measures of stress, the demand variables accounted for an additional 1% to 12% of the variance, controlling for the personal characteristics. Of the seven demand variables, all five of the caregiving situation variables and none of the two work situation variables predicted high elder-care stress. Two of those five (distance from care recipient and number of caregiving roles) did not predict in the expected direction, however. Although the literature on the effect of distance from the care recipient has been mixed, we found that living farther away from the care recipient was associated with lower stress than was living close to the recipient. Having multiple caregiving roles was also associated with decreased caregiving stress; perhaps the presence of many dependents allowed the care recipients to help one another, making the actual caregiving less burdensome. With respect to the difficulty of combining work and family, however, having multiple caregiving roles was associated, as expected, with greater difficulty, as were working more hours at one's job, providing more hours of elder care, and having an elder with special care needs. When resources were entered into the regression, all these demand predictors remained significant, except having an elder with special care needs.

As with the personal variables, the demand variables were better predictors of stress than of absenteeism. With the exception of working more hours and having multiple caregiving roles, which were associated with both high absenteeism and stress, the other demand variables predicted the two sets of outcome variables differentially.

Resource Variables

Resource variables accounted for a minimal amount of additional variance (1% to 2%) in the absenteeism variables, controlling for personal characteristics and demand variables. Of the eight resource variables, four consistently operated in the predicted direction. Having a partner (either working or nonworking), ease in finding and managing care, and satisfaction with care arrangements were associated with decreased absenteeism. A fifth variable, income, was related to both increased and decreased absenteeism. That is, those with higher incomes missed fewer days of work but had more interruptions. Perhaps those with higher incomes had job responsibilities that required them to be at work but at the same time afforded them more flexibility to accommodate interruptions while on the job. In addition, a sixth variable, having flexible schedules and family-supportive personnel policies, was related to increased absenteeism with respect to arriving late and leaving work early.

Within the stress variables, the resource variables accounted for a fairly large additional proportion of explained variance (3% to 13%), controlling for personal characteristics and demand variables. Difficulty in combining work and family was the outcome for which the resource variables explained the largest amount of variance. Again, four of the eight resource variables operated in the predicted direction: high income, flexible schedules and supportive personnel policies, ease of finding and managing care, and satisfaction with care arrangement were associated with decreased amounts of stress. Only the use of considerable formal support in caring for the elder was related to higher stress. This finding is supportive of others (Orodenker, 1990; Stoller & Pugliesi, 1989) who have found formal support to be associated with caregiver burden. Among the outcome variables, stress was predicted by the resource variables considerably better than was absenteeism. Only two resource variables consistently lowered both absenteeism and stress: satisfaction with care arrangements and ease of finding and managing care.

DISCUSSION

A number of important findings have emerged from this exploration. Here we will focus on the results that help to understand the contributors to absenteeism and stress among employed caregivers of the elderly.

As noted in previous research, being a female caregiver is more problematic than being a male caregiver (Horowitz, 1985; Stone & Short, 1990). We found that women who provided care to the elderly were more likely than male caregivers to arrive late or leave early and to experience stress. The gender differences generally remained even when resources were added. These results suggest that, for this group of caregivers, there is a need for more innovative ways of easing caregiving demands and/or bolstering the resources of female caregivers.

To address the question of what kinds of relationships contribute to greater caregiving burden, we compared those who cared for a spouse with those who cared for a parent. Previous research has indicated that, among employed providers of elder care, spousal care is a more arduous kind of caregiving (Brody, 1985; Soldo & Myllyluoma, 1983). Our findings did not confirm this research. Rather, we found that both those who cared for a spouse and those who cared for a parent were likely to miss time at work and experience stress.

We also addressed the controversy over whether younger or older caregivers experienced more difficulty—a debate that has remained inconclusive in the research literature (Cicirelli, 1981; Montgomery et al., 1985; Robinson, 1983). We found that the younger caregivers tended to miss more work and experience more difficulty in combining work and family. This finding provides support for the explanation that younger people providing elder care have unique difficulties (Montgomery et al., 1985; Robinson, 1983). Applying Neugarten's (1968) concept of a "social clock" to the experience of younger people suggests that, for them, caregiving may be more off-time and less normative than for older people.

Although several demanding aspects of work and family were considered in this study, only working more hours at one's job, the hours of care provided, and the number of caregiving roles contributed to both absenteeism and stress. Contrary to the findings of Enright and Friss (1987) that caregivers who worked the fewest hours experienced the most burden, our results clearly show that caregivers who worked the most hours were more burdened. Caregivers who work more hours are vulnerable to diminished productivity and find it difficult to combine work and family. In addition, employees who provide many hours of care are more burdened than those providing fewer hours of assistance. Thus, full-time employees and those who work overtime, as well as those who are providing many hours of elder care, are in special need of workplace supports.

The number of caregiving roles has a complex effect on absenteeism and stress. Our findings, like those of previous research, indicate that multiple roles can have both beneficial (Stoller & Pugliesi, 1989) and detrimental (Gibeau & Anastas, 1989) effects. Our employed caregivers with multiple caregiving roles were more likely to miss time at work and to express difficulty in combining work and family. They also, however, experienced less stress related specifically to their elder-care responsibilities than did those with fewer roles. It may be that some of their caregiving responsibilities offset each other, that is, some of their dependents may have been helping each other. For example, an aged mother might care for a child after school; the child, in turn, might help his grandmother with some household chores. This intergenerational help-giving can alleviate some of the employed caregiver's responsibilities.

We found that living some distance away from the care recipient was associated with less stress. In fact, as suggested by others, living with a care recipient may be particularly conflictual and burdensome (Horowitz, 1985; Stoller & Pugliesi, 1989). An analysis of these same data reported elsewhere (Chapman, Neal, & Lebow, 1988) has indicated that the optimal living distance is neither with the care recipient nor far away, but within 5 miles. This distance allows for easy access to the elder without the difficulties associated with living together.

Another finding involves formal help. Although it might appear that obtaining help from professionals would help to alleviate stress, in fact, formal help is associated with increased stress. One explanation for this finding, suggested by Stoller and Pugliesi (1989), is that employees who obtain outside help are likely to have more difficult caregiving situations. Although we attempted to control for the difficulty of the caregiving situation by including several demand measures, those measures may not have captured this dimension adequately. Another explanation, suggested by Orodenker (1990), is that the process of obtaining and maintaining outside help is itself stressful. In the words of one survey respondent:

> Because I managed my 85-year-old mentally incompetent father until his death 2 years ago, I'm pretty savvy about medical, social, and health resources in the community. These services are woefully inadequate, tremendously fragmented, and take a lot of energy to access.

In Chapter 9 we discuss services that employers can offer to help their employees locate formal service providers and alleviate some of this stress.

Two other resources—being satisfied with care arrangements, and particularly, having flexible work schedules and supportive policies—are additional areas that can be addressed in the workplace. Our findings suggest that if employers help with the provision or acquisition of quality care arrangements, they will be likely to have less stressed and more productive employees. Further, our results show that employees who have flexibility in their work schedules and family-supportive personnel policies are also likely to be less stressed. Such flexibility, however, is related to increased absenteeism, particularly in terms of arriving late or leaving early. Thus companies should recognize that if greater flexibility is to result in greater productivity among providers of elder care, it will occur because of decreased stress and improved morale and loyalty to a company that supports its employees and not because of less absenteeism from work.

REFERENCES

Abel, E. K. (1990). Family care of the frail elderly. In E. K. Abel & M. K. Nelson (Eds.), *Circles of care: Work and identity in women's lives* (pp. 65-91). New York: State University of New York Press.

American Association of Retired Persons. (1987). *Caregivers in the workplace: Survey results.* Unpublished monograph.

Archbold, P. G. (1983). Impact of parent-caring on women. *Family Relations, 32,* 39-45.

Brody, E. M. (1985, November). *The long haul: A family odyssey.* Paper presented at the annual scientific meeting of the Gerontological Society of America, New Orleans.

Brody, E. M., Kleban, M. H., Johnsen, P. T., Hoffman, C., & Schoonover, C. B. (1987). Work status and parent care: A comparison of four groups of women. *The Gerontologist, 27,* 201-208.

Brody, E. M., & Schoonover, C. B. (1986). Patterns of parent-care when adult daughters work and when they do not. *The Gerontologist, 26,* 372-381.

Cantor, M. (1979). The informal support system of New York's inner city elderly: Is ethnicity a factor? In D. E. Gelfand & A. J. Kutzik (Eds.), *Ethnicity and aging: Theory, research, and policy* (pp. 153-174). New York: Springer.

Chapman, N. J., Neal, M. B., & Lebow, W. (1988, November). *Employed caregivers in the middle: Caring for old and young.* Paper presented at the annual scientific meeting of the Gerontological Society of America, San Francisco.

Cicirelli, V. G. (1981). *Helping elderly parents: The role of adult children.* Boston: Auburn House.

Enright, R. B., Jr. (1991). Time spent caregiving and help received by spouses and adult children of brain-impaired adults. *The Gerontologist, 31,* 375-383.

Enright, R. B., Jr., & Friss, L. (1987). *Employed caregivers of brain-impaired adults: An assessment of the dual role.* Final report submitted to the Gerontological Society of America. San Francisco: Family Survival Project.

Gibeau, J. L., & Anastas, J. W. (1989). Breadwinners and caregivers: Interviews with working women. *Journal of Gerontological Social Work, 14,* 19-40.

Gibeau, J. L., Anastas, J. W., & Larson, P. J. (1987, September). Breadwinners, caregivers and employers: New alliances in an aging America. *Employee Benefits Journal, 12,* 6-10.

Health Action Forum of Greater Boston. (1989). *Eldercare: The state of the art.* Boston: Author.

Horowitz, A. (1985). Family caregiving to the frail elderly. In M. P. Lawton & C. Maddox (Eds.), *Annual review of gerontology and geriatrics* (Vol. 5, pp. 194-246). New York: Springer.

Miller, B. (1987). Gender and control among spouses of the cognitively impaired: A research note. *The Gerontologist, 27,* 447-453.

Montgomery, R. J. V., Gonyea, J. G., & Hooyman, N. R. (1985). Caregiving and the experience of subjective and objective burden. *Family Relations, 34,* 19-26.

Mutschler, P. H. (1989). *Eldercare and the collar connection: Occupation and work constraints* (Working Paper No. 52). Waltham, MA: Policy Center on Aging, Heller School, Brandeis University (Box 9110, Waltham, MA 02254-9110).

Neugarten, B. L. (1968). Adult personality: Toward a psychology of the life cycle. In B. L. Neugarten (Ed.), *Middle age and aging: A reader in social psychology* (pp. 137-147). Chicago: University of Chicago Press.

Noelker, L. S., & Poulshock, S. W. (1982). *The effects on families of caring for impaired elderly in residence.* Final report submitted to the Administration on Aging. Cleveland, OH: The Benjamin Rose Institute.

Orodenker, S. Z. (1990). Family caregiving in a changing society: The effects of employment on caregiver stress. *Family & Community Health, 12,* 58-70.

Robinson, B. C. (1983). Validation of a caregiver strain index. *Journal of Gerontology, 38,* 344-348.

Scharlach, A. E. (1989). A comparison of employed caregivers of cognitively impaired and physically impaired elderly persons. *Research on Aging, 11,* 225-243.

Scharlach, A. E., & Boyd, S. L. (1989). Caregiving and employment: Results of an employee survey. *The Gerontologist, 29,* 382-387.

Scharlach, A. E., Sobel, E. L., & Roberts, R. E. L. (1991). Employment and caregiver strain: An integrative model. *The Gerontologist, 31,* 778-787.

Select Committee on Aging. (1987). *Exploding the myths: Caregiving in America* (Committee Publication No. 99-611). Washington, DC: Government Printing Office.

Soldo, B. J., & Myllyluoma, J. (1983). Caregivers who live with dependent elderly. *The Gerontologist, 23,* 605-611.

Stephens, S. A., & Christianson, J. B. (1986). *Informal care of the elderly.* Lexington, MA: Lexington Books.

Stoller, E. P. (1983). Parental caregiving by adult children. *Journal of Marriage and the Family, 45,* 851-858.

Stoller, E. P., & Pugliesi, K. L. (1989). Other roles of caregivers: Competing responsibilities or supportive resources. *Journal of Gerontology: Social Sciences, 44,* S231-S238.

Stone, R., Cafferata, G. L., & Sangl, J. (1987). Caregivers of the frail elderly: A national profile. *The Gerontologist, 27,* 616-626.

Stone, R. I., & Short, P. F. (1990). The competing demands of employment and informal caregiving to disabled elders. *Medical Care, 28,* 513-526.

Wagner, D. L. (1987). Corporate eldercare project: Findings. In M. A. Creedon (Ed.), *Issues for an aging America: Employees and eldercare: A briefing book* (pp. 25-29). Bridgeport, CT: University of Bridgeport, Center for the Study of Aging.

Wagner, D. L., Creedon, M. A., Sasala, J. M., & Neal, M. B. (1989). *Employees and eldercare: Designing effective responses for the workplace.* Bridgeport, CT: University of Bridgeport, Center for the Study of Aging.

Wagner, D. L., Neal, M. B., Gibeau, J. L., Anastas, J. W., & Scharlach, A. (1989). *Eldercare and the working caregiver: An analysis of current research.* Unpublished manuscript.

Wilson, R. E. (1988). Intergenerational programs. In D. E. Friedman (Ed.), *Issues for an aging America: Elder care: Highlights of a conference* (pp. 37-39). New York: Conference Board.

Zarit, S. H., Reever, K. E., and Bach-Peterson, J. (1980). Relatives of the impaired elderly: Correlates of feelings of burden. *The Gerontologist, 20,* 649-655.

Zarit, S. H., Todd, P. A., & Zarit, J. M. (1986). Subjective burden of husbands and wives as caregivers: A longitudinal study. *The Gerontologist, 26,* 260-266.

6

Employees With Multiple Caregiving Roles

My husband is 68 and has Parkinson's disease. He is very dependent on me, as is his mother who is 88—she has had three operations in the last year and lived at my home for three of them. I also have my mother who is 78. My daughter has a 2-year-old which I baby-sit frequently—and is expecting another in September. It seems sometimes I am the only healthy one in the family—still I suffer from stomach problems and arthritis. I also have my son in college (22 years old) who I am supporting financially. STRESS! YES.

The previous chapters have examined caregivers of each of the care recipient groups (children, adults, and elders) separately. This chapter systematically examines the effects of having one or more caregiving roles on absenteeism and stress.

Does Caregiving Have an Impact on Employee Absenteeism and Stress?

The recent literature on multiple roles has focused on their positive as well as their negative effects. Marks (1977) referred to an "expansion" hypothesis of the effect of multiple roles—that energy can expand to accommodate the roles to which the individual is positively committed. Multiple roles may also provide multiple sources of identity and meaning for the self (Thoits, 1986). Baruch and Barnett (1986) pointed out that most research from either a role conflict or an expansion framework respectively has focused on simply the *number* of roles occupied. They argued, instead, that the impact of multiple roles may well depend on the *quality* of the experience within each role. Thus multiple roles may have positive effects to the extent that they yield a net gain of benefits over costs.

In addition, having multiple persons who depend on one for care may translate to some degree into multiple helping resources. School-age children, adults with disabilities, and elders may require assistance from employed caregivers yet also be available to help out in caring for others in the household. An older child might thus provide assistance for disabled parents or grandparents, whereas the latter might be able to provide child care for younger children. For instance, in our sample, about 38% of the older persons *receiving* some care from an employed adult also *provided* help with child or adult care, meals, or finances at least "sometimes." Such mutual exchanges are possible and likely.

Because the previous chapters have had as their focus those employees with caregiving responsibility, the comparison of those with and without caregiving responsibility has not been addressed until now. Before moving on to consider multiple caregiving roles, then, we will examine the evidence regarding the influence of holding a single caregiving role, whether for children, adults, or elders, on employee absenteeism and stress.

Employees With and Without Responsibility for Child Care. The bulk of the relevant literature, deriving largely from the multiple role tradition of research, has assessed the impact of having children in the household on working men and women. The review of the literature that follows finds rather mixed results, with the most common finding being that having children in the home is associated with better physical and mental health.

Several studies have found that the combination of employment, marriage, and parenthood is consistently associated with health and well-being (Coleman, Antonucci, & Adelmann, 1987; Gove & Zeiss, 1987; Kandel, Davies, & Raveis, 1985; Verbrugge, 1983). Most of these found that each role had an additively positive impact on health or mental health, rather than a multiplicative impact. That is, the effect of two roles was what would be predicted from adding the effects of each role when performed by itself; there was no effect of combining roles beyond that. These studies also contain evidence of the added stress of the parental role. Kandel, Davies, and Raveis (1985) reported that although on average the lowest levels of depression were found among those who had the most complex role configuration (married, employed parents), depression was exacerbated by occupying the role of parent for employees experiencing stress at work. Gove and Zeiss (1987) reported that women's happiness with their multiple roles depended on whether or not they preferred to be employed. Finally, several researchers have explored the effect not just of having children but also of having multiple children on employee well-being. Sekaran (1985) and Thoits (1986) both reported that having more children had a positive impact on the mental health of employed women but not employed men. Still, Haynes and Feinleib (1980) found that the incidence of coronary heart disease among working women increased with the number of children, especially for blue-collar workers.

Other authors have found either a small positive effect or no effect of combining work and parenthood. Baruch and Barnett (1986), Verbrugge and Madans (1985), and Waldron and Jacobs (1989) reported that parenthood had no effect on mental and physical health, although employment and in some cases marriage were associated with better mental and physical health for women. Baruch and Barnett (1986) pointed out that a higher *quality* experience in each of these roles significantly increased women's self-esteem and pleasure and decreased their depression.

Some evidence also points to instances, however, in which caring for children has a negative impact on employees. Karasek, Gardell, and Lindell (1987) found that the employed parents of very young children experienced increased fatigue and physical ailments. Employed married women, but not men, with minor children at home were found to have higher levels of depression (Cleary & Mechanic, 1983). Voydanoff (1988) found that having children in the home increased the level of reported work/family conflict for both men and women. Emlen and Koren (1984) found that employees who had children under the age of 18 living in the household had a higher incidence of absenteeism than other employees. Finally, Kessler and McRae (1982) found that employed women with children showed poorer physical health than those without children; the two groups did not differ on measures of mental health.

These conflicting findings may be due in part to differences in the outcome measures (work/family conflict vs. depression) and in the sample selection. For example, Waldron and Jacobs (1989) included only middle-aged women, whereas Bromet, Dew, and Parkinson (1990) found that it was younger, working, blue-collar wives who reported greater spillover from work to family and family to work. Such differences may reflect the greater burden of caring for younger children, the maturity of the parents, or the effects of social class and access to resources to pay for child care.

Although the findings are not consistent, the bulk of the evidence concerning child care seems to indicate that:

1. The parental role per se has either a positive or neutral effect on the physical and mental health of employees, especially women employees.
2. Although the parental role may have a negative effect for some employees (blue-collar, those with young children, or those with job stress), the effect across the total employee population is more likely to be positive or neutral than negative.

Employees With and Without Responsibility for Adult or Elder Care. Relatively little research has compared employees with and without adult or elder-care responsibilities to assess their levels of absenteeism and stress. Most of the relevant research has instead compared caregivers who are employed with those who are not employed. Thus the research is often not directly comparable with that available for child care. The few directly comparable studies, which compare employees with and without elder-care responsibility, found caregiving had negative effects on mental health and social participation (George & Gwyther, 1986) and resulted in strain on relationships with other family members (Scharlach, 1987). Scharlach and Boyd (1989) found that employees with caregiving responsibility for elders or children had more job/family conflict, missed more days of work, and took more time off during the workday than did their noncaregiving co-workers.

The larger research literature has compared caregivers who do or do not work outside the home. Employment has been found to have positive effects on stress and mental health for employed caregivers of adults with disabilities (Enright & Friss, 1987) and elders (Brody, Kleban, Johnsen, Hoffman, & Schoonover, 1987); to have no effect on either subjective burden (Montgomery, Gonyea, & Hooyman, 1985) or caregiver stress (Cantor, 1983; Miller, 1989); and to increase caregiver strain (Robinson, 1983). The inconsistencies in the findings may have arisen in part from differences in how the outcomes were conceptualized and measured and in part from differences in the comparison group used. That is, in some cases employed caregivers were compared with other caregivers who were not employed; in other cases, they were compared with other employees who were not caregivers. When caregivers with and without employment were compared, it was found that employment sometimes provided respite from particularly difficult caregiving situations, as well as additional income (Brody, 1990).

There is also ample evidence of caregivers who quit work in order to provide care to an adult or elder, thus perhaps eliminating from the work force those caregivers with the highest level of burden and conflict between work and family. Stone, Cafferata, and Sangl (1987), for example, reported that 12% of female adult children, 14% of female spouses, 5% of male adult children, and 11% of male spouses quit work to become a caregiver to an elderly parent or spouse. Brody (1990) found that women quit work or reduced their work hours due to the time conflicts involved in working and caregiving. In addition, women reported that they quit because they could not afford to purchase services for their mothers, because purchased services and help from other family members were not enough, and because their mothers would not accept paid help. Most regretted the need to leave their jobs, both because of the meaning that their work held for them and because of the financial loss.

To summarize the findings concerning caregivers of elders and adults with disabilities:

1. Studies of employees with and without caregiving responsibility for adults or elders have generally found evidence of greater stress and absenteeism among caregivers.

2. Comparisons of caregivers who are and are not employed, however, have mixed findings.

   In some cases, the job may serve as respite from caregiving responsibility instead of being simply a competing responsibility.

   As caregiving burden increases, many employees who wish to continue their caregiving role or who have limited sources of alternate care either choose to leave the work force or reduce their hours of employment.

3. Comparisons of employees with and without caregiving responsibility, and of caregivers with and without jobs, are always based on self-selected samples who have made choices about their investments of time and energy into multiple roles.

What Are the Effects of Occupying Multiple Caregiving Roles?

Many caregivers provide care for more than one type of care recipient at the same time. The combination of caregiving roles that has received the most attention is that of caring for aging parents while still having children at home. These caregivers, especially women, have been referred to as the "sandwich generation" (Miller, 1981; Shanas, 1980), and some of the resulting role conflicts have been identified. Miller (1981) pointed out that occupying the role of caregiver to aging relatives may cause role conflict since it occurs at the same time that caregivers are confronting major personal developmental issues (e.g., their own aging and the "empty nest") and when they are looking forward to a time of "relaxation and self-indulgence." The issues of timing and developmental stages are likely to be relevant to other combinations of caregiving roles as well, although less attention has been paid to them. As one of our respondents said,

> Because of the extremes in age levels in our home, from 79 down to 3 years, we seem to experience stress that is directly related to what we need to do. . . . We have a teenager, whose normal behavior is quite often not perceived as acceptable by an older brother and sister who seem to have forgotten similar past behavior. Each of us seems to have different needs from the same environment, which quite often leads to conflict. My husband and I expected this to begin a quieter and more free time of our life. Instead, because of the economy, we ended up with a live-in 3-year-old (has been with us since birth) and everything that entails. The 79-year-old, as is quite typical for elderly people with beginning senility, has behavioral patterns that quite often conflict with the household. . . . We all love each other a great deal—that's what makes it all bearable—but sometimes, jobs and school are really a nice place to escape to for some sense of balance.

Brody (1981) identified other role conflicts for middle-aged women who provide elder care. She referred to these women as "women in the middle"—in the middle not only in a generational sense but because of the various roles that they fill. They are caught between the traditional value placed on family care and the new value placed on employment and careers for women. They are also caught by the conflicting or excessive demands of multiple roles as they add employment and parent care to their customary roles as wife, homemaker, mother, and grandmother.

In addition to role conflict, role ambiguity may also be associated with the role of caregiver. In a later article, Brody (1985) pointed out that, although parent care is increasingly common, we have not as a society developed clear expectations and behavioral norms for adult children in this position. Even though we may be starting to think of caregiving for parents, other older family members, and friends as a normative life role, assumption of this role does not occur at any predictable age or stage in the life cycle. It may occur when adult children are young or old and have or do not have children of their own at home. The priorities for resolving conflicts among these roles are not clear. Thus Pratt, Schmall, and Wright (1987) found that conflicts with other obligations, including family, career, and personal well-being, were a common area of ethical concern for caregivers of dementia patients. Clear roles or moral principles that might help caregivers resolve these dilemmas were lacking. Such conflicts appear to be particularly problematic for women, who, as Gilligan (1982) argued, tend to define themselves in the context of relationships and to judge themselves with respect to their ability to care for others.

Empirical research on the effects of multiple caregiving roles is very limited. With regard to elder care, women who are both employed and caring for an elder do not significantly reduce the amount of care that they provide, whereas men do (Stoller, 1983). Stoller posited that women simply allocated less time for their own personal, social, and leisure pursuits. Despite increased labor force participation among married women, Stoller, citing a 1979 study by Hofferth and Moore, noted that wives' work weeks have simply increased instead of domestic tasks being redivided between husbands and wives. Her research found that the number and ages of children in the home had no impact on the amount of help that daughters provided to elders. By contrast, men with more children under the age of 6 provided more hours of elder care, perhaps because their wives were involved in child care. In a study of the probability of accommodating work schedules (working fewer hours, rearranging work schedules, and taking time off without pay), Stone and Short (1990) found that having child-care responsibility in addition to caring for elders did not significantly increase work accommodation.

The early study by Stoller (1983) did not assess the physical or mental health impacts of multiple caregiving roles, but one can infer considerable potential for role conflict from the number of hours devoted to work and caregiving. A more recent study by Stoller and Pugliesi (1989) assessed the association of multiple caregiving roles with two outcomes —caregiver burden and psychological distress—in a sample of caregivers to the elderly. They found that, for those providing more hours of care, employment and commitment to other nonfamily roles increased caregiver burden. At the same time, employment and involvement in nonfamily roles decreased psychological distress, a finding that supports the role expansion hypothesis (that is, that roles may increase rather than decrease available energy; Marks, 1977). Having child-care responsibility increased the caregiver burden for those providing more hours of care, but decreased the burden if the caregivers also had higher levels of emotional support from family and friends.

Stull, Bowman, and Smerglia (1991) conducted a quantitative and qualitative study of female caregivers to the elderly. Their quantitative analysis found that employment outside the home was unrelated to four measures of caregiver strain (social constraints, time constraints, interpersonal strain, and perception of the elder as demanding or manipulative) but did increase the physical strain in caregiving. In contrast to the quantitative data, however, the qualitative analysis suggested that many women found work to have a positive impact on their ability to continue in the caregiving role. The effect of the number of children in the household differed for daughters and daughters-in-law. Daughters with children present had less physical strain and fewer social constraints; they also had less depression and negative well-being than did daughters-in-law with children. Since almost two thirds of the sample had children over the age of 18 living in the home, children might well have represented a source of assistance for daughters, who are more likely to be primary caregivers, rather than a drain on their resources.

Finally, Gibeau and Anastas (1989) reported findings from a study of 77 women who were working full time while caring for an elderly family member. They found that having children at home increased the level of conflict experienced between work and family but did not increase the number of hours of work missed during the year.

In summary, the research on multiple roles is conceptually rich, but it is still empirically limited. Our review of this literature indicates that:

1. The timing of multiple role occupancy—that is, the life cycle stage at which it occurs—may be an important determinant of its effects.

2. Conflicting and historically changing role expectations offer the individual little societal guidance for resolving role conflicts.

3. The relationship between multiple roles and physical and mental health outcomes is quite complex and likely to vary depending on the outcome measure chosen.

4. Additional research concerning the interactions between levels of caregiving responsibility and competing roles may be needed to understand fully the effect of combining multiple roles.

ANALYSIS OF SURVEY RESULTS

Previous research has established some of the impacts of caregiving on work, family life, and personal well-being. Our study, however, is unique in assessing simultaneously the effects of (a) different kinds of caregiving responsibility (child, adult, elder), and (b) different combinations of these caregiving roles.

Figure 2.2 and Table 2.1 in Chapter 2 display some of the characteristics of those employees holding multiple roles. The most common multiple role combination is that of caring for a child and an elder, a combination characterizing about 9% of our sample. The other combinations (adult and elder, adult and child, and all three roles) were held by 1% of the sample or fewer. At what life stage do these combinations most typically occur? In our sample, 56% of the women employees holding multiple roles were in their twenties or thirties, although men were typically in their forties and fifties (60%). Most often, these employees had one or more children over the age of 9 (67% of men and 61% of women); a sizeable minority, however, had at least one child under the age of 9 (47% of men and 45% of women). The male and female multiple role holders also showed differences in the likelihood that they had a spouse or partner: 28% of the women did not, but only 7% of the men did not. The elders who were cared for by male employees were likely to be somewhat older than those cared for by women: 50% of the men but only 42% of the women cared for a person over the age of 75.

Effects of Dependent-Care Responsibility

The first set of analyses addresses two questions: "Do caregivers report more absenteeism and stress than noncaregivers?" and "Are there specific combinations of caregiving roles that are more likely to be associated with absenteeism and stress?"

The analytical approach taken to answer these questions was to carry out multiple regression analyses parallel to those in previous chapters, predicting absenteeism and stress from sets of variables representing personal characteristics, demands, and resources entered hierarchically. In the analyses reported here, however, a fourth set of variables was included. This final set included one or more variables representing the caregiving roles occupied. In all cases, the sample for these analyses was the entire sample of 9,573; thus employees with dependent-care responsibilities could be contrasted with those who had none. A major difference between this chapter and the preceding chapters is the inclusion of the entire sample in the analyses presented here.

The hierarchical multiple linear regression analyses entered personal characteristics on the first step, demands on the caregivers on the second, resources on the third, and the variables representing types of caregiving roles occupied on the last. Because the sample for these analyses was made up of employees with a variety of caregiving responsibilities (including none), the variables representing the demands and resources specific to the particular caregiving situation were omitted. The personal characteristics included were gender, age, ethnicity, and occupation. The demand variables were limited to the demands placed on the employee by his or her job: number of hours worked per week, and shift. The resource variables included household income, work flexibility, and a set of "dummy" variables representing whether or not the employee had a spouse or partner. Dummy variables are coded "0" and "1"; when a related set are entered together, the effect for each variable is to compare those employees coded "1" on the variable with employees coded "0" on all variables in the set. In this case, there were two variables in the set: The first coded having an employed spouse or partner as "1," and the second coded having a nonemployed spouse or partner as "1." The effect of these two variables is to compare employees meeting either of these conditions to employees having no spouse or partner (the condition that received a coding of "0" in both cases). In addition to the reported analyses, some analyses were repeated for men and women separately. The results were similar enough that only the combined analyses will be presented.

The four rows of Table 6.1 present the results of four sets of analyses conducted to examine the effects of various combinations of caregiver roles. The four analyses focus on different ways of measuring caregiving responsibility in an attempt to discover what it is specifically about multiple caregiving roles that may lead to stress and absenteeism. Each of the four rows in Table 6.1 represents a different way to measure caregiving responsibility, as detailed in the paragraphs below. Thus each row represents five multiple regression analyses (one for each outcome variable), in which the caregiving responsibility measure(s) is entered on the final step. In all cases, the table shows the percentage increase in the variance of the dependent variable (R^2 change) explained by the variable or set of variables representing caregiving roles.

TABLE 6.1   Amount of Variance in Dependent Variables Explained by Four Different Ways of Measuring Dependent-Care Responsibility

Ways of Measuring Dependent-Care Responsibility (Variable Set)	Outcome Variables				
	Days Missed	Late or Left Early	Interruptions	Personal Health Stress	Difficulty Combining Family and Work
1. Any caregiving (yes/no)	.003**	.008**	.046**	.002**	.061**
2. One to three roles	.003**	.009**	.052**	.004**	.064**
3. Seven caregiving roles	.004**	.012**	.055**	.005**	.071**
4. Child care (yes/no)	.002**	.010**	.042**	.000	.060**

* $p \le .05$; ** $p \le .01$.

Caregivers Versus Noncaregivers. The first equation compared employees with any caregiving responsibility at all (coded 1) with employees having no caregiving responsibility. For all five dependent variables, knowing that employees had caregiving responsibility significantly increased our ability to predict their absenteeism and stress scores. Thus we can conclude that having caregiving responsibility, regardless of the type or combination of types, has a consistent effect on absenteeism and stress. Furthermore, examination of the coefficients shows that, for all dependent variables, the effect is in the expected direction. That is, persons with any kind of caregiving responsibility show increased absenteeism and stress, controlling for personal characteristics, demands, and resources.

Specific Caregiver Roles. Variable sets 2 and 3 in Table 6.1 examined whether being more specific about employees' caregiving responsibilities would enable us to account for more of the variance in the dependent measures. If so, this would indicate that the different caregiving roles and combinations of roles have distinctly different relationships with the dependent measures. Thus our understanding of the relationship between caregiving responsibilities and absenteeism and stress would be enhanced by a finer differentiation among caregiving roles.

In variable set 2, the effect of the number of caregiving roles was examined. Three dummy variables were created to contrast employees with one caregiving role, two caregiving roles, and three caregiving roles with those employees with no caregiving role. Examination of the R^2 change scores (row 2 of Table 6.1) shows relatively little advantage (as measured by the amount of variance explained) in differentiating the number of caregiving roles over the simple dichotomy of caregiving-no caregiving (row 1). The largest change in R^2 was for times interrupted at work, among the absenteeism variables, and for difficulty in combining work and family, among the stress variables.

The second approach to developing a more differentiated measure of caregiving responsibilities, seen in variable set 3, developed a set of seven dummy variables: having child care only, adult care only, elder care only, both child and adult care, both child and elder care, both adult and elder care, and having all three types of caregiving roles. Again, the omitted category was having no dependent-care responsibilities. This coding scheme for the dummy variables has the effect of comparing all of the possible combinations of caregiving responsibility with having no caregiving responsibility. Row 3 of Table 6.1 shows the results of these analyses. Differentiating caregiving into the specific types and numbers of caregiving responsibilities not only consistently increased the R^2 but also increased it consistently more than did simply differentiating by number of caregiving roles (row 2). It thus appears worthwhile to keep the different types of caregiving responsibility separate in order to understand the effects of multiple role responsibilities.

Examination of the regression coefficients in variable set 3 (presented in detail later in this chapter) shows that the largest effects were for having child care only or for having child care in combination with other caregiving roles. Thus we decided to explore whether simply identifying whether employees had child-care responsibility would provide as much explanation in predicting absenteeism and stress as these more differentiated approaches to specifying caregiving roles. To explore this question, a dummy variable was created in which those with caregiving responsibility for children were coded 1 and all others were coded 0 (see row 4 of Table 6.1). In general, differentiating only those employees with children from all others (variable set 4) accounted for somewhat less variance in the dependent measures than did combining all types of caregiving responsibility into one category contrasted with no dependent-care responsibility (variable set 1). Thus it was not just child-care responsibility that was associated with absenteeism and stress. The one exception is that child-care responsibility accounted for a larger portion of the variance in the variable "arriving at work late or leaving early" than did either the single category of caregiving responsibility (variable set 1) or the number of caregiving roles (variable set 2). Thus, it appears to be largely child care that is responsible for this particular type of absenteeism.

In summary, these analyses revealed that the best fit in predicting absenteeism and stress derived from equations differentiating caregiving responsibility into the specific types and combinations of caregiving roles filled. The amount of variance explained by the caregiving variables differed by outcome variable (the least variance was explained in days missed and personal health stress) and by how caregiving responsibility was categorized. Classification into seven caregiving roles led to the strongest prediction of the outcome variables. The percentage of variance explained by caregiving roles, however, was low, ranging from a low of less than 1% of the variance (days missed and health stress), to a little more than 1% (left early or arrived late), and up to between 5% and 7% (times interrupted at work and difficulty in combining work and family).

We consistently find that occupying caregiving roles, whether one or more, increases both absenteeism and stress. This finding contrasts with a literature that is much more inconsistent and has tended to find more evidence that multiple roles are associated with positive outcomes. This inconsistency is probably due, in part, to differences in the dependent variables included in the various studies. Many of the positive findings in the literature have focused on general well-being and happiness, rather than on specific job conflicts or reports of difficulty in combining the roles. Occupying multiple roles may in fact involve satisfactions as well as costs, as pointed out by Baruch and Barnett (1986), and these conflicting feelings may be differentially reflected in the outcome measures selected. The stresses involved in providing care to children, elders, and adults with disabilities may contribute to personal growth and self-esteem at the same time that they pose difficult problems on a day-to-day basis. Horowitz (1978) and Brody (1990), for example, are among the researchers who have provided qualitative evidence of the benefits as well as the burdens experienced by some providers of elder care. Providing care to family and friends is in itself evidence that these employees are embedded in social networks and in the web of relationships and exchanges that those networks entail. At the same time, employed caregivers are caught in a conflict between these informal ties and the workplace for their limited time and commitment. The consequence may be missing a day of work, but it is more likely to be some adjustment in the work schedule (arriving late, leaving early, or interruptions from family members) that allows the employee to honor commitments to both work and family.

Seven Caregiving Roles

Since specifying particular combinations of caregiving roles predicts the most additional variance in the dependent measures, this section will present in greater detail the results of multiple regression analyses in which seven caregiving roles were included. Table 6.2 presents the results of the analyses, regressing each of the five dependent variables on personal characteristics, demands, resources, and the seven caregiving roles. Only the final step of the analysis, when all sets of variables have been entered, is reported in the table.

Personal Characteristics. The most consistent finding was that women had significantly more of all kinds of absenteeism, more health stress, and more difficulty in combining work and family. Younger employees were more likely to arrive late and leave early, to be interrupted at work, and to have difficulty in combining work and family, but they also reported less stress with their personal health. White employees were more likely to be interrupted at work, but minority employees missed more days of work and showed more health stress. Professional and managerial workers missed more days of work and reported more difficulty in combining work and family.

Demands. The only demands included in these equations were related to work, due to the lack of comparable caregiving resource measures across the caregiving subgroups. Employees working a day shift reported more of all types of absenteeism but showed no difference in stress levels. Those who worked more hours per week were interrupted more often and reported more difficulty in combining work and family.

Resources. If these variables act as resources, we would expect their regression coefficients to be negative. In other words, as resources increase, absenteeism and stress should decrease. Only 9 of the 15 significant coefficients were in the expected direction, so these variables were not acting consistently as resources. Both household income and work schedule flexibility increased rather than decreased the frequency of arriving late/leaving early and of times interrupted at work. In addition, having a working partner increased the number of days missed and the

TABLE 6.2 Effects of Personal Characteristics, Caregiving Demands, Caregiving Resources, and Multiple Roles on Dependent Variables

Predictors	Outcome Variables				
	Days Missed	Late or Left Early	Interruptions	Health Stress	Difficulty Combining Work and Family
Personal Characteristics					
Gender (female)	+	+	+	+	+
Age of employee	−	−		+	−
Ethnicity (white)	−		+	−	
Occupation (professional)	+				+
Change in R^2 at Step 1	.01**	.04**	.01**	.01**	.02**
Demands					
Hours worked				+	+
Shift (day)	+	+	+		
Change in R^2 at Step 2	.00**	.02**	.02**		.00**
Resources					
Household income	−	+	+	−	−
Work schedule flexibility		+	+	−	−
Working partner	+	−			+
Nonworking partner	−	−		−	
Change in R^2 at Step 3	.01**	.01**	.02**	.01**	.08**
Caregiving Roles					
Child care only	+	+	+	+	+
Adult care only			+	+	+
Elder care only	+	+	+	+	+
Child + adult care	+	+	+	+	+
Child + elder care	+	+	+	+	+
Adult + elder care			+	+	+
Child, adult, elder	+		+		+
Change in R^2 at Step 4	.00*	.01*	.06**	.00**	.07**
Total R^2/R^2 Adjusted	.025/.023	.080/.079	.106/.104	.028/.027	.177/.176
Overall F	12.48**	43.10**	58.20**	14.52**	106.29**
Df (reg./res.) 17,8374					

Note: Based on significant betas; "+" indicates a significant positive relationship; "−" indicates a significant inverse relationship.
* $p \leq .05$; ** $p \leq .01$.

difficulty in combining work and family. The only resource that operated consistently in the expected direction was having a nonworking partner, which decreased absenteeism and personal health stress. Both income and work flexibility, however, did function as resources in reducing personal health stress and difficulty in combining work and family.

Combinations of Caregiving Roles. Caregiving groups were represented by a set of seven dummy variables that included every combination of responsibility for one, two, or three of the types of care recipients. The variables were mutually exclusive, with "no dependent care" as the omitted (and thus the comparison) condition. All of the significant regression coefficients were in the expected direction; that is, caregiving responsibility was associated with increased absenteeism and stress. The caregiving responsibility that was most consistently and strongly associated with increased absenteeism and stress was caring for children only, followed by caring for children and elders. The size of the beta weights did not consistently increase as the number of caregiving roles increased. Two of the single roles (caring for children and caring for elders) and two of the dual roles (child plus elder and child plus adult) were significantly associated with all of the dependent variables. The remaining single role (adult), dual role (adult plus elder), and the triple role (child plus adult plus elder) were significantly associated with three of the five dependent variables.

The dependent variables most consistently predicted by the caregiving roles were times interrupted at work and difficulty in combining work and family; 5% of the variance in the former variable and 7% in the latter were accounted for by the caregiving roles. The change in the percentage of variance accounted for by the caregiving roles in the other dependent variables was statistically significant but very small (1% or less).

What can we conclude from these analyses? First, caregiving responsibilities clearly did increase absenteeism and stress when caregivers were compared with those without caregiving responsibility. Second, having either single or dual caregiving responsibility consistently increased absenteeism and stress. For single caregiving roles, 13 out of 15 coefficients (that is, three single roles by five dependent variables) predicting absenteeism and stress were significant. For dual roles, too, 13 of 15 coefficients were significant. Having all three caregiving roles was significantly associated with the outcomes in three out of the five coefficients. Interestingly, it appeared that particular caregiving roles and combinations of roles were most problematic; the simple number of caregiving roles was not the most important feature. The most difficult roles were caring for children only, elders only, or both children and elders.

Another way to represent the relative levels of absenteeism and stress experienced by the seven caregiving groups is to present graphically each group's mean absenteeism and stress scores. Figure 6.1 shows how the average scores of the caregiving employees compare with those of the entire sample of employees. Thus, the mean score of each caregiving group is represented in terms of how much higher or lower it is than the overall mean score of the sample. Because the caregiver groups were likely to differ on a number of other characteristics that also influence levels of absenteeism and stress (for example, younger people are more likely to be absent), the mean scores for each group were adjusted by controlling for personal characteristics, resources, and demands. This was accomplished by conducting multiple classification analyses with a variable representing each of the seven caregiving groups as the independent variable and the personal characteristics, demands, and resources as covariates. This analysis predicted the mean scores for each group after controlling for the effects of personal characteristics, demands, and resources.

Figure 6.1 can be inspected to address a number of questions about multiple roles. First, did those with no dependent-care responsibility have lower rates of absenteeism and stress? The answer was consistently "yes," particularly for those variables most closely reflective of work/family conflict: times interrupted at work to deal with family-related matters and difficulty in combining work and family. Second, were multiple roles associated with more absenteeism and stress than one role? The answer was "almost always," with the exceptions that those caring only for children had more difficulty in combining work and family than did those with both elder and adult care; they also missed days of work and arrived late or left early as often as several of the multiple role combinations. In addition, employees with elder-care responsibility experienced more personal health stress than those with three caregiving roles (child plus adult plus elder). Third, was occupying three caregiving roles associated with more absenteeism and stress than occupying two roles? Among those with multiple roles, having all three types of care responsibilities was associated with the highest number of times interrupted and the most days missed. Fourth, which of the dual roles were associated with the most absenteeism and stress? Among those with dual roles, those with child- and adult-care responsibilities

Deviations from Mean

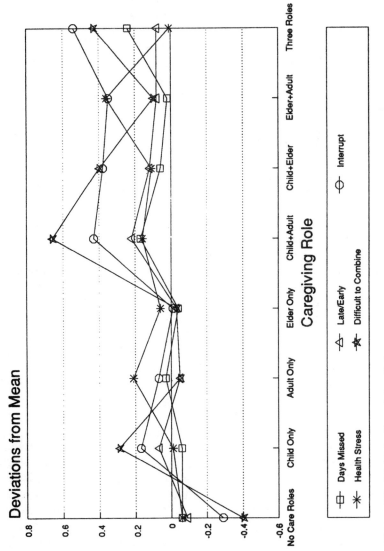

Figure 6.1. Multiple Caregiving Roles

had the highest scores for four of the five outcome measures; those with child- and elder-care duties had intermediate scores on the same four measures. Combining elder and adult care was most associated with the fifth measure, personal health stress. Fifth, which single role was the highest in absenteeism and stress? Caring for children was the most consistent single-role predictor of absenteeism and stress.

The graphic results are not always consistent with what might be expected from comparing the size of the beta coefficients among the caregiving groups. The beta coefficients that are smaller than one might expect are probably due to the small size of some of the subgroups (for example, only 54 persons held all three caregiving roles) and to differences between the caregiving groups in the variance of their scores on the dependent variables.

Interaction Effects

One limitation to the regression analyses presented thus far is that the personal characteristics, demands, and resources were entered directly into the equation, whereas their interactions with the caregiving roles have not been considered. As a result, one cannot conclude that the demands and resources presented function as such solely for caregivers. It may be, for example, that having a high income and a nonworking partner decreases absenteeism and stress for all workers, regardless of their caregiving responsibility. Within a stress model, theorists have often argued that social support functions as a buffer against stress (Gore, 1981; Thoits, 1982). Thus resources like social support might have little impact on those under minimal stress but greater impact for those experiencing high stress. This hypothesis is best tested by adding to the analysis interaction terms that multiply stress level by resources.

In the context of this chapter, stress as a predictor was represented by the number of caregiving roles, ranging from zero to three roles. This variable was entered into the regression equation after the personal characteristics, demands, and resources. Interaction terms were calculated by multiplying the number of caregiving roles by each of the 10 measures of personal characteristics, demands, and resources. These 10 interaction terms were entered in the final step of the hierarchical regression analyses. As shown in Table 6.3, the interaction terms added significantly to the prediction of arriving late or leaving early, times interrupted, and difficulty in combining work and family, although they accounted for less than 1% of the variance in all cases.

TABLE 6.3 Effects of Personal Characteristics, Caregiving Demands, Caregiving Resources, Multiple Roles, and Interaction Terms on Dependent Variables

Predictors	Days Missed	Late or Left Early	Interruptions	Personal Health Stress	Difficulty Combining Work and Family
Personal Characteristics					
Gender (female)	+	+		+	+
Age of employee		–	–	+	–
Ethnicity (white)	–				
Occupation (professional)	+	–			
Change in R^2 at Step 1	.01**	.04**	.01**	.01**	.02**
Demands					
Hours worked					+
Shift (day)	+	+	+	+	
Change in R^2 at Step 2	.00**	.02**	.02**		.00**
Resources					
Household income	–			–	
Work schedule flexibility		+	+	–	–
Working partner		–	+		+
Nonworking partner			+	–	+
Change in R^2 at Step 3	.01**	.01**	.02**	.01**	.08**
Caregiving Roles					
Number caregiving roles					+
Change in R^2 at Step 4	.00**	.01**	.05**	.00**	.06**
Interaction Terms					
Roles by gender		+	+		+
Roles by age					
Roles by ethnicity		–			
Roles by occupation		+			
Roles by hours worked					
Roles by shift			+		
Roles by income					
Roles by work flexibility		+			
Roles by working partner			–		–
Roles by nonworking partner		–	–	+	
Change in R^2 at Step 5		.00*	.00**		.01**
Total R^2/R^2 Adjusted	.025/.023	.082/.080	.106/.104	.028/.025	.170/.168
Overall F	10.33**	35.69**	47.20**	11.58**	81.64**
Df (reg./res.) 21,8370					

Note: Based on significant betas; "+" indicates a significant positive relationship; "–" indicates a significant inverse relationship.
* $p \le .05$; ** $p \le .01$.

For absenteeism, inspection of the significant interaction terms shows that women with caregiving responsibility were more likely than men to arrive at work late or leave early and were interrupted more often. White caregivers were less likely to arrive late or leave early, whereas caregiving professionals and those with flexible schedules were more likely to arrive late or leave early. Caregivers working on the day shift were more likely to be interrupted at work. Finally, caregivers with nonworking partners were less likely than those without partners to be absent (arrive late or leave early, be interrupted at work), as were those with working partners (times interrupted).

Turning to the stress outcomes, only one of the interaction terms predicting personal health stress was significant; those with nonworking partners experienced less health stress. There were three significant interaction terms predicting difficulty in combining work and family. Caregivers who were women or younger reported more difficulty, whereas caregivers with working partners reported less difficulty in combining work and family.

We can thus conclude that these demands and resources do not consistently function as such for caregivers. The finding most consistently in line with our predictions is that having a partner, whether that partner is employed or not, serves as a resource for caregivers. In addition, employed women who are caregivers are more likely than men to bear the consequences of multiple roles in the form of absenteeism and stress.

DISCUSSION

In conclusion, the results of our comparison of caregivers with non-caregivers and of our exploration of the effects of multiple roles provide evidence more in line with a "stress" or "conflict" hypothesis than an "expansion" hypothesis. That is, we found that having caregiving responsibility, especially having responsibility for more than one age group, was associated with increased absenteeism and stress rather than with the increased well-being that would be consistent with the expansion hypothesis. Our findings may be due in part to our choice of which outcome variables to include. That is, we looked specifically at productivity and stress measures but did not include well-being or life satisfaction measures that might have been more likely to reflect positive outcomes.

It appears that in addition to the number of caregiving roles occupied, the specific combination of roles has an impact on absenteeism and stress. In this chapter and in Chapter 2, three different ways of comparing caregiving role combinations have been presented. First, mean absenteeism and stress scores for each group can be compared (Table 2.1). Second, the caregiving role combinations can be included as independent variables in multiple regression analyses predicting absenteeism and stress (Table 6.2). Third, mean scores for absenteeism and stress can be predicted after controlling for the other dependent variables in a multiple classification analysis (Figure 6.1). We would argue that the third approach is the most revealing of the level of absenteeism and stress associated with caregiving roles because it controls for the differences among the caregiving groups in terms of personal characteristics, demands, and resources and is not influenced by the number of employees in each subgroup. Based on this analysis, we found that those employees with no dependent-care responsibility had the lowest levels of absenteeism and stress. Employees with responsibility for all three care groups and those with responsibility for children and adults had the most consistently elevated levels of absenteeism and stress. Among employees with only one caregiving role, caring for children was the most consistent predictor of absenteeism and stress.

Finally, the analyses including interaction terms allowed us to explore whether the effects of personal characteristics, demands, and resources on absenteeism and stress were common to the entire sample of employees or were unique to employees with caregiving responsibilities. These analyses indicated that employees with caregiving responsibilities were more likely to arrive late or leave early, be interrupted at work, and have difficulty in combining work and family than were those who were not caregivers. The combination of being a caregiver with being female was consistently associated with increased absenteeism and stress. Among the resources, having either a working or nonworking partner reduced absenteeism and stress.

REFERENCES

Baruch, G. K., & Barnett, R. (1986). Role quality, multiple role involvement, and psychological well-being of midlife women. *Journal of Personality and Social Psychology, 51,* 578-585.

Brody, E. M. (1981). "Women in the middle" and family help to older people. *The Gerontologist, 21,* 471-480.

Brody, E. M. (1985). Parent care as a normative family stress. *The Gerontologist, 25,* 19-29.

Brody, E. M. (1990). *Women in the middle: Their parent-care years.* New York: Springer.

Brody, E. M., Kleban, M. H., Johnsen, P. T., Hoffman, C., & Schoonover, C. B. (1987). Work status and parent care: A comparison of four groups of women. *The Gerontologist, 27,* 201-208.

Bromet, E. J., Dew, M. A., & Parkinson, D. K. (1990). Spillover between work and family: A study of blue-collar working wives. In J. Eckenrode & S. Gore (Eds.), *Stress between work and family* (pp. 133-151). New York: Plenum.

Cantor, M. H. (1983). Strain among caregivers: A study of experience in the United States. *The Gerontologist, 23,* 597-604.

Cleary, P. D., & Mechanic, D. (1983). Sex differences in psychological distress among married people. *Journal of Health and Social Behavior, 24,* 111-121.

Coleman, L. M., Antonucci, T. C., & Adelmann, P. K. (1987). Role involvement, gender, and well-being. In F. J. Crosby (Ed.), *Spouse, parent, worker: On gender and multiple roles* (pp. 138-153). New Haven, CT: Yale University Press.

Emlen, A. C., & Koren, P. E. (1984). *Hard to find and difficult to manage: The effects of child care on the workplace.* Portland, OR: Portland State University, Regional Research Institute for Human Services.

Enright, R. B., & Friss, L. (1987). *Employed caregivers of brain-impaired adults: An assessment of the dual role.* San Francisco: Family Survival Project.

George, L. K., & Gwyther, L. P. (1986). Caregiver well-being: A multidimensional examination of family caregivers of demented adults. *The Gerontologist, 26,* 253-259.

Gibeau, J. L., & Anastas, J. W. (1989). Breadwinners and caregivers: Interviews with working women. *Journal of Gerontological Social Work, 14,* 19-40.

Gilligan, C. (1982). *In a different voice: Psychological theory and women's development.* Cambridge, MA: Harvard University Press.

Gore, S. (1981). Stress-buffering functions of social supports: An appraisal and clarification of research models. In B. S. Dohrenwend & B. P. Dohrenwend (Eds.), *Stressful life events and their contexts* (pp. 202-222). New York: Prodist.

Gove, W. R., & Zeiss, C. (1987). Multiple roles and happiness. In F. J. Crosby (Ed.), *Spouse, parent, worker: On gender and multiple roles* (pp. 125-137). New Haven, CT: Yale University Press.

Haynes, S. G., & Feinleib, M. (1980). Women, work and coronary heart disease: Prospective findings from the Framingham Heart Study. *American Journal of Public Health, 70,* 133-141.

Hofferth, S. A.,& Moore, K. A. (1979). Women's employment and marriage. In R. E. Smith (Ed.), *The Subtle revolution: Women at work* (pp. 99-124). Washington, DC: The Urban Institute.

Horowitz, A. (1978, November). *Families who care: A study of natural support systems of the elderly.* Paper presented at the meeting of the Gerontological Society of America, Dallas.

Kandel, D. B., Davies, M., & Raveis, V. H. (1985). The stressfulness of daily social roles for women: Marital, occupational and household roles. *Journal of Health and Social Behavior, 26,* 64-78.

Karasek, R., Gardell, B., & Lindell, J. (1987). Work and non-work correlates of illness and behaviour in male and female Swedish white collar workers. *Journal of Occupational Behaviour, 8,* 187-207.

Kessler, R. C., & McRae, J. A., Jr. (1982). The effect of wives' employment on the mental health of married men and women. *American Sociological Review, 47,* 216-227.

Marks, S. R. (1977). Multiple roles and role strain: Some notes on human energy, time and commitment. *American Sociological Review, 42,* 921-936.

Miller, B. (1989). Adult children's perceptions of caregiver stress and satisfaction. *Journal of Applied Gerontology, 8,* 275-293.

Miller, D. A. (1981). The "sandwich" generation: Adult children of the aging. *Social Work, 26,* 419-423.

Montgomery, R. J. V., Gonyea, J. G., & Hooyman, N. R. (1985). Caregiving and the experience of subjective and objective burden. *Family Relations, 34,* 19-26.

Pratt, C., Schmall, V., & Wright, S. (1987). Ethical concerns of family caregivers to dementia patients. *The Gerontologist, 27,* 632-638.

Robinson, B. C. (1983). Validation of a caregiver strain index. *Journal of Gerontology, 38,* 344-348.

Scharlach, A. E. (1987). Role strain in mother-daughter relationships in later life. *The Gerontologist, 27,* 627-631.

Scharlach, A. E., & Boyd, S. L. (1989). Caregiving and employment: Results of an employee survey. *The Gerontologist, 29,* 382-387.

Sekaran, U. (1985). The paths to mental health: An exploratory study of husbands and wives in dual-career families. *Journal of Occupational Psychology, 58,* 129-137.

Shanas, E. (1980). Older people and their families: The new pioneers. *Journal of Marriage and the Family, 42,* 9-15.

Stoller, E. P. (1983). Parental caregiving by adult children. *Journal of Marriage and the Family, 45,* 851-858.

Stoller, E. P., & Pugliesi, K. L. (1989). Other roles of caregivers: Competing responsibilities or supportive resources. *Journal of Gerontology: Social Sciences, 44,* S231-S238.

Stone, R. I., Cafferata, G. L., & Sangl, J. (1987). Caregivers of the frail elderly: A national profile. *The Gerontologist, 27,* 616-626.

Stone, R. I., & Short, P. F. (1990). The competing demands of employment and informal caregiving to disabled elders. *Medical Care, 28,* 513-526.

Stull, D. E., Bowman, K., & Smerglia, V. (1991, October). *Women in the middle: A myth in the making?* Revised version of paper presented at the 1990 annual scientific meeting of the Gerontological Society of America, Boston.

Thoits, P. A. (1982). Conceptual, methodological, and theoretical problems in studying social support as a buffer against life stress. *Journal of Health and Social Behavior, 23,* 145-159.

Thoits, P. A. (1986). Multiple identities: Examining gender and marital status differences in distress. *American Sociological Review, 51,* 259-272.

Verbrugge, L. M. (1983). Multiple roles and physical health of women and men. *Journal of Health and Social Behavior, 24,* 16-30.

Verbrugge, L. M., & Madans, J. H. (1985). Social roles and health trends of American women. *Milbank Memorial Fund Quarterly/Health and Society, 63,* 691-735.

Voydanoff, P. (1988). Work role characteristics, family structure demands, and work/family conflict. *Journal of Marriage and the Family, 50,* 749-761.

Waldron, I., & Jacobs, J. A. (1989). Effects of multiple roles on women's health—Evidence from a national longitudinal study. *Women and Health, 15,* 3-19.

7

Synthesis of Research Findings: Comparison of Child, Adult, Elder, and Multiple Caregiving Roles

I have been a single parent of four minor children who are now grown and on their own. In the past, child care was a monumental problem which drained my finances. My youngest child is preparing now to leave home in the near future, so it is getting easier. . . . Flexible work hours and use of sick leave have been the most helpful personnel practices. Affordable child care would have relieved a lot of stress had it been available in the past. I frequently left my children in the care of my oldest daughter or they were "latchkey kids" who were left unsupervised for a few hours after school. These are very poor alternatives—stressful for me, bad for kids. I also have a brother who is quadriplegic and alcoholic. He is frequently suicidal. I provide him with some help in transportation to doctors' appointments, therapy, but mostly just lots of emotional support. He has lived with me on and off over the past years but is now making arrangements to leave the Portland area to live with a close friend. It looks like I will finally be able to devote my energy to my career and my relationship.

Thus far in this book, we have examined the predictors of absenteeism and stress for employees with children, those caring for adults with disabilities, and those caring for elders. We have also explored the effects of having any dependent-care responsibilities at all, compared with having none, and of giving care to more than one type of dependent. In this chapter, we summarize and synthesize what we have learned. We highlight the major findings of our own study concerning the predictors of absenteeism and stress for employees who care for each of the types of dependents and for those who have multiple types of caregiving responsibilities; we then compare the significant predictors for the three caregiving groups. We also look at how well the conceptual framework that we employed in the study functioned overall as a predictive model for absenteeism and stress. The goal is to identify those variables that should generally be considered when designing and targeting programs and policies to assist employees who have caregiving responsibilities.

Prior to this synthesis, however, let us review a few key points concerning the conceptual model and how it was employed in the analyses. The conceptual model developed for use in this study posited that outcomes measuring absenteeism and stress would, after controlling for employees' personal characteristics, be predicted by demands from both the employees' work and caregiving situations and by family- and work-related resources that assist in coping with those demands. For each of the three caregiving groups—employees with children, employees caring for adults, and employees caring for elders[1]—hierarchical multiple regression analyses were conducted for each of the six dependent, or outcome, measures. The personal characteristics variables were entered in the first step of the analyses, demand variables in the second, and resource variables in the third.

In our model, we posited no specific directional relationship between the personal characteristics and the dependent variables. Positive relationships were expected between the demand variables and the dependent variables, whereas negative relationships were hypothesized between the resource variables and the dependent variables. The demands of the work and caregiving situations were thus expected to be associated with more absenteeism and stress (i.e., positive relationships were posited), whereas resources found within employees' work and family situations were expected to be associated with less absenteeism and stress (i.e., negative relationships were hypothesized).

Chapter 6 examined the effects of occupying multiple caregiving roles and comparing employees with and without caregiving responsibility: A set of multiple regression analyses included interaction terms. These analyses addressed the question of whether the demands and resources functioned as such solely for caregivers or whether they also functioned as demands and resources for employees who had no caregiving duties. These terms were calculated by multiplying the number of caregiving roles by those measures of personal characteristics, demands, and resources that were available for all employees surveyed (i.e., including those without caregiving responsibilities). We hypothesized that family and workplace demands would prove to be particularly problematic for caregivers and that work and family resources would be particularly helpful to caregivers.

To aid in the comparison of the significant predictors of absenteeism and stress for the three caregiving groups, we offer a graphic representation in Tables 7.1 and 7.2. These tables condense the data presented in the three chapters devoted to each of the caregiving groups (Chapters 3, 4, and 5). Table 7.1 summarizes the findings pertaining to the absenteeism outcomes, whereas Table 7.2 summarizes those pertaining to the stress outcomes. These tables present data for only the third and final step, that is, when all of the independent variables had been entered into the analysis performed for each outcome variable for each caregiving group. In addition, the findings from the comparisons of employees with and without caregiving responsibilities are summarized in these tables. These comparisons represent interaction effects; significant effects are denoted by the word *interaction* in Tables 7.1 and 7.2.

In Tables 7.1 and 7.2, only the direction of the relationship is indicated; the standardized beta for each relationship is not specified. Positive relationships, where a higher value for the predictor variable is associated with an increase in the outcome variable, are denoted in uppercase letters for each caregiving group. Negative relationships, where a higher value for the predictor variable is associated with a decrease in the outcome variable, are indicated with lower-case letters (see Note 1 to Tables 7.1 and 7.2).

The total number of independent variables presented in Tables 7.1 and 7.2 is 26, but not all were used in the analyses for each of the three caregiving groups (child, adult, elder) or in those examining the interaction effects with number of caregiving roles. For example, the independent variable "caring for parent" applies only to analyses predicting the outcomes for employees caring for adults or elders. In addition, some variables, although not precisely identical for the three groups, are considered so here for purposes of comparison. For example, providing for special care needs (used in the adult- and elder-care analyses) and having a child with a disability (used in the child-care analyses) are considered comparable. Variables specific to a particular group are so indicated on the tables, as are variables considered equivalent across groups. Variables used in all analyses (child, adult, elder, and interaction) are indicated by the word *all* in the first column.

RELATIVE IMPORTANCE OF THE INDEPENDENT
VARIABLES FOR THE THREE CAREGIVING GROUPS

In the next several paragraphs, we highlight the relative importance of each of the independent variables for predicting absenteeism and stress among employees in each of the three caregiving groups. In addition, for certain of these independent variables, we summarize the findings concerning the extent to which they interact with the number of caregiving roles held by employees to produce a significant effect above and beyond that for employees in general.

Personal Characteristics

Gender. Being a female was consistently related to higher levels of stress and absenteeism for all three groups but especially for employees with children. There also were consistent interaction effects. Specifically, female employees with caregiving responsibilities were more likely than men to arrive at work late or leave early, to be interrupted at work, and to experience difficulty in combining work and family.

Age. The age of the employee had mixed effects within and across groups, but it was a predictor of absenteeism and stress for all three groups. Younger employees were more likely to experience absenteeism. This is consistent with long-standing research findings that older workers experience less job turnover, fewer accidents, and less absenteeism than younger workers (Riley & Foner, 1968, cited in Palmore, 1977). In our study, younger employees caring for children and elders were more likely to be interrupted at work, and younger employees with adult-care and elder-care duties reported higher levels of difficulty in combining work and family. Moreover, there was a significant interaction effect. An employee who was both young and a caregiver was particularly likely to experience difficulty in combining work and family. This may result from younger caregivers being "off-time"—not expecting to be caregivers for adults or elders at this young age (Neugarten, 1968).

At the same time, older employees with child- or adult-care, but not elder-care, duties experienced significantly more personal health stress. One might expect employees providing elder care, who were on average 4 to 5 years older than those caring for children or adults, to experience

TABLE 7.1 Significant Predictors of Absenteeism Among Employees With Child-, Adult-, and/or Elder-Care Responsibilities

Predictors	Absenteeism		
	Days Missed	Late or Left Early	Interruptions
Personal Characteristics			
Gender (female) (all)	CHILD	CHILD ELDER INTERACTION	ADULT INTERACTION
Age of employee (all)		Child Adult Elder	Child Elder
Ethnicity (white) (all)		Interaction	CHILD
Occupation (professional) (all)	CHILD	INTERACTION	
Caring for parent (A & E only)	ELDER		
Caring for spouse (A & E only)			ADULT ELDER
Caring for adult child (A only)			
Demands			
Hours worked (all)			CHILD ELDER
Shift (day) (all)	ADULT	CHILD ELDER	CHILD ADULT ELDER INTERACTION
Number cared for (A & E)/Number of children < age 9 (C)			
Number of caregiving roles (all)		CHILD ELDER	CHILD ELDER
Distance from recipient (A & E)/ Extra travel time for child care (C)		CHILD	CHILD

			ELDER
Hours of care provided (A & E)/ Age of youngest child (C)			
Special care needs (A & E)/ Child with disability (C)	CHILD		
Child-care cost as % of household income (C only)			
Total hours of out-of-home care (C only)	CHILD		
Resources			
Household income (all)	Child Elder	CHILD	CHILD ELDER
Work schedule flexibility (all)		CHILD ELDER INTERACTION	CHILD
Working partner (all)	CHILD	Child Elder Interaction	CHILD Interaction
Nonworking partner (all)		Child Elder	Interaction
Informal support (A & E)/ Informal support from kin (C)			
Number of children aged 9 to 17 (C only)			CHILD
Child has self-care arrangement (C only)			CHILD
Formal support (A & E only)			
Ease finding/managing care (A & E)/ Ease finding/continuing care (C)	Elder	Child	Child
Satisfaction with care (all)		Child	Child Adult Elder

Note: Upper-case letters indicate a significant positive standardized beta (i.e., there was a statistically significant direct relationship between the two variables); lower-case letters indicate a significant negative standardized beta (i.e., there was a statistically significant negative, or inverse, relationship between the two variables). The analyses adding the interaction terms included all employees in the sample, and not all employees had a valid value for the outcome variable, "caregiving stress" (i.e., those with no caregiving duties); thus, no analyses with interaction terms were conducted for that outcome variable.

TABLE 7.2 Significant Predictors of Stress Among Employees With Child-, Adult-, and/or Elder-Care Responsibilities

Predictors	Stress		
	Personal Health Stress	Caregiving Stress	Difficulty Combining Work and Family
Personal Characteristics			
Gender (female) (all)	CHILD ELDER		CHILD ELDER INTERACTION
Age of employee (all)	CHILD ADULT		Adult Elder Interaction
Ethnicity (white) (all)			
Occupation (professional) (all)		CHILD	
Caring for parent (A & E only)		ADULT ELDER	ELDER
Caring for spouse (A & E only)		ADULT ELDER	ELDER
Caring for adult child (A only)			
Demands			
Hours worked (all)			ELDER
Shift (day) (all)			
Number cared for (A & E)/Number of children < age 9 (C)		ADULT ELDER	
Number of caregiving roles (all)	CHILD	CHILD Elder	CHILD ELDER
Distance from recipient (A & E)/Extra travel time for child care (C)		CHILD Adult Elder	CHILD

Hours of care provided (A & E)/Age of youngest child (C)		Child ELDER	ELDER
Special care needs (A & E)/Child with disability (C)	ADULT	ADULT ELDER	
Child-care cost as % of household income (C only)		CHILD	CHILD
Total hours of out-of-home care (C only)			CHILD
Resources			
Household income (all)	Elder		
Work schedule flexibility (all)	Child Elder	Child	Child Adult Elder
Working partner (all)			Interaction
Nonworking partner (all)	Interaction	Child	ADULT
Informal support (A & E)/Informal support from kin (C)		CHILD	Adult
Number of children ages 9-17 (C only)			
Child has self-care arrangement (C only)		Child	Child
Formal support (A & E only)		ELDER	
Ease finding/managing care (A & E)/Ease finding/continuing care (C)	Child	Child Elder	Child Elder
Satisfaction with care (all)	Child Adult	Child Adult Elder	Child Elder

Note: Upper-case letters indicate a significant positive standardized beta (i.e., there was a statistically significant direct relationship between the two variables); lower-case letters indicate a significant negative standardized beta (i.e., there was a statistically significant negative, or inverse, relationship between the two variables). The analyses adding the interaction terms included all employees in the sample, and not all employees had a valid value for the outcome variable, "caregiving stress" (i.e., those with no caregiving duties); thus, no analyses with interaction terms were conducted for that outcome variable.

more rather than fewer health problems. Perhaps these older employees' expectations about their personal health were lower than those of younger employees, causing them to report less stress in this area.

Ethnicity. Ethnicity was a significant predictor for only one of the six outcome variables—interruptions at work—and for only one group—employees caring for children. White employees caring for children were more likely to be interrupted. There was also one significant interaction effect: The combination of belonging to a minority group and being a caregiver was associated with an increased likelihood of arriving late for work or leaving early, compared with other employees. It should be noted that ethnic minorities comprised a very small proportion of the sample (7%); this small proportion may have had the effect of limiting the number of statistically significant predictor variables.

Occupation. Occupation, specifically being a professional, manager, technician, or administrator, was a significant predictor only for employees caring for children; professionals, managers, technicians, and administrators in this group were more likely to miss days of work and to experience caregiving stress. There was one significant interaction effect: Caregivers who were professionals, managers, administrators, or technicians were significantly more likely than other employees to arrive late or leave work early.

Caring for a Parent, Spouse, or Adult Child. Three variables—caring for parent, for spouse, or for adult child—were included only in the analyses of employees with adult- or elder-care duties. Caring for a parent and caring for a spouse were consistent predictors of absenteeism and stress for both groups; caring for an adult child was a significant predictor for none of the outcome variables.

Caring for a parent was a significant predictor of days missed, difficulty in combining work and family, and caregiving stress for employees caring for elders; for employees caring for adults, it was a significant predictor for caregiving stress only. Caring for a spouse was a significant predictor of interruptions at work and caregiving stress for both those caring for elders and those caring for adults. Employees caring for an elder who was a spouse also reported more difficulty in combining work and family.

Demands

Hours Worked. This variable was a significant predictor for only two of the outcomes and two of the caregiving groups. For employees caring for elders, working more hours was a significant predictor of interruptions at work and difficulty in combining work and family. For employees caring for children, working more hours predicted more interruptions at work.

Shift Worked. Working the day shift was a consistent predictor of absenteeism, but not stress, for all three groups. In addition, employees who worked the day shift and who were also caregivers were more likely to be interrupted than other employees (i.e., the interaction term was significant).

Number Cared for/Number of Children Under Age Nine. The number of persons cared for was a significant predictor of just one dependent variable—caregiving stress—for both employees caring for adults and those caring for elders. The number of children under age 9 did not significantly predict any of the outcomes for employees with children in their households.

Number of Caregiving Roles. Not surprisingly, having a greater number of caregiving roles consistently predicted higher absenteeism and stress for employees caring for children or elders. Interestingly, employees who cared for elders and also had another caregiving role reported less, rather than more, caregiving stress. Perhaps these other care recipients were assisting in the care of the elder. Having a greater number of caregiving roles was not a significant predictor for any of the outcomes for employees caring for adults.

Distance From Care Recipient/Extra Travel Time for Child Care. Extra travel time for child care, the second of these two variables and the one used in the child-care analyses, was a consistent predictor of both absenteeism and stress for employees caring for children. That is, employees who needed to spend more time traveling to their child-care arrangement before and after work experienced more absenteeism and stress. For employees caring for elders or adults, distance from the care recipient was a significant predictor of only one outcome—caregiving stress —and the effect was in the opposite direction: Those living closer to the care recipient experienced significantly more caregiving stress. Perhaps for elders, living close increases the expectation of help. Living close by or with the elder may also be an indication of greater frailty on the part of the elder and thus increased need for assistance.

Hours of Care Provided/Age of Youngest Child. Hours of care provided, the first of these two variables, was a significant predictor of three of the six outcomes for employees caring for elders: more interruptions at work, more caregiving stress, and more difficulty in combining work and family. The number of hours of care provided was a significant predictor of none of the outcomes for employees caring for adults.

Employees having younger children were expected to experience more absenteeism and stress than those whose children were older, but this variable was a significant predictor of only one outcome—caregiving stress. Moreover, it predicted less, not more, caregiving stress.

Special Care Needs/Child With Disability. The variables special care needs and child with disability were both significant predictors, but not consistently. Employees having a child with a disability were significantly more likely to miss days of work. Employees caring for adults with special needs experienced significantly more personal health stress and caregiving stress. Employees caring for elders with special needs experienced significantly more caregiving stress.

Child-Care Cost as a Percentage of Household Income. The variable child-care cost as a percentage of income was applicable only to the analyses of data from employees with children in their households. Households who spent a higher percentage of their income on child care were significantly different in only one outcome variable—greater caregiving stress.

Total Hours of Out-of-Home Care. The variable total hours of out-of-home care was also used only in the child-care analyses and was a significant predictor of missing more days of work and greater difficulty in combining work and family. Thus providing for child care in the home proved to be less demanding than arranging for out-of-home care.

Resources

Household Income. Household income was a significant predictor of absenteeism for employees caring for children and those caring for elders, but not consistently in the same direction. For both groups of care-givers, having a higher household income was associated with missing fewer days of work but also being interrupted at work more often. For employees caring for children, a higher household income was associated with tardiness or leaving work early, whereas for those caring for elders, it was associated with less personal health stress. Having a higher household income was not a significant predictor of absenteeism or stress for employees caring for adults.

Work Schedule Flexibility. Having more work schedule flexibility was an important predictor of both absenteeism and stress, especially for employees caring for children and those caring for elders. Although consistently predicting less stress it predicted more absenteeism. Thus, work schedule flexibility appears to be a resource that relieves stress, but it may do so by increasing absenteeism.

Working Partner. Having a working partner was a predictor of the three absenteeism outcomes, especially for employees with children, but it predicted none of the stress outcomes. In general, having a working partner was a resource (compared with not having a partner), in that it was associated with fewer late arrivals or early departures and fewer interruptions at work to deal with family-related matters. The exception was that having a working partner significantly predicted missing more days of work for employees with children. Perhaps even more important for this discussion is that having a working partner functioned as a resource especially for employees who were caregivers (i.e., the inter-action term was significant). Caregiving employees with working part-ners reported less difficulty in combining work and family, fewer interruptions at work to deal with family-related matters, and fewer late arrivals or early departures than did those without partners.

Nonworking Partner. Having a nonworking partner was a significant predictor of at least one of the outcomes for all three caregiving groups. It served as a resource for reducing stress and absenteeism, with one exception: Employees with nonworking partners who were caring for adults found it more difficult to combine work and family. Employees with children and nonworking partners experienced less caregiving stress and arrived late or left early from work less often. Employees who had nonworking partners and were caring for elders were also late to work or left work early less often. We expect that for most employees whose partners do not work, the partner serves as the primary source of care for the care recipient, whether a child or an elder. In the case of caregivers for adults with disabilities, however, the nonworking partner is likely to be the care recipient. Thus, it appears that having a nonworking partner is a resource for employees caring for children or elders but not for employees caring for adults with disabilities. Furthermore, having a nonworking partner served as more of a resource for caregiving employees than for noncaregiving employees: Caregiving employees with nonworking partners were less likely to be interrupted and experienced less personal health stress (i.e., the interaction terms were significant).

Informal Support/Informal Support From Kin. The comparable variables informal support and informal support from kin were significant predictors of just one outcome each. Both the outcomes predicted were stress outcomes, but employees with children who had informal support from kin experienced more, not less, caregiving stress. For employees who were caring for adults, however, informal support did serve as a resource; these employees reported less difficulty combining work and family.

Number of Children Aged Nine to Seventeen. This variable, number of children aged 9 to 17 was considered as a resource only in the analyses of data from employees with children. It was a significant predictor of only one outcome, and it did not function as a resource. Specifically, employees caring for children aged 9 to 17 reported more interruptions at work.

Child Has Self-Care Arrangement. Child has self-care arrangment was another variable considered as a resource just for employees with children. With respect to stress, having a child who was looking after him- or herself was significantly associated with less caregiving stress and less difficulty in combining work and family. With respect to the work outcomes, however, having a child with a self-care arrangement meant more, not fewer, interruptions at work for the employee.

Formal Support. The amount of formal support, which was considered as a resource only for employees caring for adults or elders, was a significant predictor of only one outcome, caregiving stress, and instead of predicting less stress, it actually predicted more. Thus, it was consistent with the finding for caregivers of children that having more hours of out-of-home child care was associated with higher levels of stress. In the case of elder and adult care, the presence of formal care is likely to indicate higher levels of disability and thus more demands on the caregivers. In addition, having a greater amount of formal support is likely to require more effort on the part of the employee to manage those care arrangements.

Ease Finding, Managing, or Continuing Care. The variable ease of finding, managing, or continuing care was a significant predictor of five of the six outcomes for employees with children and half of the outcomes for employees caring for elders; for caregivers of adults with disabilities, it was not a significant predictor for any of the outcomes. It functioned as a resource in all cases: Employees caring for either children or elders who reported ease in finding, managing, and/or continuing their care arrangements consistently reported less absenteeism and stress.

Satisfaction With Care. The satisfaction with care variable, which represented satisfaction with the arrangements made for the care of the child, adult, or elder while the employee was at work, was another very important predictor. Satisfaction with care significantly predicted five of the six outcomes (the exception was days of work missed), and it served as a resource for all three caregiving groups, lowering their absenteeism and stress.

SIGNIFICANT PREDICTORS OF ABSENTEEISM AND STRESS FOR THE THREE CAREGIVING GROUPS

Employees Caring for Children

Examination of Tables 7.1 and 7.2 reveals that for employees with children, the variables significantly associated with the outcome measures of absenteeism and stress most consistently included having more caregiving roles, satisfaction with child care, ease in finding and continuing child-care arrangements, and work schedule flexibility. With the exception of work schedule flexibility, where greater flexibility was associated with less stress but more absenteeism, the demand and resource variables tended to operate in the hypothesized directions. All but 1 (number of children under age 9) of the 22 independent variables used in these analyses were significant predictors of at least one of the dependent variables.

Employees Caring for Adults With Disabilities

Conversely, for employees with adult-care responsibilities, considerably fewer of the independent variables were significant predictors of the outcomes. Tables 7.1 and 7.2 show that fewer than half of the 22 independent variables used in these analyses were significant predictors of one or more of the outcome variables. The variables most often significantly associated with the outcome measures for this group included age, caring for one's spouse, working a day shift, caring for someone with special care needs, and satisfaction with care arrangements for the adult while the employee was at work. To the extent that directional predictions were made, each of these variables was related to the outcome variables that it predicted in the expected direction. In addition, consistent with previous research showing the reliability of older workers, being older was associated with fewer instances of tardiness or leaving work early (Riley & Foner, 1968, cited in Palmore, 1977). Being older also was associated with less difficulty combining work and family but with greater personal health stress.

One possible explanation for the reduced number of significant predictors may be the much smaller number of employees with adult-care responsibilities ($n = 357$) compared with the number having children in the household ($n = 4,422$) and those providing elder care ($n = 2,241$). The relatively small number of caregivers for adults with disabilities may have had the effect of limiting the number of statistically significant predictor variables.

Employees Caring for Elders

For employees with elder-care responsibilities, of the 21 independent variables, those that most consistently predicted absenteeism and stress were dissatisfaction with care arrangements for the elder and occupying more than one caregiving role, followed by being female, being younger, caring for a parent, caring for one's spouse, providing more hours of care, and difficulty in finding and managing care. The resource variables of household income and work schedule flexibility predicted three of the outcomes, although they did not function consistently as resources, as discussed later in this chapter in the section titled Resources.

Significant Predictors for All Three Caregiving Groups

Examination of Tables 7.1 and 7.2 reveals that, of the 18 independent variables that were relevant for all of the three groups, 6 were particularly consistent significant predictors across the dependent measures. These predictors consisted of two personal characteristics variables, one demand variable, and three resource variables. The personal characteristics predictors included gender and age. The demand variable was having more caregiving roles (although it predicted none of the dependent variables for employees in the adult-care group); a second demand variable, working the day shift, was a consistent predictor of higher absenteeism but not stress. The resource variables included satisfaction with care arrangements, work schedule flexibility, and ease in finding and managing or continuing care; this latter variable, however, did not significantly predict any of the outcomes for the adult-care group. Again, as discussed in the following sections, some of these predictors, such as age and work schedule flexibility, functioned differently for the different caregiver groups or in the opposite direction from that predicted by our model.

USEFULNESS OF THE CONCEPTUAL MODEL

One way to assess the usefulness of the conceptual model developed for this study is to examine how well this model of personal characteristics, demands, and resources predicted the absenteeism and stress outcomes for each group. Table 7.3 summarizes the hierarchical multiple regression analyses presented in Chapters 3, 4, and 5 by examining the total amount of variance in each outcome variable that is explained by the conceptual model for each caregiving group. The multiple caregiving analyses are not included because they are not comparable— they include individuals who had no caregiving responsibilities as well as those who were providing more than one type of care.

As shown in Table 7.3, some of the six outcome variables were better predicted than others for the three caregiving groups. The outcome variables best predicted were caregiving stress and difficulty in combining work and family. Caregiving stress explained 23% to 36% of the variance, whereas difficulty in combining work and family explained 21% to 31% of the variance. The next best predicted outcome variable was interruptions at work, for which from 8% to 16% of the variance

TABLE 7.3 Amount of Variance in Absenteeism and Stress Explained by the Conceptual Model for Each Caregiver Group

	Absenteeism			Stress		
	Days Missed	Late or Left Early	Interruptions	Personal Health Stress	Caregiving Stress	Difficulty Combining Work and Family
Caregiver Group						
Child care	.03**	.09**	.08**	.05**	.36**	.28**
Adult care	.01	.04	.16**	.04	.23**	.31**
Elder care	.02**	.07**	.10**	.04**	.26**	.21**

** $p \leq .01$.

was accounted for by the independent variables. Least well predicted were the number of days missed and personal health stress (only 1% to 3% and 4% to 5% of the variance was accounted for by the independent variables, respectively).

The percentage of variance that we were able to explain in the outcome measures is relatively similar to previous research. Studies differ, of course, in the variables included, in their measurement, and in the sample from whom data were obtained. Some studies include only caregivers (employed or not), whereas others include only employees. A number of studies have included caregiver strain or burden as an outcome. For example, Voydanoff (1988) found that 24% of the variance in work/family conflict for men and 27% of that for women was explained by predictors that included personal characteristics, work demands, and family demands (emphasizing child care). Similarly, Gibeau and Anastas (1989) were able to explain 35% of the variance in work/caregiving conflict among caregivers to elders using caregiving demands (both for elders and children) as predictors. Stull, Bowman, and Smerglia (1991) explained from 10% to 15% of the variance in their measures of caregiver strain and caregiver well-being from predictors that included employment status and family demands (elder and child). Miller (1989) found that 25% of the variance in caregiving stress among adult children caregivers to their parents could be explained by personal characteristics and family demands. Finally, Stoller and Pugliesi (1989) were able to explain 56% of the variance in caregiver burden by including personal characteristics and family demands in the equation. Note that some of these studies report only the percentage of variance accounted for unadjusted sample size; with a small sample size (Stoller & Pugliesi, 1989, reported results for a sample of 135 respondents), the adjusted R^2 values are likely to be considerably smaller than those reported.

Studies predicting perceived health status generally are similar to our study in accounting for much less of the variance. For example, Verbrugge (1983) accounted for 5% of the variance in self-rated health; Greenberger, Goldberg, Hamill, O'Neil, and Payne (1989) accounted for from 3% to 8% of the variance in health symptoms for single women, married women, and married men. The latter study focused on work resources rather than family demands as predictors. Studies accounting for a higher percentage of the variance include that of Shinn, Wong, Simko, and Ortiz-Torres (1989), who were able to account for 27% to 28% of the variance in perceived health status using personal characteristics, perceived stressors in combining work and family, coping strategies used, social support, and work schedule flexibility as predictors. Similarly, Coleman, Antonucci, and Adelmann (1987) were able to account for from 15% to 21% of the variance in health status from employment status, parenthood status, marital status, income, and education.

Finally, with respect to absenteeism, Gibeau and Anastas (1989) accounted for 28% of the hours of work missed from predictors that included only caregiving demands. This study, however, reported only the unadjusted R^2 and had a sample of just 77 women.

Returning to Table 7.3, further examination reveals that overall the model (i.e., the independent variables included in the analyses) functioned best in predicting outcomes for the child-care group, followed by the elder-care group. The model was somewhat less effective in predicting outcomes for the adult-care group; indeed, the amount of variance predicted for this group was not significant for three of the six outcomes. Still, for two outcomes—difficulty in combining work and family and interruptions at work—the predictor variables accounted for proportionately more of the variance for this group than for employees with either child- or elder-care responsibilities.

In sum, the model used was more successful in predicting the outcomes measuring stress than it was in predicting those measuring absenteeism. The two outcomes best predicted were two of the three stress measures. Furthermore, for four of the six outcomes, the model was most useful in predicting outcomes for employees with child care; for the remaining two outcomes, it functioned best for employees with adult care.

The research described here does have a number of limitations that affect its generalizability, however. These limitations concern both the study sample and the response rate to the survey. With respect to the latter issue, the response rate of 34%, although not low for mailed surveys of this nature, is still low when one wishes to generalize to the population of employees, as 64% of those employees surveyed did *not* respond.

Furthermore, there were particular segments of the employee population that were either over- or underrepresented. In particular, employees in professional, administrative, managerial, or technical positions were overrepresented in the sample. Also, perhaps not surprisingly, given that individuals in these types of positions tend to earn higher wages, the employees who responded had relatively high household incomes. Women were slightly overrepresented.

Ethnic and racial minorities were underrepresented in the sample. Employees in certain industries also were underrepresented. Although companies were chosen to represent all types and sizes of companies, the response rate among employees in industries such as retail was lower than that for employees in other industries, probably due to the number of part-time and young employees in retail.

Although probably not underrepresented in our sample in terms of their numbers in the population, the group of employees caring for adults with disabilities was relatively small compared with the numbers of employees with minor children and those caring for elders. This reduced size may have resulted in fewer of the predictor variables attaining statistical significance for this group.

The last issue with respect to the sample is that it was drawn exclusively from employers in the Portland, Oregon, metropolitan area, which may limit its generalizability in ways other than the above-listed specific limitations in the sample would indicate. For example, communities differ in terms of the resources available to assist employees with caregiving responsibilities.

The instrumentation used in the study also had some limitations, due largely to the fact that it was designed for needs assessment, not hypothesis-testing, purposes. In particular, there were some measures that were not consistently available for all three caregiving groups, such as the extent to which worry about one's caregiving responsibilities interfered with the employee's social and emotional needs or work performance. Because we chose to include in our analyses only those measures available for employees in each of the three caregiving groups, our conceptual framework was not as comprehensive as we would have liked. As will be further discussed, it is likely that the amount of variance predicted could have been increased had we included additional measures.

In addition, although employees were asked specifically if they had any responsibility for caring for elders or adults with disabilities, no similar item was available pertaining to employees and their caregiving responsibilities for minor children. Employees were classified as caring for children simply if they had children living in their household. This classification ignores the degree of responsibility the employee assumed for the care of the child or children, his or her relationship to the children, and any responsibility for children not living in his or her household, such as might occur with a noncustodial parent.

Finally, another limitation of the study is its cross-sectional nature. Since data were gathered at only one time, and generally covering only a brief period of time (i.e., the past 4 weeks), certain crises and less common events related to caregiving responsibilities are probably underrepresented in the data. Also, the experiences of employees who previously were caregivers of children, elders, or adults with disabilities are not represented at all. With respect to employees with elder- or adult-care responsibilities, a survey of employees in a hospital system (Neal, 1990) found that 12% of the employees responding had had elder- or adult-care duties in the past.

Accounting for the full extent of absenteeism or time loss in all its forms would require many additional predictors, such as illness, alcoholism and other chronic conditions, job satisfaction, labor relations, specific job descriptions, company policies, and differences in how work is structured. Prediction would also be improved if the outcome measures could accurately record more than a 4-week period of time in the lives (and caregiving-related crises) of employees.

In general, the analyses offer support for the model and basic hypothesis: When controlling for personal variables (such as gender), outcomes (such as employees' difficulty combining work with family responsibilities) are predicted by the variation in specific work demands and family demands, yet are ameliorated by specific resources, again both within the workplace and the family.

This is a fruitful model for examining the impact of the responsibilities for caregiving on work and family life. It leads to an understanding of the demands that make life difficult and to an identification of the resources that can make it less difficult. "Resources" point us in the direction of conditions, policies, or interventions that can be implemented to make outcomes more favorable for employed caregivers.

With these limitations in mind, the following summary and implications are offered.

SUMMARY AND IMPLICATIONS

The synthesis of our research that is presented in this chapter reveals that:

1. Occupying a caregiving role, whether one role or multiple caregiving roles, increased both absenteeism and stress among employees. Thus interventions to assist employees who have caregiving responsibilities, regardless of type, are warranted.

2. Particular caregiving roles and combinations of roles (beyond simply the number of caregiving roles occupied) are especially problematic. In our study, when personal characteristics, demands, and resources were controlled using multiple classification analysis, as depicted in Figure 6.1 (see Chapter 6), the most difficult roles were caring for children and adults or caring for all three groups. This implies that special efforts to target employees in these caregiving situations should be mounted.

3. There were both similarities and differences in the variables that predicted the outcome measures for each of the three caregiving groups. The similarities point to variables that affect the three groups in comparable ways. Thus efforts to assist employees who are caregivers, whether for elders, adults, or children, can be aimed at all three groups uniformly and simultaneously. The differences in the significant predictors of the outcomes for the three groups imply the need for a differential targeting of interventions.

4. The personal characteristics and the demand variables that were associated with negative outcomes for the three groups, as revealed in Tables 7.1 and 7.2, provide an indication of those employees who should be targeted for assistance. Our findings show that:

   Female caregivers, in particular, and employees with multiple caregiving roles could especially benefit from program or policy interventions.

   Among employees with adult- or elder-care responsibilities, those caring for spouses and, to a somewhat lesser extent, parents have particular difficulty and might benefit from special attention.

   Programs or policies to assist employees working the day shift could be beneficial for reducing all three types of absenteeism.

   Among employees with children, those having to spend the most time in travel to their child-care arrangements appear to need particular attention.

Employees caring for adults with special needs (e.g., the adult wanders or is confused, disruptive, aggressive, or cannot manage activities of daily living) experience more personal health and caregiving stress and might benefit from intervention.

Similarly, employees spending the greatest number of hours each week caring for elders could potentially benefit from special programs or policies.

5. The resource variables may also be useful in identifying and targeting certain employees for services, depending on the desired outcome.

If lowered stress is desired, for example, employees with less work schedule flexibility and lower incomes could be targeted for assistance.

At the same time, resources such as work schedule flexibility and higher household income may be associated with higher rates of absenteeism. For example, our findings suggest that increasing work schedule flexibility would have positive effects on reducing stress for employees, yet it might also increase their absenteeism. Ideally, then, this flexibility would include tolerance of interruptions at work and of occasional instances of arriving at work late or leaving early. Without such tolerance, it seems likely that the potential benefits of lowered stress might be reduced.

6. Other resource variables, too, including partner status, satisfaction with care, ease of finding and managing care, can provide an indication of the extent to which intervention may be needed or desirable. Our findings indicate that:

Employees who do not have a partner, working or nonworking, are lacking a valuable resource; our findings suggest that these employees should be targeted for assistance.

Efforts to increase employees' satisfaction with the care given, regardless of the type of care recipient (child, adult, or elder), probably would be associated with decreases in stress and absenteeism.

Efforts to aid employees in finding, managing, or continuing care would also be of assistance, especially to those caring for children or elders. Such efforts might involve improving the quality of care, lowering the cost of care, and/or increasing the accessibility of care.

The specific services or policies designed to increase satisfaction with care and ease of finding, managing, or continuing care might, however, need to differ by group.

7. Finally, the analyses conducted revealed that the conceptual framework was most useful in predicting two stress measures—difficulty in combining work and family and caregiving stress—and one absenteeism measure — interruptions at work due to family-related matters. Our greater ability to predict these kinds of outcomes probably stems from the specific focus of these measures on the work-family interface and their direct association with caregiving responsibility. Future research concerning employees and

their family caregiving duties is likely to have greater predictive success if it examines outcomes directly related to the dual employment-caregiving roles. Other outcomes, such as days of work missed, may be affected by numerous variables, such as employee illness, that may or may not be related to employees' caregiving responsibilities.

This section of the book has described the research literature concerning employees with children, employees caring for adults with disabilities, and employees caring for elders, as well as those with multiple caregiving roles. In addition, the results from our survey of employees have been presented. We have summarized these results across the caregiving groups and indicated subgroups that might particularly benefit from employer initiatives to lower employees' stress and/or absenteeism. The next section of the book focuses on types of programs and policies in the workplace that can be implemented to help employees to balance their work and their family responsibilities.

NOTE

1. It is important to remember that the three caregiving groups—child, adult, and elder—were not mutually exclusive. For example, someone included in the child-care group was also included in the elder-care group if she or he had both types of responsibilities.

For a comparison of employees with only one type of caregiving responsibility (i.e., mutually exclusive groups) and employees with no dependent-care responsibilities, see Neal, Chapman, Ingersoll-Dayton, Emlen, and Boise, 1990.

REFERENCES

Coleman, L. M., Antonucci, T. C., & Adelmann, P. K. (1987). Role involvement, gender, and well-being. In F. J. Crosby (Ed.), *Spouse, parent, worker: On gender and multiple roles* (pp. 138-153). New Haven, CT: Yale University Press.

Gibeau, J. L., & Anastas, J. W. (1989). Breadwinners and caregivers: Interviews with working women. *Journal of Gerontological Social Work, 14,* 19-40.

Greenberger, E., Goldberg, W. A., Hamill, S., O'Neil, R., & Payne, C. K. (1989). Contributions of a supportive work environment to parents' well-being and orientation to work. *American Journal of Community Psychology, 17,* 755-783.

Miller, B. (1989). Adult children's perceptions of caregiver stress and satisfaction. *Journal of Applied Gerontology, 8,* 275-293.

Neal, M. B. (1990). *Family caregivers in the helping professions: A survey of employees of a major urban health care system.* Study conducted for the Administration on Aging (award number 90AT0419) and Good Samaritan Hospital and Medical Center under the auspices of The Gerontological Society of America's Fellowship Program in Applied Gerontology. Obtain by writing to author at Institute on Aging, Portland State University, P.O. Box 751, Portland, OR 97207-0751.

Neal, M. B., Chapman, N. J., Ingersoll-Dayton, B., Emlen, A. C., & Boise, L. (1990). Absenteeism and stress among employed caregivers of the elderly, disabled adults, and children. In D. E. Biegel & A. Blum (Eds.), *Aging and caregiving: Theory, research, and policy* (pp. 160-183). Newbury Park, CA: Sage.

Neugarten, B. L. (1968). Adult personality: Toward a psychology of the life cycle. In B. L. Neugarten (Ed.), *Middle age and aging: A reader in social psychology* (pp. 137-147). Chicago: University of Chicago Press.

Palmore, E. (1977). Facts on aging: A short quiz. *The Gerontologist, 17,* 315-320.

Riley, M. W., & Foner, A. (1968). *Aging and society: An inventory of research findings* (Vol. 1). New York: Russell Sage.

Shinn, M., Wong, N. W., Simko, P. A., & Ortiz-Torres, B. (1989). Promoting the well-being of working parents: Coping, social support, and flexible job schedules. *American Journal of Community Psychology, 17,* 31-55.

Stoller, E. P., & Pugliesi, K. L. (1989). Other roles of caregivers: Competing responsibilities or supportive resources. *Journal of Gerontology: Social Sciences, 44,* S231-S238.

Stull, D. E., Bowman, K., & Smerglia, V. (1991, October). *Women in the middle: A myth in the making?* Revised version of paper presented at the 1990 annual scientific meeting of the Gerontological Society of America, Boston.

Verbrugge, L. M. (1983). Multiple roles and physical health of women and men. *Journal of Health and Social Behavior, 24,* 16-30.

Voydanoff, P. (1988). Work role characteristics, family structure demands, and work/family conflict. *Journal of Marriage and the Family, 50,* 749-761.

PART III

Policies, Benefits, and Services in the Workplace

8

Employer Responses to Employees' Dependent-Care Responsibilities: Policies and Benefits

A few years ago, during the illness and death of my daughter, I was able to arrange my work schedule to meet the family needs. Those needs varied from time to time over 1½ years, and I was given the needed flexibility. However, all of this was arranged on an informal basis. Not all supervisors are as accommodating, even when [employer] needs would allow flexibility. I feel that there should be a code provision, directive, or other written means to encourage reasonable flexibility and compassion in providing for the extraordinary needs of the employee.

In this chapter and the next, we review the various types of supports that employers have implemented in an effort to assist employees who have family responsibilities. This chapter focuses on two kinds of employer supports: policies regarding work schedule arrangements and employee benefits. The next chapter addresses services provided by or through employers to their employees with dependent-care responsibilities. In some cases, these supports have been developed specifically to help employees to manage their work and their family duties. In other cases, these policies, benefits, and services apply to the entire work force but may serve to make it easier for employees to balance work and family demands.

Shifts in the composition of the labor force, as well as other social, economic, and technological trends, have led to increased interest in family-responsive policies, benefits, and services in the workplace (Aldous, 1990). Bowen (1988, p. 183) has referred to such policies, benefits, and programs as "corporate supports for the family lives of employees." We will describe these supports and, where data are available, report on their effectiveness. Our goals are (a) to describe a range of types of supports, analyzing some of their advantages and disadvantages, and (b) to discuss factors affecting the prevalence of these supports among employers. Although we provide examples of employers who have implemented employer supports, especially in our discussion of services in Chapter 9, other sources should be consulted as well.[1]

Several possible organizing frameworks exist for considering the range of employer responses to employees' family responsibilities. Our framework draws upon the work of Kamerman and Kingston (1982), Auerbach (1990), Scharlach, Lowe, and Schneider (1991), Creedon and Tiven (1989), and Wagner, Creedon, Sasala, and Neal (1989). This framework consists of three major categories, shown in Table 8.1. These categories include (a) policies concerning work schedule and leave, (b) benefits, and (c) services. These categories are not mutually exclusive; there is some overlap, some blurring of the lines.

Policies can be thought of as the formal or informal ways in which employees' work and leave schedules are handled (Ontario Women's Directorate, 1990). Policies provide the parameters for dealing with certain situations, for example, whether an employee can use his or her sick leave to care for a child who is ill. Generally, except for paid leave (e.g., sick, vacation, or personal), policies involve no direct compensation or cash benefit. We include the various forms of paid leave here as policies because their primary effect is added flexibility in work scheduling, not compensation related to employment.

Benefits refer to forms of compensation, direct or indirect, that provide (a) protection against loss of earnings, (b) payment of medical expenses associated with illness, injury, or other health-care needs, or (c) paid released time for vacations or personal needs. Benefits may also include provision of payment (full or partial) for other services, such as legal, educational, or dependent-care services (Kamerman & Kingston, 1982).

Services are specific programs provided directly by or through the employer that address a particular employee need in a specific way. Services are a tangible form of help but not direct compensation. In our framework, services differ from benefits in that the employer, rather than the employee, chooses the approach (i.e., specific service) to meet a given type of need. Thus when the employee chooses the type of service to be purchased, subsidized, or discounted to meet his or her particular

TABLE 8.1   Employer Supports for Employees With Dependent-Care
                Responsibilities

Support Options	Policy	Benefit	Service
Part-time job options (e.g., part-time work, job-sharing, voluntary reduced time, phased retirement)	X		
Flextime, compressed work week	X		
Flexplace	X		
Relocation policies	X		
Sick, vacation, or personal leave (paid)	X		
Parental/family leave	X		
Medical/emergency leave	X		
Health, dental, life, other insurance		X	
Unemployment insurance, worker's compensation		X	
Federal/state tax credits (publicizing of)		X	
Dependent-care reimbursement plan		X	
Subsidized dependent-care reimbursement plan		X	
Long-term care insurance, other insurance		X	
Subsidized care/vouchers		X	X
Discounts for care		X	X
Education			X
Resource and referral			X
Counseling			X
Case/care management			X
On-site care center			X
Resource development			X

family-related needs, the support is considered a benefit. When the
employer makes this choice, the support is considered a service. As a
result, as shown in Table 8.1, we have designated subsidies and discounts for care as both benefits and services.

   In general, the three categories of employer support options—policies, benefits, and services—involve different levels of employer involvement and investment, with policies representing the least involvement and services the most, and benefits and policies representing the
most cost. Another dimension is the scope of coverage. Policies, as well
as many benefits, are helpful to all employees, whether or not they have
caregiving responsibilities. Some benefits and all services are tailored
specifically to employees with particular needs—in this case, needs
related to employees' dependent-care responsibilities.

POLICIES

Policies, formal and informal, set the parameters for the way in which work is structured. Our research and that of others has shown that flexibility in the structure of work, including the number of hours worked and how work is scheduled, is one of the most important types of support that employers can provide for employees with dependent-care responsibilities. Employer options for enhancing work flexibility include reducing the number of hours worked, changing where work is done, and initiating alternatives regarding how work is scheduled—over a day, week, month, or year. Flexibility is also enhanced when employees are allowed to exercise autonomy with respect to each of these dimensions (Christensen & Staines, 1990). Training managers to increase their sensitivity to the needs of employees who have dependent-care responsibilities and to educate them about formal family-responsive policies that are in place is another important element for enhancing flexibility. The following paragraphs discuss these support options and their advantages and disadvantages both for employers and for employees.

Reducing the Number of Hours Worked

Hours may be reduced by working part time, sharing jobs, using voluntary reduced time (V-time) or phased retirement, and making use of various leave policies.

Options for Part-Time Work. Employees who work part time may be temporary or permanent employees; they may work parts of days, weeks, months, or years (U.S. Department of Labor, undated). The advantages to employers of part-time workers include the possibilities of recruiting from a larger labor pool, adjusting the work force to fit the work load, retaining workers who might otherwise quit work, providing sufficient coverage for peak periods, and achieving higher productivity (U.S. Department of Labor, undated; Zedeck & Mosier, 1990, citing Bureau of National Affairs, 1986, and Nollen, 1980). The disadvantages to employers include extra costs due to fixed per-employee labor costs, and perceptions by employers that part-time workers are less committed to their jobs than are full-time workers (U.S. Department of Labor, undated).

For employees who are caregivers, working part time instead of full time can provide needed income, additional hours to devote to caregiving, and a break from caregiving. The disadvantages can include reduced or nonexistent benefits, reduced income (and sometimes pay scale), lower retirement income (a smaller pension and a lower income base on which Social Security benefits are calculated), and fewer opportunities for career advancement. In the words of one employee in our study,

> I'm hoping to go part time so I can spend more time with my child. I'm not sure if my supervisor will agree to this, however. One reason that I have for not going part time is because my health insurance would not cover any other members in my family . . . I'm a little scared to do this with an infant. But I also feel as if I'm missing a very important time in my child's life, and I really want to work part time.

Job sharing—when two persons share one full-time position, separate but related assignments, or unrelated assignments reflected on a single budget line—is another example of part-time work. The U.S. Department of Labor (undated) noted several advantages of job sharing for employers, including the broader range of skills and experience that can be brought to a shared position, the retention of employees, and continuity should one person leave. For example, Stautberg (1987, cited in Zedeck & Mosier, 1990) reported that Steelcase, Inc., found that its job-sharing program has enabled the company to avoid the need to hire temporary workers to cover for vacations and leaves. The disadvantages for employers include resistance by managers, difficulty in evaluating individual employees whose jobs overlap (U.S. Department of Labor, undated), and difficulty in restructuring many jobs to enable them to be held by two people (Zedeck & Mosier, 1990, citing Olmsted, 1977). The primary advantage to employees is that such job-sharing programs make available additional opportunities for part-time work. The disadvantages to employees include those described above for employees working part time, especially perceived inequities in benefits (U.S. Department of Labor, undated).

A third form of part-time work is voluntary reduced time, or "V-time" (Christensen & Staines, 1990; U.S. Department of Labor, undated). V-time is an annual agreement for the number of hours worked, which is usually less than full time, so that during some weeks more hours are worked than during others (Christensen & Staines, 1990). V-time permits employees to reduce the number of hours they work (and consequently their pay) by 5% to 50% for some period of time, usually 6 to 12 months (U.S. Department of Labor, undated). Benefits and seniority are retained on a prorated basis. This option has been used by employers as an alternative to layoffs and as a means of assisting employees to meet educational, family, or personal needs (U.S. Department of Labor, undated). V-time can be particularly useful to employees with newborn or newly adopted children and to employees caring for adults or elders undergoing crises and needing additional time and attention from their employee caregiver. The disadvantages include those listed above for part-time work.

A fourth form of part-time work consists of phased retirement, based on years of service or age (U.S. Department of Labor, undated). Some phased retirement plans involve placing the retiring employee in a mentorship position and having him or her train the replacement employee. The use made of the retiring employee's knowledge in such mentorship programs is an obvious advantage to employers (U.S. Department of Labor, undated). The disadvantages for employers include the cost of developing a phased retirement program, especially one involving mentorship, and the possible need to change pension formulas (U.S. Department of Labor, undated). For employees, phased retirement generally means a reduced pension. Nonetheless, this option meets the needs of employees who wish to make a gradual transition to retirement. It may be especially useful for employees with adult- or elder-care responsibilities who might otherwise be forced to quit their jobs entirely as their responsibilities come to require increasing amounts of their time.

Options for Leave Policies. Options that result in a reduced number of hours worked also include leave policies. Several such policies have been formulated by employers, including sick leave, family illness days or hours, personal leave, and family leave. Leave may be paid or unpaid.

Sick leave and short-term disability insurance protect employees from the temporary loss of income when they become ill or experience a disability that prohibits them from working. The Social Security Administration (cited in U.S. Department of Labor, undated) reports that nearly two thirds of workers on wages or salaries have sick leave protection.

Some employers have initiated "family illness days," an expansion of the definition of sick leave to include time off to care for ill family members. This option recognizes that employees must sometimes take time off from work in order to provide such care (Ontario Women's Directorate, 1990; Scharlach et al., 1991). These days (typically 3 or 4 per year) may be included in employees' normal sick leave allotments, or they may represent additional days off. As one employee in our study reported,

> Our company policy makes it impossible to stay home with a sick child with sanctioned sick leave. Therefore, every single mother I know who works for the company pretends to be sick instead of taking time without pay. I feel with 2 months of accrued sick leave that we ought to feel free to use this benefit.

And another employee commented,

> If there is any official policy concerning staying home with a sick child, it's never been publicized here at work. Being a professional and a woman, I don't feel I even have the liberty to ask if I could stay home with my sick child, and she's had to stay by herself on occasion when she's really been ill.

"Family illness hours," a variation on the theme of family illness days, is a leave option that allows employees to take their leave an hour at a time (Scharlach et al., 1991). This option is especially useful for caregivers of elders, who must sometimes take their elder to medical or other appointments but who do not need to take an entire day off for this purpose (Scharlach et al., 1991).

Personal leave (days or hours) is time off that may be used for whatever personal or family needs the employee may have (Allis, 1989, cited in Scharlach et al., 1991; Ontario Women's Directorate, 1990). For example, vacation and sick leaves can be combined into flexible time-off packages that employees can use for any purpose. In addition, vacation times can be split into smaller blocks of time to provide more flexibility (Ontario Women's Directorate, 1990). Scharlach et al. (1991) noted that Allis (1989) advocated replacing sick and family illness days with personal days. The rationale is that such a leave policy formally recognizes the importance of employees' personal responsibilities and needs while conveying trust that employees will use their leave to benefit both themselves and their employer (Scharlach et al., 1991).

Family leave options involve temporary leaves of absence, paid or unpaid, for the birth or adoption of a child or for the care of an ill or disabled family member (Christensen & Staines, 1990). Such leave options protect the job of the employee while she or he is away for a specified amount of time. Employees may be unable or reluctant to use this leave if it is unpaid or if they fear that the progress of their careers will be jeopardized (Zedeck & Mosier, 1990, citing Halcrow, 1987). As one employee remarked,

I would like to see employees with caregiving responsibilities be allowed more flexibility in use of sick and vacation time and to not be in jeopardy of job status if extended leave is required. I think that caregiving tasks are usually taken on by women and are expected by "society" to be taken on by women for no compensation even at the risk of jeopardizing their jobs. Anything that can make it easier for working [outside the home] women and men to fulfill their responsibilities for unpaid caregiving should be tried.

Several states have passed parental leave statutes, and the federal government and many other states are considering family leave statutes.

Maternal, paternal, parental, and family leave options have several advantages to employers and employees alike. They may help employees adjust to their new role as parents. They may also aid in retaining employees, preserve employers' "training investments" in employees, and reduce caregiving-related expenses for employees. When mandated by the government, however, a disadvantage of such leave options is that employers' flexibility of response is curbed. Another disadvantage is that it may be difficult for small businesses to find or train temporary replacement employees (U.S. Department of Labor, undated).

Changing Where Work Is Done

Several options concern the place of work. These options involve doing paid work at home or at some other site away from the office. They are referred to as flexplace, flexiplace, or telecommuting (Christensen & Staines, 1990; U.S. Department of Labor, undated; Zedeck & Mosier, 1990). For employers, these options offer the possibility of recruiting or retaining workers unable or unwilling to commute, such as persons with disabilities or parents with young children. Another advantage is possible improvements in productivity because of workers' ability to do their work whenever they wish and because of fewer distractions (U.S. Department of Labor, undated). Other advantages include reduced costs for office space and fuller use of computer resources gained by extending the workday (U.S. Department of Labor, undated; Zedeck & Mosier, 1990). The disadvantages of flexplace options for employers include (a) the changes necessary in supervision and evaluation techniques when employees work at home, (b) resentment by employees whose jobs do not permit them to work at home, and (c) the special safeguards needed to preserve job security, pensions and other benefits, and job advancement rights of off-site workers (U.S. Department of Labor, undated).

Flexplace options provide several advantages for employees, including reduced commuting and greater access to their families. Working at home, however, may not reduce work-family difficulties if there are preschool children in the household (Christensen, 1988, cited in Christensen & Staines, 1990). Additional disadvantages to employees may include increased work-family conflict due to the lack of physical boundaries between work and home (Zedeck & Mosier, 1990, citing Shamir & Salomon, 1985), a greater risk of burnout since start and stop times for work are not specified (Zedeck & Mosier, 1990, citing Hamilton, 1987), and the perception by their family that they are not working because they are not at an office.

Related to flexplace options are relocation policies, which also have the potential to be supportive of families. As Kingston (1990) pointed out, relocation policies can be reformed to become "family-friendly" by minimizing the number of required transfers or by including job-finding services for employees' spouses in the new location. In addition, policies against nepotism could be dispensed with, thereby allowing spouses to work for the same company (Kingston, 1990).

Increasing Flexibility in the Work Schedule

There are two main options for increasing the flexibility of employees' work schedules. The first is allowing employees to work a compressed workweek; the second is flextime.

Compressed Workweek. The compressed workweek is a work-scheduling method that allows an employee to work "full time," but in less than the standard 5 days per week, 8 hours per day (Cohen & Gadon, 1978). Typically, the employee works 4 longer days and either shortened hours or no hours on the 5th day (Christensen & Staines, 1990; Olmsted & Smith, 1989). Compressed workweeks are used most often by employers attempting either to decrease the cost of operating capital equipment or to improve the allocation of labor time (Olmsted & Smith, 1989).

This work-scheduling option has received mixed reviews from employers and employees. The advantages for employers may include decreases in absenteeism, tardiness, and turnover; improvements in employee morale and in recruitment (for those employees who like the compressed work schedule); and improvements in staffing (the concentrated time off makes employees more willing to work shift and weekend assignments and to work during peak times of activity) (Olmsted

& Smith, 1989). Other advantages for employers may include more efficient utilization of plants and equipment (because start-ups and shutdowns are less frequent), reductions in labor cost per unit (due to reduced start-ups and shutdowns, reduced trips to and from the worksite, and better staffing during peak periods of activity), and reduced utility costs (because some or all operations can be scheduled when the costs of utilities are lower) (Olmsted & Smith, 1989). Some employers report an increase in productivity when compressed workweeks are used, but others note a decline in productivity toward the end of long shifts due to employee fatigue. Similarly, although improved employee morale may result from the initiation of a compressed workweek, morale may deteriorate for those employees who do not like the longer workdays (Olmsted & Smith, 1989). Also, tardiness may be a problem for some employees who become fatigued and/or have family responsibilities (Cohen & Gadon, 1978). Other disadvantages for employers may include problems with scheduling and coverage and difficulties in internal and external communications (Olmsted & Smith, 1989). Another difficulty is that in some states wage and hour legislation requires that employees working more than 8 hours per day be paid overtime premiums. Finally, opposition may be faced from labor unions. Some unions are concerned about the fatigue that may be faced by employees working long days and the effects on employee health, and some labor union contracts specify both a 40-hour week and an 8-hour day (Olmsted & Smith, 1989). Also, the extended period of time off makes "moonlighting" more plausible, a practice that is often opposed by unions both for safety reasons and because it reduces the overall number of individuals who are employed (Christensen & Staines, 1990; Cohen & Gadon, 1978; Olmsted & Smith, 1989; Tepas, 1985).

For employees, a primary advantage of the compressed workweek is that it allows workers an extra day at home (Kamerman & Kingston, 1982; Olmsted & Smith, 1989). Other advantages may include improved morale (for those who like the schedule), more family time on the weekends, and less commuting time and cost (because there are fewer trips to work and the longer workdays mean travel to and from work during nonpeak hours) (Olmsted & Smith, 1989). When flexible schedules are in place, the "rush hour" is spread out, transportation facilities may become less crowded, air quality is improved, and accident rates decrease due to driving under less stressful conditions (Winett & Neale, 1980). Another advantage to employees of the compressed workweek may be the increased opportunity to moonlight (i.e., take a second job)

(Cohen & Gadon, 1978; Tepas, 1985). Disadvantages for employees may include decreased morale (for those who dislike the longer workdays) and increased fatigue (especially for some older workers and working parents) (Olmsted & Smith, 1989). Also, this work schedule may place employees out of synchronization with other family members' schedules (Kamerman & Kingston, 1982). Furthermore, employees have less time on workdays to share in family activities (Kamerman & Kingston, 1982; Olmsted & Smith, 1989). Finally, the longer workdays may increase employees' daily exposure to toxic substances and/or physical hazards in the work environment (Tepas, 1985).

Flextime. The second, broader type of work schedule option, called flextime or flexitime, involves a work schedule with flexible starting and quitting times. Five components are characteristic of flextime programs. There are core hours during which employees must be present. There are "flexi-hours" or "bandwidths" at the start and the end of the workday during which employees can vary their starting and stopping times. The length of the lunch hour can be varied. Starting and stopping times may be changed daily (referred to as a "sliding" or a "gliding" schedule), weekly, monthly, or, even less frequently, with prior notice (called "flexitour"). Finally, employees may be permitted to vary the length of their workday and to accrue time to be taken off in the future (Christensen & Staines, 1990). The flextime programs affording the most flexibility are (a) those that have short core hours, large bandwidths, and lunch hours that can be lengthened or shortened, and (b) those that allow the banking, or saving up, of hours and those that permit daily schedule variation. Currently, U.S. flextime programs tend not to offer maximum flexibility (Christensen & Staines, 1990).

From an organizational standpoint, flextime schedules are humane and can develop a climate of trustworthiness (Winett & Neale, 1980). This climate can result in several advantages to the employer, including higher morale; increased productivity; decreased incidence of tardiness, unnecessary absences, and use of leave time; reduced overtime; facilitation of cross-training; and increased time during which the public can be served (due to the larger bandwidth of starting and ending times) (U.S. Department of Labor, undated; Winett & Neale, 1980). Such changes can result in considerable savings for the organization (U.S. Department of Labor, undated).

The disadvantages of flextime to employers may include occupational constraints; specifically, flextime is not well suited to some types of jobs, such as assembly line work or other work that requires employees to function as a team, work that is supervisory, or reception work (Nollen, 1982, cited in Christensen & Staines, 1990; Zedeck & Mosier, 1990). Another disadvantage is that supervisors may be reluctant to implement it due to the greater complexity of scheduling and the more participatory style of supervision that flextime encourages (Christensen & Staines, 1990; U.S. Department of Labor, undated; Zedeck & Mosier, 1990). Legal constraints produced by laws concerning overtime and maximum hours present another difficulty for employers considering using flextime. Union resistance may be problematic as well, since some unions believe that flextime actually results in a longer work week and fewer available jobs, that it decreases the need for overtime and the availability of overtime premiums, and that it facilitates moonlighting (Christensen & Staines, 1990). Still other disadvantages for employers include possible difficulties in communicating with and supervising employees and in covering work during the entire workday (U.S. Department of Labor, undated; Zedeck & Mosier, 1990). Finally, there are costs associated with the heating and cooling of facilities as hours of operation are extended (Zedeck & Mosier, 1990, citing Bureau of National Affairs, 1986).

Flextime is popular with employees because of the increased control and flexibility in work schedules that it affords to all employees, regardless of their family situations (Bohen & Viveros-Long, 1981, cited in Zedeck & Mosier, 1990; U.S. Department of Labor, undated). It offers greater personal freedom and increased opportunities for participating in educational, recreational, social, and family activities, as well as the chance to share dependent-care responsibilities with a spouse and to reduce reliance on external dependent-care arrangements (Winett & Neale, 1980). An additional advantage for employees may be easier commuting (Winett & Neale, 1980; Zedeck & Mosier, 1990, citing Bohen & Viveros-Long, 1981).

Equitable access to an employer's flextime program, however, is an issue. Mellor (1986, cited in Christensen & Staines, 1990) found that employees who were male, who were white, or who worked as managers and professionals were most likely to have access to flextime. Another disadvantage of flextime for employees is that it may have limited utility for employees who have small children (Zedeck & Mosier, 1990) or other dependents if the bandwidths are narrow (for example, only 1 or 2 hours).

In their review of the literature concerning the actual impacts of flexible work schedule programs (flextime, specifically) that had been enacted, Winett and Neale (1980) found positive organizational and environmental effects, as described above, but negative as well as positive personal and social effects. Their results indicate that flextime programs may have allowed working parents to spend more time with their families in the afternoon and evening, but only because they got up earlier in the morning. Parents who participated in flextime programs did indicate lessened difficulty in coordinating several aspects of their home and work lives.

In weighing the evidence for and against flextime, Christensen and Staines (1990) gave this option mixed reviews. Although they concluded that "no compelling case can be made for flextime solely on the grounds of employers' conventional concerns with organizational effectiveness, organizational membership, or job attitudes" (p. 475), they also noted that "employers have come to recognize that it is in their best interests to incorporate employees' family needs into management decision making" (p. 475). Their review of evaluations of flextime did reveal it to be advantageous from the family's perspective (i.e., in terms of the amount of time spent in family roles and in the types and amount of perceived interference between work and family life) but "not as beneficial as often hoped in resolving work/family conflicts" (p. 475).

Management Training

Management training, although not a direct form of alternative work scheduling, is an indirect and important form of assistance related to family-supportive policies (Raabe & Gessner, 1988; Scharlach et al., 1991; U.S. Department of Labor, undated). Although formal family-responsive work scheduling and leave policies may be in place, employees will not realize their intended benefits unless they are understood and appropriately implemented by supervisors and managers. Furthermore, many decisions about work schedule and leave are made informally. Managers who are not sensitive to the needs of employees who have family-care responsibilities may not allow employees the informal flexibility that can be so useful when one is attempting to manage both work and family roles.

Scharlach et al. (1991, p. 81, citing Trost, 1989) noted that a study by Bank Street College found better physical and mental health among workers to be associated with "having a supervisor who is supportive about family-related matters." This same study found that because some supervisors wanted all of their employees to work from 9 a.m. to 5 p.m., they refused to permit employees to use the company's policy of flexible scheduling. Writing specifically about elder-care policies, Scharlach et al. (1991, p. 81) asserted that without training of supervisors and managers, "actual elder care practices end up being determined by the attitudes and experiences of individual supervisors rather than by the formal elder-care policy designed by a company's decision makers."

In their study of the family-supportive policies of New Orleans employers, Raabe and Gessner (1988) found (a) a distinction between "formal" (written) and "informal" (unwritten) policies, (b) a distinction between policies (formal or informal) and practices, and (c) variations in the scope of policies and programs (i.e., whether they were organization-wide or applicable only to certain departments and/or levels of employees). They pointed out that the "varying and amorphous nature of organizational practices undermines employee planning and problem-solving" (p. 200). They also cited several studies indicating the importance of a sense of control over one's situation for improving coordination of work and family roles, and they have argued that written and clearly communicated workplace policies can assist in this regard by enhancing employees' planning capabilities. Raabe and Gessner (1988) further asserted the importance of sensitivity and responsiveness on the part of individual supervisors, advocating training for managers and supervisors about the problems and solutions to work-family conflicts in order to "mandate and bolster added supervisor flexibility and responsiveness in particular situations" (p. 200).

BENEFITS

Benefits comprise the second type of supports that employers may provide for their employees. Typically, employee benefits plans have several features. First, they provide protection against the loss of earnings (income maintenance) when regular earnings are lost as a result of death, injury, illness, disability, retirement, or loss of job. Second, they typically cover payment of the medical expenses associated with illness, injury, or other health-care needs. Third, they provide paid released time for vacations, holidays, and personal needs. Finally, certain nonmedical services (e.g., legal, educational, or mental health) may be covered or may be provided as benefits directly to employees (Kamerman & Kingston, 1982). As noted earlier, in this book we are treating those specific dependent- or family-care services that are directly provided or subsidized by employers as a separate category, "services." These services are described in Chapter 9.

Most employees are eligible for a set of benefits that their employer chooses to offer to its employees, in addition to those benefits that are required legally (e.g., federal [FICA], state, and local social insurance) (Dobson, Hoy, & van Schaik, 1988). Although benefits packages vary, the majority include health insurance, life insurance, participation in a pension plan and/or profit sharing, paid holidays, vacations, and sick leave, and short-term disability. Some employees receive additional benefits, such as for dental care, vision care, dependent care, long-term disability, and liability insurance (Dobson et al., 1988).

There are two basic types of benefits plans. The first type includes those composed of an identical set of benefits for all employees in a given company; this is the "standard" or "traditional" approach to benefits plans. The second type is the "flexible" or "cafeteria" approach, in which employees choose among two or more benefits with respect to all or part of the employer's contributions for employees' benefits (Dobson et al., 1988; Meyer, 1983).

The following paragraphs discuss in greater detail the flexible benefits concept and the types of flexible benefits plans and describe those particular benefit options that are especially relevant as supports for employees who have dependent-care responsibilities.

Flexible Benefits Plans

Flexible or cafeteria benefits plans are designed to permit employees to choose from a "menu" of benefits or cash compensation (Canan & Mitchell, 1991). Such plans recognize that individual employees' benefits needs differ depending on the employee's age, salary, and family status. A major portion of the costs of the benefits is paid by the employer by establishing a "flexible benefit allowance" of a certain dollar amount. This allowance is large enough to pay the full cost of those benefits (called basic or core benefits) that the employer feels all employees should have, such as medical insurance and death benefits. Every employee must choose these basic benefits (one exception is when an employee's spouse has medical coverage for the family through his or her employer, so additional medical coverage is not needed). Remaining benefits dollars can then be used to purchase additional benefits, or they may be taken in cash. This cash is subject to both federal income and FICA taxes. If the cost of benefits selected by an employee is higher than the allowance, the employee is responsible for that cost, usually through salary reduction (i.e., a portion of their salary before taxes is used to fund the optional benefits of their choice) (Canan & Mitchell, 1991). For employers, flexible benefits plans have several advantages. First, such plans can improve employee satisfaction with benefits, since they can better meet a variety of employee needs (Canan & Mitchell, 1991; Griffes, 1983; Meeker & Campbell, 1986). Second, when optional benefits are funded through salary reduction (i.e., payroll deduction, before taxes), employers can better manage the costs of benefits because employees can elect lower levels of coverage (e.g., if their spouse has benefits through his or her employer). Since cost increases are borne by employees themselves, employees are made aware of the costs of health care and can become more discriminating consumers (Meeker & Campbell, 1986; U.S. Department of Labor, undated; Zedeck & Mosier, 1990). Plans funded through salary reduction are cost effective for employers, despite their start-up and administrative costs, because they lower employers' payroll taxes (since such taxes are not paid on the portions of employees' salaries that have been traded for nontaxable benefits) (Meeker & Campbell, 1986; U.S. Department of Labor, undated). A third advantage of flexible benefits plans for employers is that benefits of use only to particular groups of employees (e.g., parents of young children) can be offered without raising questions of inequity, since other employees can choose alternate benefits (U.S. Department of Labor, undated; Zedeck & Mosier, 1990). Related to this point, it should be noted that federal tax law dictates that all benefits must be available on substantially the same terms to all employees; there are tax consequences if a benefit discriminates in favor of highly compensated employees (see Canan & Mitchell, 1991, for a discussion of nondiscrimination rules and nondiscriminatory classification tests). Fourth, the pressure from employees for new benefits can be accommodated without great additional cost since such benefits can be added as choices to employees without expanding the employer's total contribution for benefits (Griffes, 1983). Also, benefits that are no longer of interest to employees can be easily eliminated as choices (Griffes, 1983).

The primary disadvantages to employers of flexible benefits plans can be the complexities of benefit administration and communication (Griffes, 1983) and their cost of administration and implementation (Griffes, 1983; U.S. Department of Labor, undated), although this cost is decreasing with greater experience with such plans. In addition, adverse selection is likely to occur (i.e., those most likely to use a particular benefit will elect that benefit, thus increasing the utilization rate for the benefit). As a result, the cost of a flexible benefit plan may exceed the cost of a conventional plan (Griffes, 1983).

For employees, flexible benefits plans are advantageous because they allow employees to choose benefits that suit their needs and those of their family (Canan & Mitchell, 1991; Scharlach et al., 1991; U.S. Department of Labor, undated). Another advantage to employees is that, because certain expenses are paid using pretax dollars, employees' income taxes can thereby be reduced (Canan & Mitchell, 1991; Meeker & Campbell, 1986). A disadvantage is the potential for lack of equity in the use of salary reductions (payroll deductions) to pay for optional benefits: This form of plan is more attractive to employees with higher pay than to those who earn less, who may need all the income earned to meet monthly expenses (Meeker & Campbell, 1986). Another disadvantage resulting from the use of salary reduction to fund additional benefits is the accompanying reduction in Social Security benefits that will be experienced upon retirement or disability (Canan & Mitchell, 1991).

Flexible Spending Accounts

Flexible spending accounts, also called benefit reimbursement accounts, are those into which employees can allocate either their own pretax dollars or credits or flexible benefits dollars given to them by their employer to pay for certain expenses not covered under the standard package, such as additional medical expenses; dental, legal, dependent care; or other expenses (Canan & Mitchell, 1991; Seltz & Gifford, 1982). Flexible spending accounts may be available to employees as one option of their cafeteria plan. Alternatively, they may be made available by employers independently of the benefits plan as a service to employees. Of particular relevance here is the dependent-care reimbursement account, also known as a dependent-care assistance plan or program.

Dependent-Care Assistance Plans. Authorized under Section 129 of the Internal Revenue Code, dependent-care assistance plans (DCAPs) are a mechanism through which employers can help employees who have dependent-care responsibilities and who must purchase dependent care or related services in order to be gainfully employed (Canan & Mitchell, 1991). Although dependent-care assistance plans may or may not involve direct employer contributions, these plans are available only when set up by employers for employees; thus, we have included them here in our discussion of employee benefits.

Dependent-care assistance plans are established for reimbursement of dependent-care expenses incurred by the employee for household services or for the care of a "qualifying individual" so that the employee can work. Qualifying individuals include dependent children under the age of 13 as well as spouses or dependents who are unable to care for themselves, regardless of age, and who regularly spend at least 8 hours each day in the employee's household. A qualifying individual can be an eligible dependent even if that person cannot otherwise be claimed as a dependent because she or he has more than $1,900 of income (Canan & Mitchell, 1991).

Most DCAPs are intended to qualify both as nondiscriminatory cafeteria or flexible benefits plans and as dependent-care reimbursement plans. When they are a part of a flexible benefits plan, the purpose of the DCAP is to provide employees with a choice between reimbursement for certain dependent-care expenses and cash compensation (Canan & Mitchell, 1991).

DCAPs may take various forms, but there are two principal types (Scharlach et al., 1991). In one, the employer directly subsidizes a portion of the employee's caregiving expenses, such as for child care or adult day care (Scharlach et al., 1991). Such a subsidy is generally an option within a flexible benefits plan, where the employee chooses to use his or her flexible benefit dollars for this benefit. Examples of subsidies for specific types of child and elder care are presented in the next chapter.

The second, more prevalent type of DCAP that employers may establish does not involve funding by the employer (Meeker & Campbell, 1986; Scharlach et al., 1991). Instead, it is funded completely through salary reduction (Meeker & Campbell, 1986). In this type of DCAP, employees set aside a portion of their salary before taxes (Scharlach et al., 1991). These DCAPs, too, tend to be one component of a flexible benefits plan.

In both types of DCAPs, the employee elects a dollar amount of coverage, up to $5,000 for the year ($2,500 in the case of married individuals filing separately) (Canan & Mitchell, 1991). When an employee chooses this benefit, a "reimbursement account" is established. As expenses are incurred and paid, the employee obtains reimbursement by submitting a claim form. Assuming the expense is an eligible one, the employee receives a check for the amount claimed, and the amount is subtracted from his or her account (Canan & Mitchell, 1991).

Both types of DCAPs have tax advantages. The funds set aside by employees to be placed in a dependent-care reimbursement account are not taxable to employees (i.e., the employee's taxable income is reduced by the amount deducted for the DCAP), resulting in a lower base on which Social Security and income tax are paid (Canan & Mitchell, 1991; Meeker & Campbell, 1986). Employers, too, pay lower payroll taxes, as the amount deducted from employees' salaries for a DCAP is not subject to these taxes. When employers contribute to an employee's DCAP (e.g., through subsidies), this cost qualifies as a deductible business expense to the employer (Creedon & Tiven, 1989; Meeker & Campbell, 1986; Scharlach et al., 1991, citing New York Business Group on Health, 1986). Furthermore, as Meeker and Campbell (1986, p. 22) noted, even employers who do not contribute to their employees' DCAPs "can take advantage of the federal tax laws to help their employees meet expenses and reap the benefits of a more stable, productive work force" simply by making available a dependent-care assistance plan to their employees.

There are, however, several limitations associated with DCAPs. One of these is that not all caregiving-related expenses are eligible for reimbursement. For example, only expenses incurred as a result of the employee's working can be reimbursed. In addition, care must be provided by someone other than an employee's dependent (e.g., child or nonemployed spouse) (Scharlach et al., 1991). Also, in order for care-related expenses to be reimbursed, receipts or invoices indicating the care provider's name, place of business, and Social Security or tax identification number must be submitted (Canan & Mitchell, 1991; Scharlach et al., 1991). This requirement effectively eliminates care provided by in-home care providers who are willing to earn less than the minimum wage to avoid reporting their earnings to the IRS (Scharlach et al., 1991). Scharlach et al. (1991, citing Adolf, 1988) noted that 50% to 70% of child-care providers do not report their earnings to the IRS.

Another disadvantage is the $5,000 limit on funds that can be placed in flexible spending accounts of any type, including DCAPs (U.S. Department of Labor, undated). At the same time, dollars placed in such accounts will be of little or no use if the services that they are intended to purchase are unavailable in the community or in short supply. Furthermore, each year, the employee must specify the amount that is to be deducted from his or her gross salary or wages; these dollars are forfeited if they are not spent by the end of the year (Canan & Mitchell, 1991). As pointed out by Scharlach et al. (1991), estimating the amount of money that should be set aside in such an account is particularly difficult for employees caring for dependent elders, whose needs for assistance fluctuate, as compared with employees caring for young children, whose needs are fairly predictable. Finally, the requirement that the dependent spend 8 hours a day in the employee's home has made DCAPs less useful for employees with elder-care responsibilities, most of whom do not share a household with the elder whom they are assisting (Scharlach et al., 1991).

Despite these limitations, given the tax advantages for both employees and employers, Meeker and Campbell (1986) concluded that on balance, "There is good reason for employers to provide their employees with dependent-care assistance in the form of an employee benefit" (p. 22).

Tax Credits

Dependent-Care Tax Credits. In addition to Dependent-Care Assistance Plans, a federal tax credit for employment-related expenses incurred also is available to individuals who have dependent-care responsibilities for children, adults with disabilities, or elders. At least 34 states also have state dependent-care tax credits (Biegel, Schulz, Shore, & Morycz, 1988), most of which are tied to the federal tax credit (Creedon & Tiven, 1989). Even though employers have no direct role in the provision or implementation of these credits, because employers can actively publicize the availability of the credits (Meeker & Campbell, 1986), we have included them in our discussion.

The federal dependent-care tax credit reduces the amount of income taxes (but not FICA) the employee owes by a percentage of the expenses the employee has incurred as a result of his or her dependent-care responsibilities. This percentage varies depending on the combined income of the employee and his or her spouse; it is a maximum of 30% of those expenses per dependent up to certain dollar limits (in 1991, $2,400 for one dependent and $4,800 for two or more dependents) (Canan & Mitchell, 1991; Meeker & Campbell, 1986). The types of individuals for whom care may be provided and the types of expenditures eligible for favorable tax treatment are the same as those that apply to the DCAP, as specified in Section 21(b) of the Internal Revenue Code (Canan & Mitchell, 1991; Meeker & Campbell, 1986).

Although the DCAP and the dependent-care tax credit can be used simultaneously, the same expenditures cannot be claimed twice (Meeker & Campbell, 1986). Furthermore, the amount of the tax credit is reduced by the amount excluded from income under a DCAP (Canan & Mitchell, 1991). The individual employee's particular tax situation will dictate which form of assistance, the DCAP or the dependent-care tax credit, will be more advantageous for him or her to use. In general, employees with lower incomes (e.g., according to Canan & Mitchell, 1991, less than $23,000 for a couple, and less than $17,000 for a single person) will find the tax credit to their advantage, whereas the DCAP will probably be more advantageous for those with higher incomes (Canan & Mitchell, 1991). (See Canan & Mitchell, 1991, for a detailed discussion of this issue.)

According to Meeker and Campbell (1986), the tax credit is "the largest source of federal assistance to taxpayers with employment related expenses for dependent care" (p. 19), but it serves employees with dependent children to a much larger extent than it serves those with dependent adults or elders. Approximately 80% of the benefits claimed through the federal dependent-care tax credit are for child care rather than for adult or elder care (Perlman, 1982, cited in Biegel et al., 1988).

The limited use of the tax credit for adult and elder care is due in large part to the restrictive regulations that govern its use. Allowable expenditures for adult or elder care include only those that "assure the well-being and protection of the employees' qualifying spouse or dependent" (Meeker & Campbell, 1986, p. 18; Canan & Mitchell, 1991). Care may be provided inside or outside the employee's home, although the dependent adult must regularly spend at least 8 hours every day in the employee's household. Moreover, all eligible expenses must be work related (i.e., the taxpayer must have been employed or looking for work when the expenses were incurred), and if the taxpayer is married, his or her spouse must also have been employed or have been a full-time student or a disabled qualifying individual. Further limiting the use of the tax credit for adult or elder dependent care is that this care often qualifies as a medical deduction as well, and expenses may not be counted twice (i.e., as medical expenses and as dependent-care expenses) (Meeker & Campbell, 1986).

The tax credit provides greater benefits to taxpayers with lower incomes; thus, it is of most use to lower- and middle-income families (Biegel et al., 1988; Creedon & Tiven, 1989; Meeker & Campbell, 1986). Since fewer Social Security taxes are paid as a result of the salary reduction, however, Social Security benefits received in the future may also be lower (Canan & Mitchell, 1991). In addition, employees with lower incomes are often not able to receive the 30% maximum tax credit, since they cannot afford to spend as much for dependent care as is necessary to qualify for that percentage credit (Meeker & Campbell, 1986). Furthermore, since the tax credit is not refundable, it is not available to families who owe no taxes or who do not itemize deductions (Osterbusch, Keigher, Miller, & Linsk, 1987; Stipek & McCroskey, 1989). Another disadvantage of the tax credit is that unpaid work, such as caregiving by family members, is not an allowable cost, and the maximum of 30% of expenditures that can be claimed may not be an adequate incentive for use of the credit (Osterbusch et al., 1987). Finally, many individuals do not know about the availability of the tax credit and therefore do not make use of it (Schmidt & Tate, 1988).

Earned Income Tax Credit. In addition to the dependent-care tax credit, the earned income tax credit also is available. The earned income credit is a special federal tax credit that is available to families who have earned incomes and adjusted gross incomes below a certain level ($21,250 in 1991) and who have one or more children who live with them (Internal Revenue Service [IRS], 1991). Not related to the amount actually paid by the family for child care, the earned income credit is composed of three different credits: the basic credit (available to all those meeting the above-described income and children in the household requirements); a health insurance credit (for those who paid health insurance premiums that included coverage for one or more children); and an extra credit for a child born in that tax year (this latter credit is available only to those who did not choose to take the dependent-care tax credit). Generally, the earned income credit is applied for directly by individuals on their federal tax returns; the tax liabilities of these individuals then are less. Employees expecting to be eligible for the earned income credit, however, may have their withholding reduced (i.e., they may pay less tax initially) by completing Form W-5 (Earned Income Credit Advance Payment Certificate) and giving it to their employer. The earned income tax credit is useful only to employees with low incomes (IRS, 1991). As with the dependent-care tax credit, many individuals and families do not understand or know about the availability of the earned income credit and therefore do not make use of it.

Long-Term Care Insurance

Another form of employee benefit is group long-term care insurance for employees, their spouses, and sometimes their parents and parents-in-law, and/or retirees and their spouses (Neal, 1990; Scharlach et al., 1991; U.S. Department of Labor, undated). This insurance may be offered as an add-on option to a standard employee benefits package or as an optional benefit among others in a flexible benefits plan. Long-term care is "a set of health, personal care, and social services delivered over a sustained period of time to persons who have lost or never acquired some degree of functional capacity" (Kane & Kane, 1987, p. 4). Thus it refers to care needed by persons of any age who have physical or mental limitations. The cost of such care can be prohibitive, whether delivered in the home or in an institutional setting: Latest estimates of the cost of nursing home care for one year range between $30,000 and $40,000 ("An Empty Promise," 1991). As Meiners (1983, p. 74) has noted with respect to long-term care for the elderly, "even those persons with personal resources that are quite adequate for a normal retirement will not be able to pay for long-term care should it become necessary."

Insurance products to cover the costs of long-term care, therefore, are being developed, including group products that can be offered by employers to their employees. Scharlach et al. (1991, citing Health Insurance Association of America, 1990) have noted that 118 major insurance companies were offering a long-term care policy as of December 1989, and that 12 of these companies had a group policy. Examples of employers offering a group long-term care insurance policy include Procter & Gamble, Northeast Utilities, John Hancock, University of Southern California, Household International, Army and Air Force Exchange Services, Ford Motor Company, Monsanto, Levitz, Ball Corporation, and the State of Maryland (Neal, 1990).

Typically, when employers offer group long-term care insurance to their employees, the benefit consists of the opportunity to purchase the insurance at group rates (Neal, 1990). Such insurance may cover home health services, respite care, and day care, as well as nursing home care (U.S. Department of Labor, undated).

A study of the rationale for employers' decisions to offer group long-term care insurance revealed a number of motivating factors (Neal, 1990). The first of these was interest and need expressed by employees. The second was decision makers' general or personal awareness of the need for such insurance. The third was the availability of group products, and the fourth factor was the low cost involved. Since employees pay the premiums, the employer's only costs are those associated with administering the program. The fifth factor named was the competitive advantage that employers felt the benefit gave them in terms of employee productivity, retention, and recruitment. The sixth factor was related to some employers' sense of social responsibility or the opportunity the benefit afforded to help employees. Finally, public relations advantages, including company pride and a sense of being on the leading edge, were a motivating factor.

Employers also identified some potential disadvantages to implementing group long-term care insurance (Neal, 1990). Among these were liability concerns because the tax implications of this benefit were not clear, at least at that time, and because data about claims were sparse. For example, if an employer promoted a product and told employees/retirees that they would be covered, the employer was liable if a particular condition was ultimately not covered. In addition, it was not clear whether premiums could be deducted or if the benefits themselves were taxable. The need for employers to learn about long-term care and the features of policies was a further concern, as was the need for employers and employees to recognize the current lack of long-term care coverage by existing health insurance and Medicare. A related disadvantage was the difficulty of communicating both the need for the insurance and information about the features of policies. The relatively high cost of premiums to employees, especially to older employees, was cited as another limitation. Possibly related to cost, as well as to the complexity of this insurance, is a history, albeit limited, of low utilization rates to date. Fears of an eventual shift of the cost of the premiums from the employee to the employer were also mentioned as a disadvantage. Yet another was the difficulty of finding a stable carrier of group long-term care insurance. Finally, employers cited the need to be prepared for the emotional issues raised by discussions of needs for long-term care (Neal, 1990).

From the employees' standpoint, the advantages of employer-sponsored long-term care insurance are the reduced cost, due to group rates, and the convenience of having premiums deducted directly from their paychecks (Scharlach et al., 1991). The disadvantages are the relative newness of the products (thus a lack of history and experience with them), the exclusion in some policies of preexisting conditions, and the cost of premiums, even at group rates.

Finally, an employer support option related to group long-term care insurance is expansion of employees' health and dental care coverage to include the health and dental care expenses of elderly parents (Ontario Women's Directorate, 1990). This coverage can be offered in a fashion similar to group long-term care insurance; that is, the employer simply makes group rates available to employees, who then have the cost of premiums deducted from their salaries.

SUMMARY

In this chapter, we have described several work schedule and leave policies, as well as types of employee benefits plans and particular benefit options that may be of assistance to employees who have family-care responsibilities, as summarized in Table 8.1. The following chapter (Chapter 9) describes specific services that employers may provide or subsidize for their employees with child-care, adult-care, or elder-care duties. At the end of that chapter, we discuss factors affecting the implementation of all three types of supports—policies, benefits, and services. We also make recommendations for future research and suggest specific steps that employers can take to assist employees in balancing their work and family lives.

NOTE

1. Additional sources to consult for examples of employer supports for employees with family responsibilities include the Bureau of National Affairs (1988), Wagner, Creedon, Sasala, and Neal (1989), Scharlach, Lowe, and Schneider (1991), Subcommittee on Human Services (1990), and the Ontario Women's Directorate (1990), as well as *The Wall Street Journal* and *The New York Times*.

REFERENCES

Adolf, B. (1988). The employer's guide to child care. New York: Praeger.

Aldous, J. (1990). Specification and speculation concerning the politics of workplace family policies. *Journal of Family Issues, 11,* 355-367.

An empty promise to the elderly? (1991). *Consumer Reports, 56,* 425-442.

Allis, J. M. (1989). *Child care programs for health organizations: Decision making and implementation.* Ann Arbor, MI: Health Administration Press.

Auerbach, J. D. (1990). Employer-supported child care as a women-responsive policy. *Journal of Family Issues, 11,* 384-400.

Biegel, D. E., Schulz, R., Shore, B. K., & Morycz, R. (1988). Economic supports for family caregivers of the elderly: Public sector policies. In M. Z. Goldstein (Ed.), *Family involvement in the treatment of the frail elderly* (pp. 157-201). Washington, DC: American Psychiatric Press.

216   POLICIES, BENEFITS, AND SERVICES

Bohen, H. H., & Viveros-Long, A. (1981). *Balancing jobs and family life: Do flexible work schedules help?* Philadelphia, PA: Temple University Press.

Bowen, G. L. (1988). Corporate supports for the family lives of employees: A conceptual model for program planning and evaluation. *Family Relations, 37,* 183-188.

Bureau of National Affairs. (1988). *33 ways to ease work/family tensions—An employer's checklist* (Special Report No. 2). Rockville, MD: Buraff. (Product Code BSP-84)

Canan, M. J., & Mitchell, W. D. (1991). *Employee fringe and welfare benefits plans: 1991 edition, including coverage of the Omnibus Budget Reconciliation Act of 1990.* St. Paul, MN: West.

Christensen, K. E., & Staines, G. L. (1990). Flextime: A viable solution to work/family conflict? *Journal of Family Issues, 11,* 455-476.

Cohen, A. R., & Gadon, H. (1978). *Alternative work schedules: Integrating individual and organizational needs.* Reading, MA: Addison-Wesley.

Creedon, M. A., & Tiven, M. (1989). *Eldercare in the workplace.* Washington, DC: National Council on the Aging.

Dobson, A., Hoy, E. W., & van Schaik, C. (1988). *Trends in employee benefit design: Issues for NEA affiliates.* West Haven, CT: National Education Association.

Griffes, E. J. E. (1983). Appendix 2: Flexible compensation discussion paper. In E.J.E. Griffes (Ed.), *Employee benefits program: Management, planning, and control* (pp. 280-287). Homewood, IL: Dow Jones-Irwin.

Halcrow, A. (1987). Should business alone pay for social progress? *Personnel Journal, 66*(9), 58-73.

Hamilton, C. (1987). Telecommuting. *Personnel Journal, 66*(4), 90-101.

Health Insurance Association of America. (1990, March). Sixth annual private long-term care insurance conference, Orlando, FL.

Internal Revenue Service. (1991). *Earned income credit* (Publication 596, Catalog No. 15173A). Washington, DC: Government Printing Office.

Kamerman, S. B., & Kingston, P. W. (1982). Employer responses to the family responsibilities of employees. In S. B. Kamerman & C. D. Hayes (Eds.), *Families that work: Children in a changing world* (pp. 144-208). Washington, DC: National Academy Press.

Kane, R. A., & Kane, R. L., with Reinardy, J., & Arnold, S. (1987). *Long-term care: Principles, programs, and policies.* New York: Springer.

Kingston, P. W. (1990). Illusions and ignorance about the family-responsive workplace. *Journal of Family Issues, 11,* 438-454.

Meeker, S. E., & Campbell, N. D. (1986). Providing for dependent care. *Business and Health, 3*(7), 18-22.

Meiners, M. R. (1983). The case for long-term care insurance. *Health Affairs, 2,* 55-79.

Meyer, M. (1983). *Flexible employee benefit plans: Companies' experience.* New York: The Conference Board.

Neal, M. (1990, November). *Employer-sponsored long-term care insurance: Factors in decisions to offer.* Paper presented at the annual scientific meeting of the Gerontological Society of America, Boston.

New York Business Group on Health. (1986). *Employer support for employee caregivers.* New York: Author.

Nollen, S. D. (1980). What is happening to flextime, flexitour, gliding time, the variable day? And permanent part-time employment? And the four-day week? *Across the Board, 17*(4), 6-21.

Nollen, S. D. (1982). *New work schedules in practice: Managing time in a changing society.* New York: Van Nostrand Reinhold.

Olmsted, B., & Smith, S. (1989). *Creating a flexible workplace: How to select and manage alternative work options.* New York: AMACOM, a division of American Management Association.

Ontario Women's Directorate. (1990). *Work and family: The crucial balance.* Toronto: Author. (Available from Consultative Services Branch, Suite 200, 480 University Avenue, Toronto, Ontario, M5G1V2; ph. 416-597-4570)

Osterbusch, S. E., Keigher, S. M., Miller, B., & Linsk, N. L. (1987). Community care policies and gender justice. *International Journal of Health Services, 17,* 217-232.

Perlman, R. (1982). Use of the tax system in home care: A brief note. *Home Health Services Quarterly, 3,* 280-283.

Raabe, P. H., & Gessner, J. C. (1988). Employer family-supportive policies: Diverse variations on the theme. *Family Relations, 37,* 196-202.

Scharlach, A. E., Lowe, B. F., & Schneider, E. L. (1991). *Elder care and the work force: Blueprint for action.* Lexington, MA: Lexington Books.

Schmidt, S. E., & Tate, D. R. (1988). Employer-supported child care: An ecological model for supporting families. In L. A. Bond & B. M. Wagner (Eds.), *Families in transition: Primary prevention programs that work* (pp. 49-67). Newbury Park, CA: Sage.

Seltz, C., & Gifford, D. L. (1982). *Flexible compensation: A forward look.* New York: American Management Associations.

Shamir, B., & Salomon, I. (1985). Work-at-home and the quality of working life. *Academy of Management Review, 10,* 455-464.

Stautberg, S. S. (1987). Status report: The corporation and trends in family issues. *Human Resource Management, 26,* 277-290.

Stipek, D., & McCroskey, J. (1989). Investing in children: Government and workplace policies for parents. *American Psychologist, 44,* 416-423.

Subcommittee on Human Services of the Select Committee on Aging, U.S. House of Representatives. (1990). *Sharing the caring: Options for the 90s and beyond* (Committee Publication No. 101-750). Washington, DC: Government Printing Office.

Tepas, D. I. (1985). Flexitime, compressed workweeks, and other alternative work schedules. In S. Folkard & T. H. Monk (Eds.), *Hours of work: Temporal factors in work-scheduling* (pp. 147-164). New York: John Wiley.

Trost, C. (1989, January 10). Boss' backing vital to family benefits. *The Wall Street Journal,* p. B1.

U.S. Department of Labor, Office of the Secretary, Women's Bureau. (Undated). *Work and family resource kit.* Washington, DC: Author. (Available from Clearinghouse on Implementation of Child Care and Elder Care Services; ph. 1-800-827-5335)

Wagner, D. L., Creedon, M. A., Sasala, J. M., & Neal, M. B. (1989). *Employees and eldercare: Designing effective responses for the workplace.* Bridgeport, CT: University of Bridgeport, Center for the Study of Aging.

Winett, R. A., & Neale, M. S. (1980). Modifying settings as a strategy for permanent, preventive behavior change: Flexible work schedules and the quality of family life. In P. Karoly & J. J. Steffen (Eds.), *Improving the long-term effects of psychotherapy* (pp. 407-436). New York: Gardner.

Zedeck, S., & Mosier, K. L. (1990). Work in the family and employing organization. *American Psychologist, 45,* 240-251.

9

Employer Responses to Employees' Dependent-Care Responsibilities: Services

It would be very helpful if the company I work for would provide some sort of day-care facility. Both my wife and I work in the downtown core area. It makes me happy to see and be with my children and it would be very enjoyable to see them during the day at some point (like lunch hour). I don't believe that American industry realizes the full potential and happiness they can bring to their employee by providing such a service. I would be willing to pay the going market rates to have day care close to my work location. The greatest stress to many mothers and fathers is the concern about their children while at work—it does affect the work I do.

Over the past several years, the dependent-care responsibilities of employees have become increasingly salient to the workplace. Thus far, businesses have directed most of their attention toward child-care concerns. Corporate concern for workers' elder-care responsibilities has developed more slowly. Since the pioneering efforts of The Travelers Companies in 1985 to survey employees about their elder-care needs and the Travelers' subsequent development of services to address these needs, several other corporations have begun to offer similar programs. Indeed, Friedman (1986, p. 51) has speculated that elder care will become "the new, pioneering benefit of the 1990s." To date, however, few companies have offered programs designed specifically to meet the needs of employees with adult dependents who are not yet elderly.

EMPLOYER-SUPPORTED SERVICES

Employer-supported services addressing employees' dependent-care responsibilities can be organized into four categories with varying levels of employer involvement and investment. These categories are (a) education, (b) information and referral/case management, (c) counseling and support, and (d) direct services for care recipients. This chapter describes services that exemplify each of the categories and presents information about their advantages and disadvantages. An excellent resource that we cite frequently in the following discussion is a monograph by the Bureau of National Affairs (1988) entitled, *33 Ways to Ease Work/ Family Tensions—An Employer's Checklist.*

Education

The provision of education and of written materials is often the first step that companies take in assisting their employees with caregiving responsibilities (Beinecke & Marchetta, 1989). Some educational methods, such as the provision of a corporate library, require minimal resources and effort. Others, such as educational seminars and caregiver fairs, are somewhat more costly and time consuming (Bureau of National Affairs, 1988). The provision of education and written materials tends to gain visibility for the company among both employees and the outside media (Scharlach, Lowe, & Schneider, 1991).

Corporate Library. Companies can include books and videotapes on caregiving in their libraries. The Travelers Companies have added such books to their library and occasionally have articles on caregiving topics in their company publications (Bureau of National Affairs, 1988). In a demonstration project involving educational seminars for employed caregivers of the elderly, videotapes of the lectures were lent to employees who were unable to attend the seminars (Ingersoll-Dayton, Chapman, & Neal, 1990).

Newsletters and Guidebooks. An effective way to inform a large number of employees about caregiving issues is through newsletters and guidebooks (Scharlach et al., 1991). Companies are now using newsletters to provide parenting information (U.S. Department of Labor, undated) as well as child-care information (Scharlach et al., 1991). Caregiving can be covered in several different ways, such as including a single article in the company newsletter, focusing an entire issue of the newsletter on caregiving concerns, or borrowing from other publications (e.g., *Work and Family Life,* the monthly newsletter of Bank Street College) that are devoted to work and family concerns (Scharlach et al., 1991).

Guidebooks have been developed by a number of companies to provide information on caregiving, particularly with respect to elder care. Pepsico, for example, has distributed a resource guide for elder care to employees (Creedon & Wagner, 1986). The advantages of such guidebooks are that they do not require the time commitment associated with going to a lecture, they provide considerable depth, and they can be saved for rereading when needed (Scharlach et al., 1991). The disadvantages include uneven access to the guidebooks for all caregivers and an inability to address the specific concerns of individual caregivers (Scharlach et al., 1991).

Educational Seminars. Many companies have started providing educational forums for their employees. Within the child-care arena, companies have offered presentations on topics such as prenatal health, parenting skills, latchkey kids, and how to choose good child-care services (Bureau of National Affairs, 1988; Schmidt & Tate, 1988). For example, a bank in Philadelphia contracted with a firm to conduct a 6-hour seminar for employees who were concerned about day-care arrangements and about having children at home after school without adult supervision. Parents were assigned to groups according to the age of their children; in the groups, parents shared their worries and discussed possible solutions. Initially, some employees felt that such family matters were personal, and so they were reluctant to participate in the seminars. Over time, however, the positive experiences of group members encouraged the participation of others (Bureau of National Affairs, 1988).

Educational forums for caregivers of the elderly are also becoming increasingly popular in the workplace. Since most employees are unprepared for the responsibilities of elder care, seminars can provide basic information about the aging process and guidance about caregiving concerns (Scharlach et al., 1991). For example, Somerville-Cambridge Elder Services has contracted with companies in Massachusetts to provide workshops for "employees who are, or might become, caregivers, or who are concerned about their parents' and their own aging" (Aarens, 1986, p. 26). Workshop topics include myths and realities of aging, physical and social aspects of aging, and family relationships. Companies approached by Elder Services have chosen to offer the educational workshops because they believed that the workshops were more affordable than case management services.

As part of a demonstration project we conducted for employed caregivers of the elderly (Ingersoll-Dayton et al., 1990), we offered a similar educational series. Participation was associated with a significant increase in knowledge about the services available for the elderly. By the end of the series, however, employees were also missing more work, at least on a temporary basis. This increased absenteeism may have been related to the needs of employees to take time off from work to help their elders make use of the services about which they had learned in the educational series.

Caregiving Fairs. Some businesses have implemented caregiving fairs where employees may obtain information from a variety of different agencies and organizations at one time. Employees can informally stop at booths and acquire written information about specific community resources (Scharlach et al., 1991). For example, to address the needs of employees with elder-care responsibilities, The Travelers Companies brought in representatives from approximately 25 community agencies. These representatives set up booths and distributed information in the lobby of corporate headquarters in Hartford, Connecticut. The fair was attended by approximately 700 employees and retirees (Bureau of National Affairs, 1988).

While a disadvantage of caregiving fairs is their inability to provide much in-depth information on specific caregiver concerns, there are several benefits to such an approach. Specifically, they attract those who might not take part in educational seminars, and they interrupt the work schedules of employees minimally (Scharlach et al., 1991).

Information and Referral/Case Management

Some company-based programs are intended to inform employed caregivers about specific services that are available to them and their dependents and to help them locate these services. Programs that serve this function usually operate at two different levels: (a) information and referral and (b) case management.

Information and Referral. The provision of information and referral, also known as resource and referral, is a relatively inexpensive option. It is frequently the second step that companies make after providing educational and written materials to employees with dependent-care responsibilities (Beinecke & Marchetta, 1989). Companies that provide information and referral generally focus on helping their employees find child-care arrangements. This service is performed within the company or by an agency with which the company contracts, such as an employee assistance program (Bureau of National Affairs, 1988). The latter arrangement is exemplified by the Metropolitan Washington Child Care Network, toward the development of which numerous companies in the Washington, D.C., area contribute financially. The Network distributes a guidebook listing all the child-care services in the area, their telephone numbers, and suggestions for the best ways to select child-care arrangements. Further, employed parents can speak to a telephone counselor at the Network about their specific child-care needs and receive a list of child-care providers (Bureau of National Affairs, 1988). The effectiveness of such referral programs depends upon the availability and adequacy of the child-care market. A 1983-1984 federally funded study showed that resource and referral programs had a negligible effect on employed parents' productivity, suggesting that parents may continue to face interruptions at work if community child-care arrangements are inadequate and unstable (Friedman, 1987).

Recently, a few companies have started to implement similar programs for employees with elder-care responsibilities. IBM, for example, has hired a firm to implement an information and referral program. IBM employees nationwide receive personalized telephone consultations that include information about services and possible providers in their older relative's community, a handbook with more detailed information, and a follow-up call. As an indication of its usefulness, IBM employees have used the elder-care information and referral services at twice the rate of a similar child-care referral program during a comparable period (Halcrow, 1988). Beinecke and Marchetta (1989) have pointed out the differences between information and referral for child care as compared to elder care. The problems associated with elder care are often more complex than those of child care. In addition, elder care is sometimes provided at a distance. Therefore, the information and referral processes can often be more difficult and time consuming. The special difficulties associated with elder care were expressed by one respondent:

I have two parents who are in separate nursing facilities 3,000 miles away. Try finding information over that great distance! I now know how to "feel" the system so when it's time for my in-law to enter into such facilities I'll know where to go for help, money talks. It took me 3 years of working three and four jobs all the time, 7 days a week to keep them in nursing homes before [Medicaid] would take over.

Case Management. Another level of more intensive and individualized service is case management. Case management is particularly relevant to those employees with adult and elderly dependent-care responsibilities who need assistance in assessing their and their elder's multiple needs. Case management was one of the supports that we offered to employees with elder-care responsibilities in a demonstration project involving several companies (Ingersoll-Dayton et al., 1990). A care planner met with each interested employee three times to conduct a needs assessment; to present an individualized care plan that outlined the needs, goals, and resources of the employee and the elder; and to review progress on the plan. Employees who used this service experienced a significant reduction in negative affect and found the service to be helpful in providing information about caring for their elder.

Counseling and Support

Some companies provide assistance to employees who are coping with the emotional difficulties of dependent care. Programs focusing on the psychological ramifications of caregiving range from professional counseling to peer support.

Professional Counseling. Professional counseling is generally offered to employees through employee assistance programs (EAPs) either within the company or on a contractual basis or through wellness programs (U.S. Department of Labor, undated). Employee assistance programs have expanded their focus from their original mission of helping employees with alcohol problems to include an interest in assisting employees with work-family problems (Hughes & Galinsky, 1988). For example, the Richmond Employee Assistance Program was formed by a consortium of employers (companies ranging in size from 50 to 5,000 employees) in Richmond, Virginia. Among the difficulties addressed by EAP counselors are "emotional, marital and family problems, and problems connected with children and aging" (Bureau of National Affairs, 1988, p. 22).

Zedeck and Mosier (1990, citing Trice & Beyer, 1984) have pointed out the lack of research documenting the effectiveness of current EAPs, but have noted that organizations using them are convinced of their cost-saving effectiveness through decreased absenteeism. Scharlach et al. (1991) have asserted that EAP services are typically not very beneficial to caregivers of the elderly because the counselors are unfamiliar with the problems or resources for older people. They have suggested that EAP counselors need to obtain specialized training in this area and that companies should hire counselors with expertise in elder-care issues.

Support Groups. Another form of emotional assistance, support groups, involves placing employees with similar kinds of dependent-care concerns into groups that are facilitated by a professional. Support groups in the workplace enable employees to address their emotional concerns without necessitating an additional time commitment for the worker (Scharlach et al., 1991). For example, Transamerica Life Companies have sponsored two groups related to child care. One is a group for pregnant women, and the other is for new mothers. These groups, which are facilitated by Transamerica's child-care coordinator, meet during the lunch hour for 13 weeks. Some sessions concentrate on specific topics, whereas others address the immediate concerns of the participants (Bureau of National Affairs, 1988).

A similar format has been utilized for employees concerned about elder care. The University of Bridgeport worked with the EAPs of several companies to offer support groups for caregivers. Depending upon the timing of the groups, different kinds of employees attended. Female employees generally attended lunch-time support groups, whereas male management personnel were more likely to attend after-work support groups (Creedon, 1987). In our demonstration project (Ingersoll-Dayton et al., 1990), employee participation in the 8-week support groups was associated with a decrease in negative affect. A possible disadvantage of a workplace support group is that employees find it difficult to talk about emotional concerns and then return to work. Still, participants in our demonstration project stated that they felt less emotionally drained and more able to concentrate on their work after support group meetings.

Peer Support. A few companies have attempted to institutionalize the support that one employed caregiver can offer to another. For example, the Oil, Chemical, and Atomic Workers Local 8-149 and Barr Laboratories have a joint labor-management committee on work and family issues. As part of their collective bargaining agreement, designated union representatives can serve as peer counselors for union members who are experiencing work and family problems. The company allows the union members time at work to participate in such peer counseling (Bureau of National Affairs, 1988).

Our demonstration project attempted to develop a program of peer support among employees with elder-care responsibilities (Ingersoll-Dayton et al., 1990). This service was designed to pair employees who had similar caregiving situations. The caregiver "buddies" could then be in contact in person or by phone, independent of a professional, to provide each other with information and support. Employees from the companies in the demonstration project expressed little interest in this service, however, perhaps because they feared a poor match or an over-commitment of their time. Another of our approaches for encouraging peer support resulted in greater employee interest. Specifically, we worked with a small group of experienced caregivers in one company who decided to publicize their availability to co-workers in the company newsletter. This experience suggested that increasing peer support may be better accomplished by building upon existing networks rather than by developing new ones.

Direct Services for Care Recipients

Increasingly, companies are helping employees to deal with their dependent-care needs directly, by providing subsidies, vouchers, or discounts for particular services, such as alternative day-care and respite programs, or by sponsoring on-site or near-site day-care facilities. Subsidies and vouchers involve having employers pick up a portion of the costs of a service. The advantages are that such programs allow employees to select their own care arrangements; thus care services throughout the community are supported. The disadvantages for employers include the cost of such subsidies or vouchers, issues of equity that may arise if the subsidies or vouchers are available only to employees with lower incomes, and the inability of subsidies to address problems of lack of care or poor-quality care (U.S. Department of Labor, undated).

Discounts involve having employers make arrangements with particular vendors (e.g., child or adult day-care centers) to offer care to their employees at a discounted rate, such as a 10% reduction. In other words, employees can purchase care at a reduced cost. A disadvantage for employees is that discounts require the use of selected vendors. Furthermore, if the allocated slots become filled, some employees' needs will not be met. For employers, discounts are advantageous because of their relatively low cost, their limited liability, their flexibility in meeting the needs of changing numbers of employees, the minimal administration required, and the publicity they provide for the employer as the vendor promotes its services (U.S. Department of Labor, undated).

Child-Care Centers and Programs. A small number of companies and agencies have established day-care centers either at or near the workplace for their employees' children. Generally, the employer pays all or part of the expenses (Bureau of National Affairs, 1988).

One company, Merck Pharmaceuticals, helped to sponsor a center in two phases. At first, Merck provided seed money to help a group of employees establish their own child-care center. When the waiting list for the center became extremely long, Merck provided the funds to build another facility that could accommodate twice the original number of children (Galinsky & Stein, 1990).

A major disadvantage of on-site or near-site centers is the high start-up costs, making this support option unfeasible for most small businesses (Bureau of National Affairs, 1988). Other disadvantages include problems with predicting center use and demand, and the inability of centers to serve the needs of all employees with child-care responsibilities or to serve multisite companies (Bureau of National Affairs, 1988; Friedman, 1986). Further, Zedeck and Mosier (1990) have noted that such day-care centers raise concerns among companies about liability issues and among parents about "institutional care" and about subjecting their children to daily commutes to the worksite.

At the same time, there are numerous advantages for companies that are able to afford child-care centers. Karen Leibold (1990) of Stride Rite, which has an on-site child-care center, has contended that such centers result in better employee recruitment, higher morale, a more humane workplace, and excellent community relations. Indeed, such benefits to the company have been confirmed in a study comparing employees using company-sponsored day-care centers with those using alternative sources of day care and those without preschool children. Absenteeism and turnover were significantly lower for employees who used the company day-care centers (Milkovich & Gomez, 1976). The benefits to the community observed by Stride Rite as a result of its child-care center include the opportunity for more people to enter and remain in the work force, thus paying taxes, buying goods and services, and becoming contributing members of the community (Leibold, 1990). Families themselves benefit from experiencing less of the stress that results from the dearth of quality and affordable child care and appreciate the opportunity to provide their children with "a good start educationally" (Leibold, 1990, p. 21).

A day-care consortium, in which two or more employers collectively operate a day-care center, is an alternative that is particularly suitable for smaller companies. For example, in Massachusetts, the Prospect Hill Parents' and Children's Center is operated by 30 companies that are located near one another. These companies vary in size from 7 to 200 employees. Each company determines the shares that it and the employee will contribute to the cost of care. The advantages of this kind of consortium arrangement include the sharing of costs, risks, and benefits among several companies, as well as the protection from underenrollment that is afforded by a large, combined work force. A major disadvantage of consortia is the complicated negotiations required among the companies. Further, only a few employees from each company may be served because of the large combined work force (Bureau of National Affairs, 1988).

A child-care voucher system is an alternative program that allows employees to select and make their own child-care arrangements and obtain some reimbursement from their employer. In Massachusetts, Polaroid Corporation signs contracts with day-care providers chosen by the employees and pays a percentage of the cost based on the employees' incomes. Polaroid chose this reimbursement system because its work force was not centrally located, thus making an on-site day-care center impractical (Bureau of National Affairs, 1988). The advantages of vouchers and subsidies are that employees may choose their own arrangements, that several child-care services throughout the community are supported, and that administrative responsibility for the program is minimal when directed through the payroll system. If, however, the amount and/or quality of existing day-care programs in the community are inadequate, then the voucher system is not responsive to employees' child-care needs. Other disadvantages with this system include, on the one hand, its expense to the company if eligibility is not limited and, on the other hand, problems of inequity among employees if eligibility is limited (Bureau of National Affairs, 1988; U. S. Department of Labor, undated).

Sick and Emergency Day Care for Children. Employees frequently miss work when their children become sick or when their regular day-care arrangements disintegrate. One respondent to our survey described her employer's response to family sickness:

> At my job, if you call in sick, you get paid plus one black mark. If you call in because a child is sick and miss work, you don't get paid and you get a black mark anyway. If you get four black marks in 1 year, you get disciplined, that is, talk, a letter, suspension, up to being fired. That is stressful.

Some companies assist employees with sick children by helping to defray the cost of a care center for sick children. In Minneapolis, such a center, called Chicken Soup, is staffed by a nurse and a teacher who care for children aged 6 months to 12 years who are moderately ill. Businesses can contract with Chicken Soup and pay a retainer or can be billed directly for the services used by their employees. Most companies pay 50% to 75% of their employees' costs for the sick day care. According to the president of Chicken Soup, one company has estimated that their subsidy represented 15% of what it would cost to have their employees take time off from work to care for their children (Bureau of National Affairs, 1988).

Alternatively, some companies have opted to subsidize in-home professional care for sick children. For example, 3M Corporation in Minneapolis/St. Paul developed a program in cooperation with a local hospital to send health-care workers to employees' homes so that the employees could go to work. The company then reimbursed the employee for up to 75% of the costs depending on the family's income (Bureau of National Affairs, 1988).

Crises also arise for employees when regular day-care arrangements suddenly fall apart. To address this concern, a few employers, such as the Washington, D.C., law firm of Wilmer, Cutler, & Pickering, have an on-site emergency day-care facility to accommodate their employees' children. This law firm of 500 employees pays all costs of the center. Since its opening, the center's usage rate is 72%, with an average of three children in the facility per day. The center has been helpful in attracting new personnel as well as in producing a smoother work flow and more billable hours. Further, employees need to be less concerned about making their own provisions for back-up child care (Bureau of National Affairs, 1988).

After-School and Summer Arrangements. Some companies have become involved in helping employees to make after-school and summer care arrangements for their school-age children. To support a program for latchkey children in Houston, Texas, a group of corporations have contributed both money and volunteers to schools and churches throughout the Houston area. The program charges a fee for the child-care service based on a sliding scale (Bureau of National Affairs, 1988). For employees with children at home for the summer, Fel-Pro, Inc., of Skokie, Illinois, has established a summer day camp for children aged 6 to 15. The camp is available only to employees on the day shift; transportation between the plant and the camp is provided to coordinate with the beginning and end of that shift. Fel-Pro, Inc., covers most costs of the program with a minimal charge to parents. The company spokesperson has cited reduced employee absenteeism during the summer as a major corporate advantage of this program (Bureau of National Affairs, 1988). Such camps are particularly beneficial for divorced employees whose children stay with them only during the summer months. These parents have no regular day-care arrangements, and the summer camps fill this need (Friedman, 1986).

Day Care for the Elderly. The provision of company-sponsored day-care centers for the elderly is just beginning. Wang, in cooperation with the National Association of Area Agencies on Aging, is establishing a center where employees can leave their elderly relatives while the employees are at work (Azarnoff & Scharlach, 1988; Friedman, 1986). Stride Rite has recently initiated an intergenerational day-care center for both elders and children. This center is an example of a public-private partnership, in which a local, nonprofit, aging services organization provides expertise in screening potential participants who are elderly, offering referrals, and developing the curriculum and training models for the adult day-care center (Leibold, 1990).

Elderly Respite Care. In addition to day-care arrangements for their elderly relatives, employees also need respite from full-time caregiving for the times when they are at home (Bureau of National Affairs, 1988). Respite care involves care by a substitute caregiver to assist an elder or adult with disabilities when the employee needs to take a break on evenings or weekends (Scharlach et al., 1991). A few companies are considering providing their employees with assistance with respite care. For example, as part of a demonstration project at the University of

Bridgeport, Remington Products shared the cost of respite care arrangements for a few days, thus allowing employees to take a vacation (Friedman, 1986). Specifically, under this program, Remington Products paid one half of the costs incurred by employees for up to a total of 95 hours per year; costs for respite care delivered during normal working hours, however, were not reimbursable (Scharlach et al., 1991). The program was used by very few employees (Scharlach et al., 1991) and was subsequently discontinued.

Stimulating Care Resources. Many of the above-mentioned programs are major supports for employees only if quality community-based resources are available. When such resources are not available, companies may become involved in efforts to stimulate them. For example, businesses can work with community groups to increase the number of family day-care providers in areas through which employees commute to work. An example is Child Care Dallas, which is responsible for recruiting, training, and monitoring family day-care providers in the Dallas area (Bureau of National Affairs, 1988).

Alternatively, companies can contract with agencies to develop additional services, for example with a child-care center to develop family day-care satellite homes or with an agency to develop information and referral services. A day-care center at St. Luke's Presbyterian Hospital in Chicago has developed 20 family day-care satellites to accommodate a long waiting list. The center at St. Luke's is responsible for training these providers and providing back-up support if the provider is sick (Bureau of National Affairs, 1988). Another example is the previously mentioned Metropolitan Washington Child Care Network, an information and referral service toward which several companies in the Washington, D.C., area contribute (Bureau of National Affairs, 1988).

Employer assistance in stimulating quality day care can also take the form of loans to family day-care centers. For example, Steelcase, Inc., of Grand Rapids, Michigan, funds the purchase of equipment needed by their employees' family day-care providers (Bureau of National Affairs, 1988).

IMPLEMENTING POLICIES, BENEFITS, AND SERVICES

Although it is crucial to be aware of the range of services available for employees with family responsibilities, we must also consider the extent to which such initiatives are actually implemented and determine possible obstacles to the implementation of dependent-care policies, benefits, and services. For example, Hughes and Galinsky (1988) contend that although supportive services for employees with family responsibilities have expanded, only a small proportion of employees in the work force are served by them.

Kingston (1990, p. 438) concluded that American businesses have made only modest progress in instituting "family-friendly" practices. As evidence, he cited the fact that "family-friendly" initiatives are news. He asserted that, "It is illusory to expect that market solutions will deliver good or equitable family policy in the foreseeable future" (p. 438). The reasoning behind this position is that the economic benefits of such policies and practices have yet to be demonstrated. For example, one factor affecting employers' implementation of family-responsive supports is that the incentives for employer response to work-family conflict may not be as strong as they at first appear. Predicted labor shortages may be overstated and job growth is likely to occur in jobs that are low-paying and require little experience.

A second factor is that corporations themselves perceive several obstacles to the implementation of dependent-care policies, benefits, and services. The major obstacles mentioned in a survey of Fortune 500 companies include inadequate information about employees' needs, the costs associated with many types of supports, concerns about equity issues, and insufficient evidence of the long-term benefits derived from such supports (Galinsky, Friedman, & Hernandez, 1991).

Focusing on this final obstacle, it is clear that both the quantity and quality of research examining the effectiveness of family-responsive supports with respect to the "bottom lines" of business have been lacking (Raabe, 1990; Stipek & McCroskey, 1989). Some studies, however, such as that by Orthner and Pittman (1986), have linked family-supportive policies to greater job commitment and retention. These studies suggest that improved family supports will yield benefits in the areas of employee performance, morale, and retention, but more research is needed. Rigorous documentation concerning the prevalence of family supportive policies, benefits, and services is also lacking (Raabe & Gessner, 1988). Much of the research conducted to date with respect to both the family-responsiveness of American businesses and the effectiveness of the work-family supports provided has been flawed. These flaws include small samples; low response rates; and limited, unrepresentative sampling frames, such as surveys only of large employers, who may differ from smaller employers in the types of supports they can offer (Kingston, 1990; Raabe & Gessner, 1988). The lack of longitudinal, comparative data and the use of perceptions of effects rather than behavioral measures are also limitations (Raabe, 1990). Aldous (1990) has summarized the current status of family-responsive supports for employees and the forces impeding the widespread implementation of such supports as follows:

> There is less to corporate policy than meets the eye focused on media stories covering individual companies. Few businesses see it as in their self interest to institute family benefits. There is little solid research that would indicate they pay off in profitability. More surprising, however, is the lack of evidence showing how benefits ease the lives of employees with families. The few who receive them and their relatively advantaged status may account for this situation. (p. 365)

At the same time, it is important to note that there is great diversity among companies regarding their commitment to family-responsive supports. Galinsky and Stein (1990) have pointed out that there are various stages in developing such supports. They have distinguished between companies in the early stages of identifying employee needs and developing responsive programs ("Stage 1 organizations") and those that have established a comprehensive approach to employees' dependent-care needs ("Stage 2 organizations").

Galinsky and Stein (1990) have identified several features that contribute to the process of organizational change from Stage 1 to Stage 2. For example, a commitment to helping employees balance work and family responsibilities must be seen as legitimate within the organization. The head of the organization must be supportive, managers require training to be sensitive to workers' needs, and someone must be responsible for coordinating dependent-care programs. Further, the company's policies need to be reviewed regularly with an orientation toward flexibility and change.

IBM exemplifies a company that has moved from a Stage 1 to a Stage 2 organization. The company initially addressed the child-care concerns of its employees by establishing a child-care information and referral service. Later, IBM added a similar referral program for elder-care concerns. The company's movement toward even greater responsiveness to employees is apparent in its recent attempts to address the complex problem of schedule flexibility. IBM's response has involved redefining the traditional workday and allowing employees greater flexibility in the timing of their arrival to and departure from work (Galinsky & Stein, 1990).

There are many challenges for companies as they attempt to be responsive to caregivers in the workplace. Currently, most services for employees are concentrated in big businesses, so that the many workers employed by smaller companies do not have access to dependent-care assistance (Hughes & Galinsky, 1988). Thus it is particularly important to identify policies and benefits, as well as services, that smaller businesses can implement. For example, Raabe (1990, citing Hayghe, 1988) has noted that larger employers offer more child-care supports, whereas smaller ones are more likely to offer flexible leaves and alternate work patterns.

In addition, companies' policies and programs must be responsive to the composition of their work force (Scharlach et al., 1991). At present, most services offered by companies have been directed toward those with child-care responsibilities. Programs serving employees with elder care are much less numerous, and programs for those with adult-care responsibilities are virtually nonexistent. Scharlach et al. (1991) have illustrated ways in which organizations can be responsive to work force diversity in terms of elder-care responsibility:

> Companies whose employees include a large percentage of primary caregivers providing intensive day-to-day care, for instance, will benefit from respite care, support groups, and assistance in locating and paying for adult day care and other community-based support services. Companies whose employees include primarily long-distance caregivers, on the other hand, will benefit especially from informational seminars, telephone consultation that provides access to a nationwide information and referral network, and case management. (p. 61)

Clearly, the initial step that employers must take before developing such specialized programs is to assess the dependent-care responsibilities and needs of their work force.

As employers develop an increased awareness of the dependent-care needs of their employees and the benefits of assisting them, there is likely to be more commitment to providing policies, benefits, and services. Companies may respond initially by offering a few limited services directed toward specific dependent-care needs. Over time, they can gradually progress toward a more comprehensive approach, including flexible work arrangement policies and benefits that are responsive to a variety of dependent-care responsibilities.

RECOMMENDATIONS

We offer these recommendations, first for future research and second for steps to be used in implementing one or more types of family-responsive supports.

Future Research

Given the lack of current research on the prevalence and effectiveness of employer supports, demonstration projects with comprehensive evaluation components are needed to test the effectiveness of employer supports separately and in combination. Such research should include the following considerations:

1. Pre- and postcomparisons of family-responsive policies, benefits, and services should be conducted (Christensen & Staines, 1990; Raabe, 1990).
2. Research should take into consideration the fact that different policies are likely to have varying effects and relevance for different occupational groups and particular work forces (Christensen & Staines, 1990; Raabe, 1990).
3. In addition to the existence of a policy, its quality and strength (e.g., the length of maternity/parental leave) should also be considered (Raabe, 1990).
4. The extent of coverage and use of the policy/program must be taken into account (Kingston, 1990; Raabe, 1990).
5. Since formal policies can be hindered by unsupportive supervisors or organizational cultures, the informal policies and practices in place must be systematically observed (Raabe, 1990).
6. The outcome measures used and the time frame covered by these measures should be reconsidered, since, for example, the quantity of work time may not be comparable to quality work time, and short-term and long-term outcomes may differ (Raabe, 1990).
7. The effects of employer supports on the quality, as well as quantity, of family time should be considered (Christensen & Staines, 1990).
8. The interrelated effects of policies, benefits, and services must be considered (Raabe, 1990).
9. Attention should be paid to the effects on the outcomes being measured of factors other than the policies, benefits, or services under study. For example,

absenteeism due to breakdowns in child care may be lessened by the availability of an on-site child-care center, but absenteeism caused by a child's illness may not (Raabe, 1990).

Improved research is likely to provide more compelling evidence for the effectiveness of employer supports in reducing work-family conflict (Christensen & Staines, 1990). Moreover, if this research demonstrates the organizational benefits of family-responsive policies, more widespread implementation of such policies, benefits, and services may result (Raabe, 1990).

Steps Toward Implementation of Family Supports for Employees

For employers interested in developing policies, benefits, and services for their employees who are attempting to balance their work and their family lives, there are a number of steps to be taken (Denton, Love, & Slate, 1990; Galinsky & Stein, 1990; Wagner, Neal, Gibeau, Anastas, & Scharlach, 1989). The first step is for employers to assess the unique needs of their own employees. Details concerning this process are provided in the next chapter.

Once the assessment is complete, existing work scheduling policies and benefits should be reviewed to determine ways to maximize flexibility and equitable access. The services available in the community to meet the employees' identified needs should then be determined. If those services are adequate, employers can promote their use by educating employees about their existence, as well as through information and referral and case management services. If the available services are not adequate, employers can stimulate the further development of resources or initiate the provision of the service or services directly to employees.

Any services, as well as policies and other benefits offered, must be vigorously and continuously marketed, otherwise employees will not be aware of their existence when they are needed. Furthermore, managers and supervisors should be trained regarding the issues faced by employees with dependent-care responsibilities and the existing policies, benefits, and services that may assist these employees. Routine monitoring of changing benefit products and public policy developments related to dependent care is necessary. Finally, employers should periodically reassess their employees' needs and the supports made available to them in order to ensure continuing responsiveness to employees' dependent-care needs (Denton et al., 1990; Galinsky & Stein, 1990; Wagner, Creedon, Sasala, & Neal, 1989).

REFERENCES

Aarens, M. (1986). Seminars for employees on caregiving. *Aging*, No. 353, pp. 26-27.

Aldous, J. (1990). Specification and speculation concerning the politics of workplace family policies. *Journal of Family Issues, 11,* 355-367.

Azarnoff, R. S., & Scharlach, A. E. (1988, September). Can employees carry the eldercare burden? *Personnel Journal, 67,* 60-65.

Beinecke, R. H., & Marchetta, A. (1989). Employees and eldercare: A review of needs and programs. In Health Action Forum of Greater Boston, *Eldercare: The state of the art* (Part 1). Boston: Health Action Forum of Greater Boston.

Bureau of National Affairs. (1988). *33 ways to ease work/family tensions—An employer's checklist* (Special Report No. 2). Rockville, MD: Buraff. (Product Code BSP-84)

Christensen, K. E., & Staines, G. L. (1990). Flextime: A viable solution to work/family conflict? *Journal of Family Issues, 11,* 455-476.

Creedon, M. (1987). The corporate eldercare project. *Businesslink, 3,* 10.

Creedon, M. A., & Wagner, D. L. (1986). *Eldercare: A resource guide.* Bridgeport, CT: University of Bridgeport, Center for the Study of Aging.

Denton, K., Love, L. T., & Slate, R. (1990). Eldercare in the '90s: Employee responsibility, employer challenge. *Families in Society: The Journal of Contemporary Human Services, 71,* 349-359.

Friedman, D. E. (1986). Eldercare: The employee benefit of the 1990s? *Across the Board, 23*(6), 45-51.

Friedman, D. E. (1987). *Family-supportive policies: The corporate decision-making process* (Report No. 897). New York: The Conference Board.

Galinsky, E., Friedman, D. E., & Hernandez, C. A., with Axel, H. (1991). *Corporate reference guide to work-family programs.* New York: Families and Work Institute.

Galinsky, E., & Stein, P. J. (1990). The impact of human resource policies on employees: Balancing work/family life. *Journal of Family Issues, 11,* 368-383.

Halcrow, A. (1988). IBM answers the elder care need. *Personnel Journal, 67,* 67-69.

Haygue, H. V. (1988, September). Employers and child care: What roles do they play? *Monthly Labor Review, 111,* 38-44.

Hughes, D., & Galinsky, E. (1988). Balancing work and family lives: Research and corporate applications. In A. E. Gottfried & A. W. Gottfried (Eds.), *Maternal employment and children's development: Longitudinal research* (pp. 233-268). New York: Plenum.

Ingersoll-Dayton, B., Chapman, N., & Neal, M. (1990). A program for caregivers in the workplace. *The Gerontologist, 30,* 126-130.

Kingston, P. W. (1990). Illusions and ignorance about the family-responsive workplace. *Journal of Family Issues, 11,* 438-454.

Leibold, K. (1990). Sharing the caring. In Subcommittee on Human Services, Select Committee on Aging, House of Representatives, *Sharing the caring: Options for the 90s and beyond: A policy forum* (Committee Publication No. 101-750, pp. 20-27). Washington, DC: Government Printing Office.

Milkovich, G. T., & Gomez, L. R. (1976). Day care and selected employee work behaviors. *Academy of Management Journal, 19,* 111-115.

Orthner, D. K., & Pittman, J. F. (1986). Family contributions to work commitment. *Journal of Marriage and the Family, 48,* 573-581.

Raabe, P. H. (1990). The organizational effects of workplace family policies: Past weaknesses and recent progress toward improved research. *Journal of Family Issues, 11,* 477-491.

Raabe, P. H., & Gessner, J. C. (1988). Employer family-supportive policies: Diverse variations on the theme. *Family Relations, 37,* 196-202.

Scharlach, A. E., Lowe, B. F., & Schneider, E. L. (1991). *Elder care and the work force: Blueprint for action.* Lexington, MA: Lexington Books.

Schmidt, S. E., & Tate, D. R. (1988). Employer-supported child care: An ecological model for supporting families. In L. A. Bond & B. M. Wagner (Eds.), *Families in transition: Primary prevention programs that work* (pp. 49-67). Newbury Park, CA: Sage.

Stipek, D., & McCroskey, J. (1989). Investing in children: Government and workplace policies for parents. *American Psychologist, 44,* 416-423.

Trice, H. M., & Beyer, J. M. (1984). Employee assisted programs: Blending performance-oriented and humanitarian ideologies to assist emotionally disturbed employees. *Research in Community and Mental Health, 4,* 245-297.

U.S. Department of Labor, Office of the Secretary, Women's Bureau. (Undated). *Work and family resource kit.* Washington, DC: U.S. Department of Labor. (Available from Clearinghouse on Implementation of Child Care and Elder Care Services; ph. 1-800-827-5335)

Wagner, D. L., Creedon, M. A., Sasala, J. M., & Neal, M. B. (1989). *Employees and eldercare: Designing effective responses for the workplace.* Bridgeport, CT: University of Bridgeport, Center for the Study of Aging.

Wagner, D. L., Neal, M. B., Gibeau, J. L., Anastas, J. W., & Scharlach, A. (1989). *Eldercare and the working caregiver.* Unpublished manuscript.

Zedeck, S., & Mosier, K. L. (1990). Work in the family and employing organization. *American Psychologist, 45,* 240-251.

10

Assessing Employee Needs

My employer has a lot of working mothers. It would seem very beneficial
to the company to have an in-house day-care service.

In this chapter, we examine the methodology for assessing employee
needs through employee surveys, focus groups, and dependent-care task
forces. These methods, along with literature reviews, evaluative studies, community-resource surveys, and other kinds of research, are part
of a corporate decision-making process that has been described usefully
by Friedman (1987).

In assessing employee needs, many companies start from a point at
which they know surprisingly little about their employees, at least in
terms of their family responsibilities. For years, employers have tried
not to know about the family baggage of their employees, much less to
help them carry it, and have even been required by law not to ask about
such responsibilities when hiring employees. As a result, organizations
have lacked the kinds of information that would help in planning
employee-benefits programs or in thinking about policies dealing with
dependent care. Recently, however, employee "needs assessment," in
one form or another, has become an increasingly familiar undertaking
by employers across the United States. As more organizations have
begun to examine the links between work, family, and dependent care,
their commitment to "family-friendly" policies has gone through stages
(Galinsky, Friedman, & Hernandez, 1991), their understanding and assessments becoming deeper, more extensive, and more sophisticated.

Much of the information that appeared in Chapters 3 through 6 was
derived from company efforts to assess employee needs. In those chapters,
however, we addressed scientific questions that often went beyond what

companies needed to know for the decisions at hand. Studies done for the purpose of assessing employee needs usually have the modest purpose of seeking better information that will help in making the next decision facing the organization. The realities of that purpose define such studies, their methods, and their variables. Needs assessment tends to be oriented toward the future and focused on policy. Less often is the purpose to evaluate the impact of a past decision. Assessing needs differs from evaluating programs, and experimental studies of the impact of new programs are rare.

The concept "need" may be defined as the lack of basic conditions that employed members of families require in order to meet successfully their responsibilities with regard to work, family, and dependent care. The logic of assessing needs reflects a process of reasoning about problems and solutions. We make inferences about needs from the problems that people have when their basic requirements for life are lacking and from the services, policies, and other solutions that either alleviate those problems or prevent them from occurring in the first place.

This chapter concentrates on the kinds of questions that have been addressed in assessing employee needs. It also provides illustrations of how the answers have contributed to understanding of needs and to making decisions about solutions. The chapter begins by describing needs assessment as a methodology and ends by summarizing the range of concerns about dependent care that have emerged from assessments of employee needs.

METHODS OF ASSESSING NEEDS

As companies embark on assessing their employees' needs, they can benefit from an increasing wealth of information on what other companies have discovered. National organizations that can assist them in this endeavor include The Conference Board, Families and Work Institute, Catalyst, Bureau of National Affairs, Work/Family Directions, The National Council on Aging, and the American Association of Retired Persons, as well as research centers and universities. It is helpful to be able to take advantage of what others are doing and learning, but eventually companies find that there is no substitute for a needs assessment applied to their particular business and their own unique work force. Each of the methods commonly used for assessing employee needs— employee surveys, focus groups, and task forces—has special advantages, although these are complementary approaches. These methods also provide the context for specific descriptive, evaluative, or experimental studies that are narrower in scope.

Employee Surveys

Employee surveys can gain anonymous information about the work force that is not contained in personnel records. Employee surveys make it possible to obtain an analyzable set of data from the usually disparate domains of work and family. Such surveys, which are especially useful in larger companies, provide a demographic perspective on the extent of needs in a work force or of the use of a benefit, and they allow inferences about needs from systematically collected data. An effective variation is for groups of large and small businesses, agencies, and unions in a single community all to conduct work force surveys at the same time; in this way, a composite community profile is created to which individual employers can compare themselves. By thus compiling a broader profile of employees' family-care needs, communities can identify strategies that should be pursued collectively, since many of the family-care problems identified through employee surveys are beyond the ability of any one employer to solve by itself.

One survey methodology that has proved successful involves distributing a four- to six-page questionnaire anonymously to the entire work force. Return rates of 70% or higher can be expected when the survey enjoys strong internal support and is filled out on the job. Simple random samples that are representative of the work force as a whole are not as useful (and may be equally costly) as anonymous batch distribution to all employees. The latter provides ample cell sizes for comparing the many subgroups within the employee population that have different demographics and dependent-care responsibilities.

Experience in needs assessment also points to the advisability of avoiding (or at least not relying on) subjective questions about preferences of the "If we had an on-site child-care center, would you use it?" variety. These kinds of questions yield untrustworthy estimates of future behavior, and if followed, the answers often result in the underenrollment of apparently popular options. The reason is that program options may sound attractive in the abstract but in reality may not fit well into family life or may compete with alternatives that are currently in use. Moreover, employers may be reluctant to raise expectations for options that may not be feasible. It is more useful to ask about what employees are currently doing, what kinds of dependent-care arrangements they are using, and how well they are managing. This kind of information provides a realistic point of departure for making reasonable inferences about need and feasible policies.

Focus Groups

Focus groups are an effective technique that is widely used in market research and increasingly applied to work-family issues (Friedman, 1987). Focus groups are group interviews of up to 2 hours that provide focus on a topic yet still have enough flexibility to explore it, allowing researchers to gain insights from the group interaction that may not emerge from individual interviews or surveys (Morgan, 1988). This method of inquiry can combine a depth of exploration of employee concerns with an adequate discussion of the organizational context to reveal how company policies affect individual employees. The focus group is a fruitful method for understanding how systems work.

Focus groups can be used effectively in small or large companies. The groups typically consist of six to eight employees when the aim is to elicit intense participation (Morgan, 1988), or up to 12 employees when a quicker reaction is sought from more people. The number of groups needed for a reliable study depends on the size and homogeneity of the organization. Groups tend to be more vocal when composed of employees from similar backgrounds, such as all supervisors, all nurses, or all mechanics, and possibly when men and women are separated. The groups should not include social cliques, friendships, or combinations of bosses with those vulnerably subordinate to them.

Task Forces

Task forces created by companies and agencies to think about work-family issues help to develop an understanding of these issues within the organization and provide a more sustained consideration of problems and solutions. The composition of the task force is thus important. Without being unwieldy in size, it should represent supervisors as well as rank and file, men as well as women, and various regional and ethnic interests. If a task force is to succeed, however, it must have committed leadership, and its members must couple their personal investment in the issues with creative minds.

In some communities, a public-private task force can be effective in exploring community partnerships to address employees' family-care needs. A community task force can give voice to the interests of small agencies or businesses, such as a group of downtown merchants. In the process of assessing the work-family needs of their employees, employers eventually become acutely aware that dependent-care problems require community solutions.

Whichever methods are adopted, needs assessment usually means a five-step process: (a) assimilating relevant background information from the literature, experts, and organizations specializing in the issues; (b) collecting information about the work force—employees' jobs, work schedules, family demographics, patterns of child care, adult care, and elder care, and the problems that employees are having in carrying out their work and family responsibilities; (c) analyzing the interrelationships among variables and comparing subgroups within the work force; (d) making reasonable inferences about "needs"; and (e) thinking through possible policies, services, and other solutions to problems that may be feasible for different kinds of employees within the context of the organization.

CRITICAL ISSUES IN CONDUCTING
EMPLOYEE NEEDS ASSESSMENTS

Companies beginning to assess employee needs often start out with a simple, skeptical desire to establish whether or not their employees' family responsibilities really do pose a problem for the company. Is the need exaggerated or being minimized? Does it affect many or just a few? Which employees are affected most? What is the nature and magnitude of the need? How should data about potential problems be interpreted, and how can the need to address a problem be inferred from such data? Among all the problems, which ones deserve priority? The remainder of this chapter illustrates the kinds of questions that are raised in assessing needs and also describes the logic employed in answering them. Unattributed references to needs assessment studies refer to unpublished work by one of the authors, Arthur Emlen.

Sizing Up the Scope of Employees' Dependent-Care Needs

Often the first concern is to determine the scope of employees' dependent- or family-care needs. How many employees are affected by dependent-care issues in a particular work force? Companies are often surprised to learn the magnitude of the dependent-care responsibilities affecting their work force. For example, Friedman (1991) reported that child care became a "mainstream issue" for DuPont when the company found that 70% of all employees with children under age 13 said that they were using some form of child care outside the home. For a West Coast hospital chain, it came as a revelation to learn that 62% of its collective work force had some kind of a dependent-care responsibility, with 47% having children living at home and 22% of employees caring for, looking after, looking in on, or in some way helping out a family member or friend who required assistance due to frailty or disability (Emlen, Koren, & Louise, 1987). In that work force, 7% had responsibilities at both ends of the age spectrum—a group that represented 15% of parents and 34% of those with adult or elder care. Suddenly the potential scope and relevance of dependent care as a workplace issue acquired magnitude for the corporation. A young work force has proportionally more children, and an older work force has more elder-care responsibility, but in repeated surveys, the sum of dependent-care responsibilities has been apt to fall within a range of 60% to 65% of employees who have one or the other kind of care responsibility, including a small percentage caring for adults with disabilities. Still, each worksite is different in ways that can affect priorities. At the same West Coast hospitals, variation in elder-care responsibilities across 20 sites was striking, ranging from 11% to 33%.

It is important to note that, for some categories of interest, a needs assessment may turn up numbers that are smaller than expected. Companies know how much they pay their employees but usually not what their employees' household incomes are. Thus, in a large West Coast regional bank in which 73% of employed mothers had personal incomes of less than $20,000, only 19% had household incomes that low. Employed mothers with low household incomes stood out sharply in a two-tier work force in which the great majority had higher incomes; the company decided that the numbers of their low-income minority were small enough and their problems acute enough to justify subsidizing their dependent-care reimbursement plans on a sliding scale.

The Politics of Need and Equity

Assessing the scope of needs may raise questions about the extent of political support for a work-family policy within an organization. A governmental agency in the power industry, the Bonneville Power Admin-istration, wanted to start an on-site child-care center but wondered whether the idea had widespread support. Questions gave way to a realistic assess-ment of support when two thirds of the work force said that starting such a center was a good idea. Not surprisingly, the support varied according to the family circumstances of the employees. Approval came from 89% of mothers with children under the age of 9 (who were most likely to benefit), from 67% of single women who were not parents, and even from 52% of fathers of children aged 9 to 17 whose wives were not employed. Thus the lowest percentage of approval, which came from the fathers in "traditional" families, who comprised 5% of the work force, still represented more than half of that group of employees. The agency was able to construct its on-site child-care center knowing that the idea enjoyed widespread political support, even among those who would not be using it themselves.

At another company with many sites, however, a task force looked at a flat graph showing that all age groups of employee children were represented nearly equally. As a result, they backed away from consid-ering on-site child-care facilities or adopting any benefit that would serve only a single age category. This is because the introduction of any benefit that is designed for the needs of a special category of employees may raise questions of fairness or equity. Some benefits are universal. For example, all employees have teeth and need dental coverage. Some employees, including employees who raise their children without day care or a second income and employees who have no children, vocally express resentment of subsidies for others whose lives and decisions are different. As one of our survey respondents who did not have children put it:

> It seems to me that companies should reward people who do not take time off work for family-related problems. No compensation is made in this area whatsoever. My patience is growing very short with people who are constantly missing work due to their children. At least the time should be made up. It shouldn't just be an added gift. It is not fair to expect people who do not have children to do double the work.

Within a complex work force, however, there is more equity in the fabric of benefits and perquisites than may at first appear from a consideration of a single issue. This is especially true if companies have implemented a cafeteria of benefits in their plan and if a longer term perspective is taken. Many dependent-care benefits deal with relatively brief episodes in a work career. Parental leaves and leaves to deal with a seriously ill parent are two such benefits that are short-lived costs that may have long-term pay-offs. One of the values of assessing the family-related needs of the entire work force is that it broadens the field of employees who are recognized as benefiting, immediately or potentially, from a range of policy options. Many companies believe that they are strengthened politically when they broaden their concern beyond child care to all types of family-care responsibilities or beyond leaves for one reason to leaves for other urgent family emergencies.

Analyzing the Needs of Subgroups

Questions about the scope of needs quickly focus on particular subgroups within the work force, or on a comparison of subgroups, since many companies have special issues that they are interested in researching. Such issues may include whether different kinds of employees (e.g., full time versus part time) have different dependent-care needs, or which employees are best able to take advantage of a benefit. For example, Merck & Co. wanted to learn more about dual-career couples and single parents (Friedman, 1991). IBM wanted to know how the relocation of dual-career couples would affect future staffing (Friedman, 1991). U.S. Bancorp wanted to know if child-care needs in small towns were the same as those experienced by employees in urban areas (Emlen, Koren, & Yoakum, 1990). Corporate motivations to assess needs may be inspired by a desire to marshal evidence for an initiative already favored or, alternatively, by a desire for evidence about the limitations of a policy option that a vocal group may be demanding, such as for an on-site child-care center.

The methodology for assessing employee needs relies heavily on simple analyses comparing differences between carefully delineated categories of employees. A corporate audience will examine a percentage difference and assess whether it is big enough to consider making policy changes. For the hospital chain, it was important to examine separately all the full-time employees with elder care. Those who found it difficult to some degree to combine work and family were twice as likely as those without such concerns to report difficulty in knowing where to turn to get help for elder care. The findings were seen as relevant in assessing the needs of this single important category of employees. Similarly, among the hospitals' full-time employed mothers who said that paying for child care was difficult or very difficult, 91% reported difficulty finding child care. Thus, as frequently happens when assessing needs, narrowing the scope of attention to particular groups reveals more acute needs than those found on average for the work force at large.

Making Inferences About the Nature of Need

To shift from questions about the scope and magnitude of need to questions about the nature of needs requires comparing subgroups or categories of employees with respect to the "outcomes" that may arise from the problems or difficulties experienced by these different groups of employees. Needs are inferred from these differences. For example, the finding that single parents report somewhat higher absenteeism rates than employees who have an employed spouse or partner leads to a recognition that single parents have less flexibility in dealing with child care or other family emergencies. This is because they have less ability to afford child care and have fewer alternatives in family resources for sharing daily child-care responsibilities.

Assessments of employee needs usually have been efforts to establish the relevance of employees' work and family-care needs to "bottom-line" issues that may have a bearing on organizational effectiveness and productivity (Friedman, 1991). Nevertheless, problems of interpretation beset all the means that have been commonly used to assess employee needs. "Outcomes" such as absenteeism, stress, and difficulty in combining working with family responsibilities do not directly measure productivity. They have, however, served usefully when analyzed in relation to variables such as dissatisfaction with care arrangements, disruptions of care arrangements, difficulty in knowing where to turn for help, or the many demands or lack of resources identified in earlier chapters.

Interpreting Absenteeism. One kind of assessment that has caught corporate attention because of its presumed relevance to bottom-line productivity issues is the relationship between dependent-care responsibilities and absenteeism. Since 1982, a number of investigators have measured employee self-reports of time loss, in the form of days missed, times late, times leaving early, and interruptions at work during the previous 4 weeks or some other period of time (Emlen, 1982; Emlen & Koren, 1984; Fernandez, 1986; Friedman, 1991; Galinsky, 1988;

Neal, Chapman, & Ingersoll-Dayton, 1988). These measures are fruitful to use in work-family studies, but not because they provide valid direct indicators of productivity, which is a complex and elusive concept that is not easily measured (Googins, Gonyea, & Pitt-Catsouphes, 1990). Instead, measures of time loss are sensitive to both work and family issues. As we saw in earlier chapters, job requirements and flexibility in work schedules account for wide variation in absenteeism rates, but so do differences in employees' dependent-care responsibilities and care arrangements.

Using measures of absenteeism in assessing employee needs poses a number of problems of interpretation. The forms of time loss are not correlated with each other, except for a weak relationship between being late and leaving early; each kind of time loss is apparently adaptive to different jobs and types of dependent-care arrangements (Neal, Chapman, Ingersoll-Dayton, Emlen, & Boise, 1990). Measures based on 4-week samples of absenteeism fail to capture some of the incidence of time loss associated with the occasional nature of family crises. More troublesome, the measures fail to record compensation for time loss, voluntary extra effort or overtime, or periods of intense work activity. Personal performance and productivity may go in cycles or at a steady pace. Time loss or time worked is not equivalent to level of effort or productivity, which involves product quantity and quality.

One of the problems with absenteeism as a proxy indicator of productivity is that a short-term loss in productivity may result in a longer term gain in productivity. For example, there is evidence that, for many employed parents, at least a little absenteeism to deal with family emergencies is a safety valve that may help to prevent stress in many companies (Emlen, 1987) and be inversely related to turnover (Rubin, Weinstock, Chetkovich, & Schlichtmann, 1989). Therefore assessments of the consequences of dependent-care arrangements should probably discount the cost of absenteeism by the gains from reduced stress or less turnover, which is more costly than absenteeism because of company investment in employee skill, knowledge, and training. Another perspective on absenteeism to bear in mind is that some jobs realistically allow more absenteeism than others, so that an organization's informal policy of tolerating some absenteeism when it is possible and needed allows those employees a measure of flexibility. Thus as an employee-needs issue, some companies have recognized that vigorous attempts to control absenteeism may have negative trade-offs.

Sources of Perceived Stress. Among the concerns that have received the most attention in assessments of employee needs are employee reports of the worry, difficulty, or stress that they experience in various areas of life. For employers, these measures have face validity even though they are somewhat ambiguous. Although perceived stress may reflect the difficulty that employees have in some area of their lives, it also may reflect which area of life is of primary concern or importance to them. For example, university students who were parents rated schoolwork and finances, but not jobs, as the sources of highest stress (Emlen & Emlen, 1991), just as employees in work force surveys invariably rate job stress highest.

When employers see the different levels in stress that employees report as arising from different areas of their lives, they are impressed by the fact that stress about child care and adult dependent care is comparable with other sources of stress, such as personal health, health of family members, and family relationships, even if not as high or frequent as the stresses of job and finances. Likewise, employers are attentive when they see more stress being reported by those employees who have dependent-care responsibilities. Such findings strengthen the inference that concrete difficulties in finding, arranging, and maintaining care arrangements do spill over into worries that may be carried to work.

The Need for Flexibility. When family emergencies occur, or regular medical appointments for family members must be kept, the flexibility to attend to these needs has to come from somewhere. The three major possible sources of flexibility are in the shared division of labor in the family, latitude in job requirements and the ways that work is structured, or in accommodation by care providers in the community. Thus the assessment of employee needs has increasingly focused on the need for flexibility. Some companies have stated that flexibility to deal with family emergencies is a matter of policy, and they encourage managers and supervisors to carry out the policy sympathetically (Galinsky et al., 1991). Assessment of flexibility has been a focus of surveys, often yielding wide variation among organizational units and leading to the decision to focus on training supervisors to be more sensitive to employees' family-related needs.

Needs Related to Community Resources for Caregiving. Employee needs assessments persistently point to a lack of community resources to support employees in finding supplemental care of satisfactory quality. This deficiency is most pronounced for child care. Extensive dissatisfaction with current child-care arrangements is linked to the perception that child care is difficult to find, a perception that has been reported by one half to three fifths of employed mothers in companies and communities of all kinds (Emlen & Koren, 1984; Emlen, Koren, & Yoakum, 1990). This perception is many-faceted. It reflects real shortages in the supply of child care, dissatisfaction with quality of care, inadequate information, absence of referral mechanisms or networks to make child care and services accessible, reticence and inexperience in making care arrangements, uncertainty about what to look for and how to evaluate what is observed, and ambivalence about the larger family decisions about work, career, child rearing, and parental roles (Emlen, 1987). For parents, these decisions and tasks get easier with time and experience, but those employees with care responsibilities for elders or for family members with disabilities often face increasingly complex and difficult decisions, sometimes suddenly. They too may be without sufficient community support or available resources.

Meeting dependent-care needs requires contributions by communities as well as by families and employers. It is a shared responsibility. When employers recognize how many employees are dissatisfied with their child-care arrangements or have difficulty in finding child care, they realize that a solution to the available care "out there" in the community requires more than families can do by themselves and more than any one employer can do by itself. This recognition has led many employers to purchase dependent-care resource and referral services for their employees and also to support community-wide efforts to increase the availability of better resources (Shellenbarger, 1991). For example, reinforced by the results of its needs assessment, U.S. Bancorp decided to do what it could as a bank by initiating a program to make loans available for the improvement of care facilities to be used by the community at large.

SUMMARY AND CONCLUSIONS

In this chapter we have described the methodologies that may be used by employers in assessing employees' dependent-care needs. We also have discussed some of the issues that often arise in making such assessments. Finally, we have identified the major needs that must be met for employees to be able to balance their work and their caregiving responsibilities.

1. Anonymous surveys of all employees regarding their dependent-care responsibilities and the strategies they have used to balance their work and family responsibilities are one technique for assessing employees' needs.
2. Focus groups are effective techniques for exploring in depth employee concerns and responses to existing and potential company policies.
3. Task forces may help provide more sustained consideration of problems and solutions. Members should represent the diverse interests of the work force, including those of line staff and supervisors, men and women, and members of ethnic groups. Community members may also be included.
4. Needs assessments typically have five steps: assimilating background information, collecting information about the work force, analyzing the data, making inferences about needs, and thinking through possible solutions.
5. In developing work-family policies, employers need to be attentive to issues of equity in addressing the diverse needs of their employees, including those without dependent-care responsibilities.
6. In analyzing the data collected, employers should examine the needs of specific subgroups, such as single parents and dual-career couples, in their data analysis.
7. Needs assessments should carefully choose outcome measures such as stress or absenteeism from which inferences regarding need can be made. Caution should be exercised in interpreting absenteeism, since some absenteeism may reduce stress. The presence of flexibility in work schedules and personnel policies, both formal and informal, should also be assessed.
8. Employers should be alert to indications of gaps in needed resources in the community and, when possible, try to work with community agencies to help create those resources.
9. The process of assessing employee needs has led to substantial agreement regarding the basic needs that must be met for employees successfully to balance work and family life, to care for family members, and to be productive in their work. These needs are:

   Flexibility: the need for sufficient flexibility in meeting the concurrent demands of work and family;

   Accessibility: the need to find, establish, and maintain arrangements for supplemental care of family members that fits in with family life and work schedules;

   Availability: the need for an adequate supply of services and supplemental care resources in the community;

Quality: the need for care arrangements with which employees can be satisfied and that have favorable effects on family members;

Affordability: the need to be able to pay for the care and services that are required to meet work and family-care responsibilities.

These are the major recognized needs that have emerged from assessing employees' abilities to balance work, family, and caregiving. It is no accident that these needs have come to be identified as national policy goals as well. As noted in Chapters 8 and 9, some employers are already seeking to reach these goals—that is, to meet these basic employee needs by designing family-friendly policies, benefits, and services. In the next chapter, we will identify some specific strategies that can be implemented to address these needs.

REFERENCES

Emlen, A. C. (1982). *When parents are at work: A three-company survey of how employed parents arrange child care.* Washington, DC: Greater Washington Research Center.

Emlen, A. C. (1987, August). *Child care, work and family.* Paper presented at the meeting of the American Psychological Association, New York.

Emlen, A. C., & Koren, P. E. (1984). *Hard to find and difficult to manage: The effects of child care on the workplace.* Portland, OR: Portland State University, Regional Research Institute for Human Services.

Emlen, A. C., Koren, P. E., & Louise, D. (1987). *1987 dependent care survey: Sisters of Providence: Final report* (Vol. 1). Portland, OR: Portland State University, Regional Research Institute for Human Services.

Emlen, A. C., Koren, P. E., & Yoakum, K. S. (1990). *1990 dependent care survey: 15 employers of Lane County, Oregon.* Portland, OR: Arthur Emlen & Associates, Inc., and Portland State University, Regional Research Institute for Human Services.

Emlen, M. D., & Emlen, A. C. (1991). *Aiding student parents at Portland State University.* Portland, OR: Arthur Emlen & Associates, Inc., and Portland State University, Regional Research Institute for Human Services.

Fernandez, J. (1986). *Child care and corporate productivity: Resolving family/work conflicts.* Lexington, MA: Lexington Books.

Friedman, D. E. (1987). *Family-supportive policies: The corporate decision-making process* (Report No. 897). New York: The Conference Board.

Friedman, D. E. (1991). *Linking work-family issues to the bottom line* (No. 962). New York: The Conference Board.

Galinsky, E. (1988, March). *Child care and productivity.* Paper presented at the Child Care Action Campaign Conference on Child Care and the Bottom Line, New York.

Galinsky, E., Friedman, D. E., & Hernandez, C. A., with Axel, H. (1991). *The corporate reference guide to work-family programs.* New York: Families and Work Institute.

Googins, B. K., Gonyea, J. G., & Pitt-Catsouphes, M. (1990, December). *Linking the worlds of family and work: Family dependent care and workers' performance.* Final report to the Ford Foundation. Boston, MA: Boston University, Center on Work and Family.

Morgan, D. (1988). *Focus groups as qualitative research.* Newbury Park, CA: Sage.

Neal, M. B., Chapman, N. J., & Ingersoll-Dayton, B. (1988). *Elder care, employees, and the workplace: Findings from a survey of employees.* Portland, OR: Portland State University, Regional Research Institute for Human Services and Institute on Aging.

Neal, M. B., Chapman, N. J., Ingersoll-Dayton, B., Emlen, A. C., & Boise, L. (1990). Absenteeism and stress among employed caregivers of the elderly, disabled adults, and children. In D. E. Biegel & A. Blum (Eds.), *Aging and caregiving: Theory, research, and policy* (pp. 160-183). Newbury Park, CA: Sage.

Rubin, V., Weinstock, P. J., Chetkovich, C. A., & Schlichtmann, L. (1989). *Employer-supported child care: Measuring and understanding its impacts on the workplace: Final report.* Report for the U.S. Department of Labor. Oakland, CA: Berkeley Planning Associates.

Shellenbarger, S. (1991, October 17). Companies team up to improve quality of their employees' child-care choices. *Wall Street Journal,* p. B1.

PART IV

Implications
and Recommendations

11

Where Do We Go From Here?
Suggestions for Practice, Policy,
and Research

This past year our youngest left home, and my husband's mother has become more dependent. Last year my husband's father became seriously ill, which required us to both take time off 3 times—during his illness, his move to residential retirement (all in Chicago), and to arrange to attend his funeral. Over the past 7 years his mother has had several surgeries and hospitalizations. Until 2 years ago I had or we had traveled to L.A., then 2 years ago she moved here. Now we have taken on more of the daily chore type things for her such as shopping, meal preparations, and occasionally go to the doctor with her when she needs emotional support as well as mere transportation. She doesn't feel well most of the time. In this past week, my husband's brother and his wife and children have moved to Oregon to also be available to care for her after a recent hospitalization . . . . So this is middle age!

In this book, we have examined the growing interest in work-family issues, presented a conceptual framework for understanding some of the implications of informal care responsibilities for employed individuals, reviewed the literature, and presented findings from our own study regarding absenteeism and stress among employees with dependent-care responsibilities—for children under 18, adults with disabilities, and/ or frail elders. We have also described some of the methods that employers may use to identify the needs of their employees and to make decisions about what actions to take. Furthermore, we have detailed policy and program options that some employers have instituted at the workplace to ease work-family conflict for their employees. We have noted the

255

fact that, despite the mounting interest in the impacts of family on work and vice versa, employer response to employees' family responsibilities has not been widespread. Although several companies have established themselves as leaders in this area and implemented extensive programs, these front-runners have been in a different league from most organizations—they are large employers competing in the global economy for future work forces. Smaller companies and organizations, which employ the bulk of the American work force, have not been as family-responsive. Several issues related to practice and policy then arise. Is a response to the needs of employed caregivers warranted? If so, which employed caregivers are most in need of assistance? What programs and policies should be implemented, and by whom? In this chapter, drawing on the findings of our study, we address these questions and make recommendations for practice, policy, and future research.

CRITICAL ISSUES IN DEPENDENT-CARE PRACTICE AND POLICY

Is a Response to Employed Caregivers Necessary?

The first issue is whether some form of response to employees' dependent-care responsibilities is really necessary. As we reported in Chapter 6, our findings clearly indicate that employees who have dependent-care responsibilities of any type experience more absenteeism and stress than those who have no such responsibilities. Because our sample consisted entirely of employed individuals, we could not address other important impacts of dependent-care responsibilities on work, such as quitting work, changing jobs, or not entering the work force. Considerable evidence of such negative impacts does exist in the literature, and we received anecdotal testimony in the form of volunteered comments that employees wrote on their surveys. For example, one employee wrote, "You might ask—if I had adequate and safe child care, would my spouse work?—YES!" In light of our findings, therefore, we conclude that many, although not all, individuals who are employed and caring for dependent family members or friends could benefit from some form of assistance to help them in managing their dual employment and caregiving roles.

Which Employed Caregivers Should Be Targeted?

A second issue concerns to whom the response should be addressed. Based on our findings, employees with simultaneous responsibility for individuals in each of the dependent-care groups—children, adults with disabilities, and elders—had the most consistently elevated levels of absenteeism and stress, followed by those caring for both children and adults with disabilities. Employees with only one caregiving role experienced relatively less absenteeism and stress. Among those employees with only one caregiving role, however, employees caring for children experienced the most absenteeism and stress. These groups of employees would thus appear to be those most in need of assistance. At the same time, it is important to remember that there is wide variation in the degree of responsibility (or demands) and in resources within each of these caregiving groups. It is the combination of demands and resources, as well as other factors, that affects how well individuals are able to manage their employment and caregiving roles.

Furthermore, employees in certain specific circumstances appear to need particular attention, based on the quantity and poignancy of the written comments that they volunteered. Many of the solutions that come most readily to mind do not address these employees' problems. For example, when we think of the child-care needs of employees, we often focus on child-care centers as a solution. Such centers rarely address the problems that arise for employees with school-aged children, since children must have some means of getting to the center after school is over for the day, and older children must be willing to go to the center. Employees who have latchkey children (that is, children who are unattended by adults after school until their parents return home from work) report that their productivity drops dramatically from the time the child is due home to quitting time. Likewise, summer vacations, teacher planning days, holidays, and so forth pose additional hardships for working parents. As one employee wrote:

> My boy is 7 years old. He has been staying alone for 1 ½ hours every workday since the beginning of the school year. He is in the first grade. This is an uncomfortable situation for us. We do not have anyone who would be willing to baby-sit for that length of time; it would not be worth their while. Now that summer vacation is coming, we are desperately looking for someone to come to our house to baby-sit. This has been going on for 2 months, and I have been unsuccessful. I have 6 more days until school is

out. If I do not find anyone, he will have to go stay with his grandparents 30 miles away, and we won't see him until the weekends. This is not a good family practice.

Another difficult circumstance occurs when an employee works shifts that change on a daily, weekly, or irregular basis. This practice usually requires the employee to make different dependent-care arrangements each time the work shift changes. For example, some employees and their partners have purposely chosen their work shifts specifically so that one parent can be available to take care of the child or children while the other works, and vice versa. Sometimes shifts change unpredictably, creating nearly constant uncertainty about how long a care arrangement will remain adequate. One employee wrote:

My husband works 4 p.m. to 12 a.m., and I work 8 a.m. to 4 p.m. so that we can share the child-care responsibilities. It's very difficult for us because we only get to see each other on our days off. . . . When our next bid for shifts goes around my unit, there is a very great likelihood that I will be bumped to the 4 to midnight shift. Then I will either have to quit my job (which I cannot afford) or my little boy, who will start kindergarten next fall, won't ever get to see his folks. And who would pick him up and get him to the baby-sitter?

Also posing particular difficulties is the need to take unplanned, sometimes extended, periods of time off to care for ill adults, elders, or children. Some employers and managers are understanding; others are not. As one employee noted, "Because I get 'comp' time, I can scoot out for my mother's needs sometimes. However, you don't win great ratings with your supervisor if she or he is on to your 'family problems.' " Another employee reported:

In March, my mother (age 58) suffered massive heart attacks. My employer gave me a leave of absence from work. My husband and I moved my mother into our house, and I took care of her until she passed away 7 months later. She did not go to the hospital except for special tests prescribed by her doctors. I am most grateful for those special months. I returned to work in November.

Care of sick children also presents problems. Some employees are not allowed to take time off for this reason, and they fear for their jobs if they do take such time off. Others, especially women, are attempting to move up the career ladder and fear that their progress will be hampered if they report that they must stay home to care for a sick child. One employee wrote:

> This company allows only some time off for child illness—the more you need, the less chance you'll still have a job. It was very hard to stay home with a sick child knowing your boss, because of company policies, expected you to be at work every day.

Several employees pointed out the special problems of employees with older children in their teens and beyond. As one employee noted, "You can experience more time loss due to a problem teenager than is often experienced with younger children, and you have less control . . . . Also, the financial stress of paying for a college education equals that of paying a sitter."

The informal, rather than formal, nature of policies concerning work schedules and time off can itself be problematic, although it may also be viewed as helpful. Several employees noted their good luck in having sympathetic managers who "let" them rearrange their schedules or take unscheduled time off and then make it up. Such informal arrangements, because they hinge on individual managers or departments, can create stress for employees who are not favored by a particular manager or for employees who may wish to change departments but fear that another manager might not be so understanding of their family situation. As one employee reported:

> I used to work for a [department] which allowed me to work a half hour extra per day and then when I had 8 hours accumulated, I used that time to see my lawyer, visit and check on my parents, get my hair cut, etc. This [department] . . . caused me so much stress that I had to transfer. I told my parents that I had stayed there many years because of the flextime, which I felt would eventually be used to take them shopping, to the doctor, etc. I had to tell them that I could no longer stand to work for this [department], that it was affecting my health, and I would give them money for taxi fare. The [department] I now work for is structured regarding time.

Finally, there is the issue of the hours of operation of educational, health, and social service institutions and agencies. The hours when these organizations are open often conflict with the standard 8:00 a.m. to 5:00 p.m. workday. Day-care facilities, schools, doctors' offices, social welfare agencies, and so forth are usually not open early enough in the morning or late enough in the evening. As one employee with multiple caregiving responsibilities noted, "Agencies are wonderful, but we need the time to use them . . . I used all family illness, emergency, personal (and some time unpaid) leave for the first time this year." Particularly difficult is the situation in which care arrangements for children or other dependents must be found for nights and weekends, often with little or no prior notice:

> Just try and get child care at 10 p.m. at night when you've been ordered in to work—if you don't attend work, you have disobeyed a direct order. If you show up, you either need to bring the child or leave them unattended, or be sick.

What Types of Programs and Policies Should Be Implemented and by Whom?

A third issue concerns what types of responses to employees' dependent-care responsibilities should be made and by whom. We have discussed the types of supports that can be provided for employees by employers. We have offered a strong rationale for employers' assistance to employees attempting to balance their work and their family responsibilities. At the same time, along with others (e.g., Kingston, 1990; Kamerman & Kingston, 1982), we also suspect that this rationale is not sufficiently compelling to ensure that all employers will voluntarily provide supports for employees with family responsibilities.

Moreover, we think that the responsibility for helping employees to balance their work and their family lives should not fall entirely on the shoulders of employers. Instead, we believe that responsibility should be shared by families, employers, and the community as a whole, with support for all from state and federal policy. State and especially national policy has a bearing on what employers can do, enabling or disabling them. In the process, these policies also enable or disable families. In short, employers cannot address this problem alone. Changes at the societal, family, and individual level are necessary as well. Some of these changes are elaborated by an employee specifically concerned with assisting employees who have small children:

> If I held the purse strings, I would spend my money on funding infant-care programs; offer money to have care providers to receive special infant-care training; push for more types of part-time "gradual return" options for parents

so that full-time care would not be required prior to 18 months; convene a business-employee caregiver-university/college/high school symposium to explore ways to elevate the status of child-care provider in our society; and force economic partnership between business, private foundations, and employees that would provide better salaries to child-care providers. This would greatly reduce staff turnover, attract better candidates, and improve the quality of child care in general. All of which would make for happier, less stressed children and parents!

Table 11.1, which is an expanded version of a table developed by Emlen (1991), provides examples of strategies for improving care for dependents and easing work-family conflict. These are strategies that can be implemented by the three domains having primary responsibility in this regard: the family, the workplace, and the community. The strategies are organized according to the policy goal, as identified in Chapter 10, that they address. The policy goals address the basic needs, identified through needs assessments of employees, that must be met for employees successfully to care for family members and to be productive in their work. They include (a) availability—the need for an adequate supply of services in the community, supplemental care resources by employers, and assistance with and planning for caregiving within the family; (b) accessibility—the need to be able to find, establish, and maintain arrangements for supplemental care of family members that fits in with family life and work schedules; (c) quality of care and services— the need for care arrangements with which employees can be satisfied and that have favorable effects on family members; (d) flexibility and manageability—the need in all three domains for sufficient flexibility and adaptability for meeting the concurrent demands of work and family; and (e) affordability—the need to be both willing and able to pay for the care and services that are required to help employees meet their work and family-care responsibilities.

For example, to foster the policy goal of improving the availability of dependent-care arrangements, a family strategy is to share domestic and caregiving responsibility, as Glasse (1990, p. 5) has noted, between "husbands and wives, sons and daughters, men and women." An employer strategy is to provide part-time work options. A community strategy is to extend the hours of operation of schools and social and health services.

The typology of policy strategies listed in Table 11.1 focuses attention on ways in which each the efforts of each of these domains may

TABLE 11.1 Policy Goals and Strategies for Improving Dependent Care

	Domains of Primary Responsibility		
	Family	*Workplace*	*Community*
Basic Aims:	to nurture the economic and psychosocial well-being and contributions of its members	to develop an economically strong organization that produces quality goods and services and contributes to the well-being of society	to develop community resources and environments supportive of individuals, families and economic activity
Policy Goals		*Policy Strategies*	
Availability	share domestic and caregiving responsibility enhance sibling care (children) involve members outside nuclear unit (adults/elders) make use of family leave plan for the long-term needs of members (disabled children/adults/elders)	support development of care options in the community provide family leave provide part-time work option support on-site or near-site care facilities	establish a resource and referral (R & R) service recruit and retain care providers (e.g., through paying adequate wages, providing training and support) eliminate unnecessary restrictive zoning requirements for location of care facilities reduce liability insurance premiums for care providers
Accessibility	learn to be an effective consumer	purchase or support resource and referral (R & R) services develop an in-house network and communication linkage to community resource and referral services	extend hours of operation of schools, social and health services underwrite a community-wide R & R serving all neighborhoods develop a demand-responsive supply of care for the ages, hours, locations, and special types of care needed
Quality	learn to be an effective consumer think through values and standards	support corporate and community initiatives to promote quality of care promote employee choice among care options	through R & R, give support and consultation to consumers through R & R, give support and consultation to care providers

262

	Family	Employer	Community/Government
Flexibility & Manageability	understand that quality may cost more and be willing to pay for it identify care options that best meet the individual needs of family members work out a division of labor and/or shared caregiving responsibility live close to work have back-up care plans for family emergencies make use of flexible work schedule options make compatible career-timing and caregiving decisions establish balance between work and family life	create policies permitting work schedule flexibility and time loss for family emergencies create options for part-time employment facilitate family leave and career breaks make available other options for restructuring of work schedule and place of work	accredit providers regulate/reduce care recipient-to-provider ratio and other threats to quality promote a range of care options encourage care providers and educational, social, health, and other services to be accommodating, conveniently located, and have extended hours enhance neighborhood safety and attractiveness through community planning, reduce distances between home, work, and care
Affordability	recognize that many dependent-care arrangements cost money use available tax credits and dependent-care spending accounts rely on care by other family members plan and save for long-term care needs of members lobby for lower income taxes for those with low incomes	pay adequate salaries, wages subsidize care for employees with low household incomes create dependent-care flexible spending accounts subsidize emergency care	generate political support for sharing the cost of care, services, programs, and policies that contribute to values and outcomes in which all domains have a stake

Note: Expanded from Emlen (1991).

lead to the achievement of desired policy outcomes. Explicit public policy may be needed to support the primary responsibilities of those three sectors of society. In the crafting of public policy, we believe that policymakers should take into account the complex situations, decisions, and behaviors of families in the context of their employment and of community resources.

By pursuing the strategies outlined in this table, as well as other related strategies, employers stand to benefit from a work force that experiences less conflict between job and family responsibilities. Family members, including those who are the recipients of care, will benefit, and society as a whole will benefit from happier, healthier employees and families.

To encourage the implementation of these strategies, a number of "family-friendly" policies should be enacted at the national and state level. The following is a partial list of policy recommendations. Several of these are modified versions of those voiced by Lou Glasse, President of the Older Women's League, at a policy forum on elder care held by the Subcommittee on Human Services (Glasse, 1990):

1. Enact family leave legislation requiring employers to allow family members temporary unpaid leave to arrange care for their newborn or newly adopted children, chronically ill children, parents, spouses, or other elder or adult family members with disabilities (Glasse, 1990).

2. Change the U.S. Social Security system so that unpaid caregivers are not penalized, either giving credit for years spent in caregiving or not counting those years in determining benefits (Glasse, 1990).

3. Enact national legislation establishing universal health-care coverage, so that employees who drop out of the labor force to care for family members can continue to have health insurance.

4. Improve the working conditions, including pay and support, for those persons who are paid to care for employees' dependents, that is, child-care, adult day-care, and long-term care providers (Glasse, 1990).

5. Mandate that long-term care insurance policies provide for respite and in-home care as well as care in nursing facilities (Glasse, 1990).

6. Change the eligibility criteria for dependent-care tax credits to make more families eligible to use them.

7. Encourage employers to offer flexibility in work schedules and in the number of hours worked and to initiate and formalize family-friendly policies for all employees—full and part time, management and nonmanagement.

8. Modify the hours of operation of U.S. school, health, and social service systems. As Winett & Neale (1980, pp. 408-409) have noted:

The "ideal American family," composed of the male "breadwinner," the female "caretaker," and children, is the basis for the rules and regulations that govern many of our social systems. For example, the typical school system's hours of operation assume that some [mother] is always available to watch children after 3 p.m., and of course assume that a full-time caretaker is available during the summer, numerous holidays, and "conference" days. Yet the ideal American family is now a *statistical minority*. For example, the single breadwinner family comprises only 13% of existing American households (Ramey, 1978).

NEEDS FOR FURTHER RESEARCH

Beyond implementing these recommendations for policy and practice, several issues require study through further research. One important issue is the relationship between stress, absenteeism, and productivity. The question of how much productivity is actually lost as a result of the dependent-care responsibilities of employees remains unanswered; the link between productivity, stress, and absenteeism has not been clearly established.

Related to this issue is the question of how to measure impacts on work. Historically, productivity has been difficult to measure, and its measurement has become more complex with the increasing prevalence of service-producing industries over goods-producing industries. Similarly, although the quality of work performed is difficult to measure, the impact of caregiving responsibilities on work quality should also be examined. In addition, measures of absenteeism, including those used in this study, could be improved through greater specificity, such as whether time taken off was planned or unplanned, paid or unpaid, made up for later or not, and so forth.

Still another research issue concerns the relationship between productivity and intervention—does intervention affect productivity positively? Considerably more evaluation of the impact of "family-friendly" policies and programs on employees and their work performance is needed.

Furthermore, work-family research, including that reported here, has tended to be cross-sectional in nature, examining just one brief period of time. Much knowledge can be gained from longitudinal research that follows employees with different kinds of dependent-care responsibilities to learn how resources and demands vary over time. This knowledge will help in designing programs and policies that can take into account the ebbs and flows in employees' needs. It will also improve our understanding of the utilization of programs and policies by employees.

Moreover, the predictors of absenteeism, stress, and productivity demand further attention. It is important that the scope of future work-family studies be expanded to include the social ecological context in which those studies are conducted. For example, the behavior of employees is affected by the organizational climate of the company for which they work, yet that climate is often not taken into account, in part because it is not easily captured by measures that are based solely on data obtained from employees. Likewise, one strong conclusion from employee needs assessments is that employees, families, and employers are to varying degrees at the mercy of the resources and services available (and not available) in their communities, yet service availability typically has not been considered. Future research needs to consider these organizational and community contexts.

Within companies or organizations, future research is needed on the impact of occupation and of how work itself is organized. Great variability, both between and within companies, exists with regard to one of the key policy variables of work-family research—flexibility of work scheduling. Flexibility needs to be studied, however, in relation to productivity and in the context of occupations, job requirements, and organizational policies (formal and informal) on work-family issues. Galinsky, Friedman, & Hernandez (1991) have created a scale to measure the family-friendliness of corporate policies. It would be useful to apply this scale to determine, for example, how employees in different occupations are differentially affected by corporate policies.

There are also particular characteristics of individual caregivers that require further consideration in future research. Specifically, future research must take into consideration the diversity within and across the employee-caregiver groups. One variable that has received inadequate attention is ethnicity. Our study was able to include ethnicity only as a dichotomous variable—white versus other. What similarities and differences are there among caregivers of various ethnic and racial groups with respect to family and work resources, demands, and outcomes experienced?

Another personal characteristic needing further study is household composition. Households today are extremely diverse. Only some are composed of one nuclear family with two parents and their children.

Others consist of two or more families, and may comprise not just two, but three, or even four generations. Still others are composed of single adults with no children, heterosexual or homosexual couples with or without children, an unrelated group of adults with or without children, blended families with his, hers, and their children, noncustodial parents and stepparents, and so forth. Who are the caregivers in these households? What are their resources and demands? What are the similarities and differences in outcomes experienced by employees who have caregiving responsibilities in these different types of households?

Finally, research is needed on the ways that absenteeism can be a precursor to turnover in some situations and a safety valve that prevents burnout in other situations. We found that although absenteeism increased with greater flexibility in work schedules and more understanding departmental policies concerning employees' family needs, stress decreased; perhaps the decrease in stress offset the increase in absenteeism in terms of job productivity. The question of short-term versus long-term outcomes must also be addressed. Perhaps employer tolerance of short-term absences leads employees to be more productive and committed to their jobs over the long run. These questions probably cannot be answered without considering such diverse predictors of productivity as family demands and resources, dependent-care arrangements, occupation, organizational climate, and community resources related to dependent care.

CONCLUSION

Individuals' work and family lives are inextricably intertwined. We have begun to elucidate the kinds of caregiving responsibilities and employment situations that are particularly difficult for employed caregivers. Research is needed to specify further those individual, family, work, and community conditions that are especially problematic. Policymakers need to take into account the complex situations and behaviors of families and the configuration of employment and community resources in which these situations and behaviors occur. In the meantime, families, employers, and communities can begin to implement a wide variety of strategies to maximize the availability, accessibility, quality, flexibility, and affordability of dependent-care arrangements. Through the efforts of all three sectors, with the assistance of public policy, care for dependents can be improved and work-family conflict can be eased. As one employee in our survey wrote,

> I think it is very important that, as a society, we make it easier for people to care for their responsibilities regarding their elders and children. If more people were able to do this on their own, it would reduce government costs and give the individual the satisfaction of discharging his responsibilities to parents and children, which is what I think most adults really want to do anyway. People will do better work if they are contented with their lives, and job satisfaction is only a small part of how we measure our self-worth. Besides, if it weren't for our parents, we wouldn't be here, and if it weren't for our children, all our striving would have no purpose.

REFERENCES

Emlen, A. C. (1991, May). *Rural child care policy: Does Oregon have one? 1991 legislative discussion paper.* Legislative Discussion Series. Rural Policy Research Group (Oregon State University, University of Oregon, Oregon Economic Development Department). Obtain by writing to author at Regional Research Institute for Human Services, Portland State University, P.O. Box 751, Portland, OR 97207-0741.

Galinsky, E., Friedman, D. E., & Hernandez, C. A., with Axel, H. (1991). *The corporate reference guide to work-family programs.* New York: Families and Work Institute.

Glasse, L. (1990). Who cares for the caregiver? In Subcommittee on Human Services, Select Committee on Aging, House of Representatives. *Sharing the caring: Options for the 90s and beyond: A policy forum* (Committee Publication No. 101-750, pp. 1-5). Washington, DC: Government Printing Office.

Kamerman, S. B., & Kingston, P. W. (1982). Employer responses to the family responsibilities of employees. In S. B. Kamerman & C. D. Hayes (Eds.), *Families that work: Children in a changing world* (pp. 144-208). Washington, DC: National Academy Press.

Kingston, P. W. (1990). Illusions and ignorance about the family-responsive workplace. *Journal of Family Issues, 11,* 438-454.

Ramey, J. (1978). Experimental family forms—the family of the future. *Marriage and Family Review, 1,* 19-26.

Winett, R. A., & Neale, M. S. (1980). Modifying settings as a strategy for permanent, preventive behavior change: Flexible work schedules and the quality of family life. In P. Karoly & J. J. Steffen (Eds.), *Improving the long-term effects of psychotherapy* (pp. 407-436). New York: Gardner.

Appendix A:
Model Cover Letter and
Survey Instrument

MODEL COVER LETTER

(NOTE: The model cover letter (on page 270) was provided to businesses and agencies, who used it to prepare an identical or similar letter on their letterhead. A copy of the letter then was stapled to each questionnaire, along with an envelope addressed to the "Work and Family Project, Portland State University.")

DATE

Dear Employee:

COMPANY NAME is co-sponsoring (OR participating in) a survey to determine how employees manage their family responsibilities, such as caring for children, disabled family members, and elderly relatives or friends, in addition to their work. We are one of 30 other Portland-area organizations and agencies participating in this survey, which will include about 30,000 employees.

We urge you to join in this community effort by filling out the attached questionnaire. Although this may appear to be a long form, very few people will need to fill out the entire questionnaire. The first page is relevant for *all* employees. It is important that you participate, *whether or not* you provide any of the types of care described. The Regional Research Institute for Human Services and the Institute on Aging at Portland State University, who are conducting this study, are trying to learn just *how many* employees have child-care, disabled-care, and elder-care responsibilities they are trying to fulfill in addition to their roles in the workplace. The ultimate goal of the study is to increase the information and resources available to Portland employees who are helping elderly family members.

The information you supply will be anonymous. No one at COMPANY NAME will see the individually completed questionnaires. When you complete your questionnaire, simply seal it in the attached envelope addressed to the Regional Research Institute and drop it in our interoffice mail by (DATE). The Regional Research Institute staff will then come and pick up the envelopes.

Thank you for your assistance!

Sincerely,

NAME
TITLE

**REGIONAL
RESEARCH
INSTITUTE**
for Human Services

Portland State University

EMPLOYEE SURVEY

Card Number 1–5
Card ⊡ 6

INSTRUCTIONS: Thank you for participating in our survey. Please **enter the number** of your answer to the right of each question **in the box** provided. **All responses are anonymous** and will not be seen by your employer. We appreciate your frank answers.

1. Your sex?
1. Male
2. Female ⬜ 7

2. Your ethnic background?
1. White
2. Black
3. Hispanic
4. Asian or Pacific Islander
5. American Indian or Alaskan Native
6. Other: _____ ⬜ 8

3. Your occupation?
1. Professional or technical
2. Managerial or administrative
3. Sales
4. Clerical
5. Crafts
6. Service (food, health, personal, cleaning)
7. Machine operator
8. Transport operator
9. Non-farm labor
10. Other: _____ ⬜ 9 ⬜ 10

4. Your job status?
1. Full-time
2. Part-time
3. On call ⬜ 11

5. Your job shift?
1. Days   4. Rotating
2. Nights   5. Other
3. Swing ⬜ 12

6. The number of hours per week you usually work? ⬜ 13 ⬜ 14 hours

7. The number of days per week you usually work? ⬜ 15 days

8. The amount of time it usually takes you to travel one way from home to work? ⬜ 16 ⬜ 17 minutes

9. The zip code of your home address? ⬜ 18 ⬜ 22

10. What are the ages of the people, including yourself, who live in your household? Put your age first. For infants or children under 1, put "IN."
⬜ years ⬜ years ⬜ years ⬜ years 34
⬜ years ⬜ years ⬜ years ⬜ years 46

11. If any of the above people are disabled, please circle their age above. By "disabled" we mean physically handicapped, frail, chronically ill, developmentally handicapped, or seriously emotionally handicapped. [47–70]

12. How many of the adults in your household, including yourself, work outside the home? ⬜ 71 number

13. Is one of the other adults in your household your spouse or partner?
1. Yes
2. No
3. Not applicable ⬜ 72

14. Does he or she work outside the home?
1. Yes
2. No
3. Not applicable ⬜ 73

15. What is the approximate annual gross income of your household?
1. Under $10,000   6. $40,000-49,999
2. $10,000-14,999   7. $50,000-59,999
3. $15,000-19,999   8. $60,000-69,999
4. $20,000-24,999 10. $70,000 or more
5. $25,000-29,999
6. $30,000-39,999 ⬜ 74 ⬜ 75

16. What is your own personal annual gross income?
1. Under $10,000   7. $40,000-49,999
2. $10,000-14,999   8. $50,000-59,999
3. $15,000-19,999   9. $60,000-69,999
4. $20,000-24,999 10. $70,000 or more
5. $25,000-29,999
6. $30,000-39,999 ⬜ 76 ⬜ 77

17. Are you eligible to claim any of the following other than yourself or your spouse as a dependent or exemption on your federal or state income tax return?
1. Yes
2. No
3. Don't know

Child(ren) ⬜ 78

Person(s) 65 or older ⬜ 79

Disabled adult(s) ⬜ 80

Code Number 1–5
Card ② 6

18. In the past four weeks:

How many days have you missed work? ⬜ 7 ⬜ 8 number

How many times have you been late to work? ⬜ 9 ⬜ 10 number

How many times have you left work early or left during the day? ⬜ 11 ⬜ 12 times

While at work, how many times have you been interrupted (including telephone calls) to deal with family-related matters? ⬜ 13 ⬜ 14 times

19. How much flexibility do you have in your work schedule to handle family responsibilities?
1. A lot of flexibility
2. Some flexibility
3. Hardly any flexibility
4. No flexibility at all ⬜ 15

20. How long have you worked for this employer? ⬜ 16 ⬜ 17 years ⬜ 18 ⬜ 19 months

21. Circumstances differ and some people find it easier than others to combine working with family responsibilities. In general, how easy or difficult is it for you?
1. Very easy   4. Somewhat difficult
2. Easy   5. Difficult
3. Somewhat easy 6. Very difficult
4. Somewhat difficult ⬜ 20

22. We would like to know which areas of life are creating difficulty, worry, and stress for people. In the past 4 weeks, to what extent have any of the following areas of life been a source of stress to you?

Your health:
1. No stress at all
2. Hardly any stress
3. Some stress
4. A lot of stress ⬜ 21

Health of other family members:
1. No stress at all
2. Hardly any stress
3. Some stress
4. A lot of stress ⬜ 22

Child care:
0. Not applicable
1. No stress at all
2. Hardly any stress
3. Some stress
4. A lot of stress ⬜ 23

Care for elderly or disabled adult family members:
0. Not applicable
1. No stress at all
2. Hardly any stress
3. Some stress
4. A lot of stress ⬜ 24

Personal or family finances:
1. No stress at all
2. Hardly any stress
3. Some stress
4. A lot of stress ⬜ 25

Your job:
1. No stress at all
2. Hardly any stress
3. Some stress
4. A lot of stress ⬜ 26

Family relationships, including extended family:
1. No stress at all
2. Hardly any stress
3. Some stress
4. A lot of stress ⬜ 27

PLEASE CONTINUE ON PAGE 2 →

Figure A.1. Regional Research Institute Employee Survey

Code number 1-5
Card 3 6

23. Do you have responsibilities for helping out adult relatives or friends who are ELDERLY or DISABLED? This includes persons who **live with you** OR who **live somewhere else.** By "helping out" we mean help with shopping, home maintenance or transportation, checking on them by phone, making arrangements for care, etc.
1. Yes (PLEASE CONTINUE)
2. No   (PLEASE SKIP TO PAGE 4)   [7]

24. How many elderly or disabled   [8]
persons are you currently helping?   number

The following questions concern the ONE OR TWO PERSONS YOU ARE HELPING OUT THE MOST. The boxes under "PERSON A" are for the one person you are helping or the person you are helping the most. The boxes under "Person B" are for the second person you are helping, if applicable.

25. For the one or two persons you are helping the most, please indicate their ages, sex, relationship to you and how long you've been giving them extra help. Use the numbers below to indicate relationship and sex.
Relationship to you:
1. Spouse   5. Other relative
2. Parent or step-parent   6. Friend
3. Spouse's parent or step-parent 7. Other
4. Disabled child over 18

	Person A	Person B
Relationship	[9]	[10]
Sex (1. Male 2. Female)	[11]	[12]
Age	[13 15] years	[16 18] years
Length of time you've been helping	[19 20] years [21 22] months	[23 24] years [25 26] months

26. Where does this person(s) live?
1. In his or her own home
2. In my home
3. With a relative
4. With a friend
5. In a nursing home, care facility, etc.

	Person A	Person B
	[27]	[28]

27. How far from your home does this person(s) live?
0. Person lives with me   4. 100 - 499 miles
1. Less than 5 miles   5. 500 - 999 miles
2. 5 - 24 miles   6. 1,000 miles or more
3. 25 - 99 miles

	Person A	Person B
	[29]	[30]

28. Do you claim an income tax credit for this person's care? In other words, on your federal tax return, do you claim any expenses that you pay for care such as nursing service or adult day care?
1. Yes
2. No

	Person A	Person B
	[31]	[32]

Thinking now in terms of the past year, please answer the following questions.

29. To what extent do each of the following describe the person(s) you are helping.
1. Never   4. Frequently
2. Seldom   5. Most or all of the time
3. Sometimes

	Person A	Person B
Cannot manage activities of daily living for him or herself	[33]	[34]
Wanders or is confused	[35]	[36]
Acts inappropriately, is disruptive	[37]	[38]
Is aggressive or uncooperative	[39]	[40]

30. In the past year, how often have you done each of the following for this elderly or disabled person(s)? Use the scale below and write the number of your response in the box next to each activity. For example, if you have never gone shopping for this person, put a "1" in the box next to "shopping", etc.
1. Never or seldom   5. Once a week
2. Several times a year   6. A few times a week
3. Once a month   7. Daily
4. A few times a month

	Person A	Person B
house and yard maintenance	[41]	[42]
transportation	[43]	[44]
shopping	[45]	[46]
check on by phone	[47]	[48]
fix or bring meals	[49]	[50]
personal care (dressing, bathing, etc.)	[51]	[52]
housekeeping	[53]	[54]
continuous supervision	[55]	[56]
nursing care	[57]	[58]
help with expenses (give money)	[59]	[60]
manage legal and financial affairs (write checks, fill out insurance forms, etc.)	[61]	[62]
visit, give emotional support	[63]	[64]
arrange and manage health or social services	[65]	[66]
read to, write letters, play cards with, etc.	[67]	[68]
take time off from work to do something for the person	[69]	[70]

31. In the past year, what is the greatest number of hours in a week that you have helped this person(s) in ways such as those above?

Person A	Person B
[71 72] hours	[73 74] hours

32. On average in the past year, how many hours per week have you helped this person(s)?

Person A	Person B
[75 76] hours	[77 78] hours

33. In the past year, when this person(s) has needed help, who has usually been the one who has given it or seen that it was given?
1. I have been the only one
2. I have been the main one, with some help from others
3. I have shared equally with one or more others
4. Others, with my help

Person A	Person B
[79]	[80]

Code Number 1-5
Card 4 6

34. In the past year, how often has this person(s) helped **you** by doing each of the following:
1. Never   4. Frequently
2. Seldom   5. Most or all of the time
3. Sometimes

	Person A	Person B
caring for children	[7]	[8]
preparing meals or cleaning	[9]	[10]
caring for disabled adult family members	[11]	[12]
helping out financially	[13]	[14]
other _____	[15]	[16]

PLEASE CONTINUE ON PAGE 3 →

Figure A.1. Continued

PAGE 3

35. In the past year, while you've been at work, who has helped or cared for this adult(s)? Please indicate how often **each** of the following has helped.

    1. Never   4. Frequently
    2. Seldom   5. Most or all of the time
    3. Sometimes

	Person A	Person B
	17	18
Person him or herself		
	19	20
Family members		
	21	22
Friends		
Someone who was hired (agencies or individuals like home nurse, housekeeper)	23	24
Volunteer (Meals on Wheels, church members, etc.)	25	26
Adult day care center (center providing daytime supervision, activities, etc.)	27	28
	29	30
Nursing home, care facility, etc.		

36. How satisfied have you been with these arrangements?
    1. Very satisfied
    2. Satisfied
    3. Mixed feelings
    4. Dissatisfied
    5. Very Dissatisfied

Person A	Person B
31	32

37. In general during the past year, how easy or difficult has it been for you to help out this person(s)?
    1. Very easy   5. Difficult
    2. Easy   6. Very difficult
    3. Somewhat easy
    4. Somewhat difficult

Person A	Person B
33	34

38. In the past year, how often have your caregiving responsibilities interfered with your social and emotional needs and other family responsibilities?
    1. Never
    2. Seldom
    3. Sometimes
    4. Frequently
    5. Most or all of the time

Person A	Person B
35	36

39. Do you think you will be able to continue providing care for this individual(s) for as long as is necessary?
    1. Yes, with the same help I have now
    2. Yes, but with more help
    3. Not sure
    4. No

Person A	Person B
37	38

40. In your experience, how easy or difficult has it been to **find** care arrangements for this elderly or disabled person(s)?
    0. Not relevant   5. Difficult
    1. Very easy   6. Very difficult
    2. Easy
    3. Somewhat easy
    4. Somewhat difficult

Person A	Person B
39	40

41. In your experience, how easy or difficult has it been to **manage** or **maintain** these arrangements?
    0. Not relevant   5. Difficult
    1. Very easy   6. Very difficult
    2. Easy
    3. Somewhat easy
    4. Somewhat difficult

Person A	Person B
41	42

Thinking now **in general** about your adult care responsibilities, please answer the following questions.

42. When the person(s) you are caring for needs assistance and you take time off from work, which one of the following is most likely to make this possible?
    0. I am not able to take time off work.
    1. I use sick leave.
    2. I have flexible hours.
    3. I use emergency leave.
    4. I take a day off without pay.
    5. I use vacation or personal leave.
    6. I do my work at home.
    7. Other: _____
    8. I never need to take time off for this reason.

43

43. Have you reduced the number of hours you work per week at your job in order to care for this person(s)?
    1. Yes   [44]   IF YES, how many hours per week?   [45] [46] hours
    2. No

44. How often have you worked less effectively at your job because you are worried or upset about this person(s)?
    1. Never   4. Frequently
    2. Seldom   5. Most or all of the time
    3. Sometimes

47

45. To what extent do personnel practices in your department make it easy or difficult to provide care for this person(s)?
    1. Very easy   4. Somewhat difficult
    2. Easy   5. Difficult
    3. Somewhat easy   6. Very difficult

48

46. Do you work because of your responsibilities for this person(s), either to earn extra money or for some other reason related to caregiving?
    1. Yes
    2. No

49

47. The following is a list of things that are sometimes useful to employees who are helping out an elderly or disabled person. For each one, please indicate whether you:
    1. currently take advantage of it
    2. would take advantage of it now if available
    3. would take advantage of it if available and needed
    4. probably would not take advantage of it if available or needed

Information and education (on such topics as available services, aging, coping strategies, insurance and legal issues)	50
A discussion group with others who are helping an elderly or disabled person.	51
Being paired with another person who has experienced similar problems in caring for an elderly or disabled person.	52
Individual consultation with a professional to solve problems and discover sources of help.	53
Respite care (someone to give you a break from caregiving).	54

48. People who have responsibilities for providing adult care often have difficulty knowing where to turn to get help. In general, how easy or difficult has it been for you to know where to turn?
    1. Very easy   4. Somewhat difficult
    2. Easy   5. Difficult
    3. Somewhat easy   6. Very difficult

55

PLEASE CONTINUE ON PAGE 4 →

Figure A.1. Continued

PAGE 4

49. Do you have children (under age 18) living in your household?
1. Yes
2. No
[50]

If you have **no children under 18** living in your household, please go to question 64 on page 5. If you **do have children under 18** living in your household, please complete the following questions. These questions ask about the child care and other arrangements that you currently use.

Code Number 1–5
Card [5] 6

50. Does a member of your household age 18 or over take care of any of the children while you are at work?
1. Yes
2. No
[7]

IF YES, please answer all of the questions in the box below. IF NO, skip this box.

Is this person?
1. Your spouse or partner   3. Grandparent
2. Your older child, 18 or older   4. Other
[8]

What are the ages of the children cared for by this adult member of your household? For children under 1 year, put "IN" for infant.

[9] | | | | | | | [24]
years years years years years years years years

While you are away at work, how many hours a week do you use this arrangement?
[25] [26]
hours

How satisfied are you with this arrangement?
1. Very satisfied
2. Satisfied
3. Mixed feelings
4. Dissatisfied
5. Very dissatisfied
[27]

51. Does someone come to your home to care for any of the children while you are at work?
1. Yes
2. No
[28]

IF YES, please answer all of the questions in the box below. IF NO, skip this box.

Is this person a relative?
1. Yes
2. No
[29]

What are the ages of the children who are cared for by someone who comes to your home? For children under 1 year, put "IN" for infant.

[30] | | | | | | | [45]
years years years years years years years years

While you are away at work, how many hours a week do you use this arrangement?
[46] [47]
hours

How satisfied are you with this arrangement?
1. Very satisfied   3. Mixed feelings
2. Satisfied   4. Dissatisfied
5. Very dissatisfied
[48]

What is the average weekly cost of this arrangement?
[49] [51]
dollars

52. Do you have children who look after themselves or are cared for by an older brother or sister under age 18 while you are at work?
1. Yes
2. No
[52]

IF YES, please answer all of the questions in the box below. IF NO, skip this box.

What are the ages of the children who care for themselves or are looked after by an older brother or sister? For children under 1 year, put "IN" for infant.

[53] | | | | | | | [68]
years years years years years years years years

While you are away at work, how many hours a week do you use this arrangement?
[69] [70]
hours

How satisfied are you with this arrangement?
1. Very satisfied
2. Satisfied
3. Mixed feelings
4. Dissatisfied
5. Very dissatisfied
[71]

Code Number 1–5
Card [6] 6

53. Are any of the children cared for in someone else's home while you are at work?
1. Yes
2. No
[7]

IF YES, please answer all of the questions in the box below. IF NO, skip this box.

Is this person a relative?
1. Yes
2. No
[8]

Is this a licensed or registered family daycare home?
1. Yes
2. No
3. Don't know
[9]

What are the ages of the children cared for in someone else's home? For children under 1 year, put "IN" for infant.

[10] | | | | | | | [25]
years years years years years years years years

How long have you used this child care arrangement?
[26] [27]   [28] [29]
years   months

While you are away at work, how many hours a week do you use this arrangement?
[30] [31]
hours

About how far is it from your home to this child care arrangement?
1. Next door   4. 1/2 mile   7. 4 miles
2. 1 or 2 blocks   5. 1 mile   8. 8 miles
3. 1/4 mile   6. 2 miles   9. over 8 miles
[32]

About how far is it from your work to this child care arrangement?
1. Next door   4. 1/2 mile   7. 4 miles
2. 1 or 2 blocks   5. 1 mile   8. 8 miles
3. 1/4 mile   6. 2 miles   9. over 8 miles
[33]

How satisfied are you with this child care arrangement?
1. Very satisfied   3. Mixed feelings
2. Satisfied   4. Dissatisfied
5. Very dissatisfied
[34]

What is the weekly cost of this arrangement?
[35] [37]
dollars

PLEASE CONTINUE ON PAGE 5 →

Figure A.1. Continued

PAGE 5

54. Are any of the children cared for in a child care center while you are at work? (By "child care center" we mean day care centers, nursery schools and before and after-school facilities, but **not** public kindergarten or elementary school.) 1. Yes 2. No `36`

IF YES, please answer all of the questions in the box below. IF NO, skip this box.

What are the ages of the children cared for in the center or school-based program? For children under 1 year, put "IN" for infant.

`39` [ ] [ ] [ ] [ ] [ ] [ ] [ ] `54`
years years years years years years years years

How long have you used this child care arrangement? `55` `56` years `57` `58` months

While you are away at work, how many hours a week do you use this arrangement? `59` `60` hours

About how far is it from your **home** to this child care arrangement?

1. Next door 4. 1/2 mile 7. 4 miles
2. 1 or 2 blocks 5. 1 mile 8. 8 miles
3. 1/4 mile 6. 2 miles 9. over 8 miles `61`

About how far is it from your **work** to this child care arrangement?

1. Next door 4. 1/2 mile 7. 4 miles
2. 1 or 2 blocks 5. 1 mile 8. 8 miles
3. 1/4 mile 6. 2 miles 9. over 8 miles `62`

How satisfied are you with this child care arrangement?
1. Very satisfied
2. Satisfied
3. Mixed feelings
4. Dissatisfied
5. Very dissatisfied `63`

What is the weekly cost of this arrangement? `64` `65` dollars

Code Number 1–5
Card `7` 6

55. In addition to the child care arrangements listed above, are your children involved in any other activities while you are at work? 1. Yes 2. No `7`

IF YES, please list the ages of children in each activity. IF NO, skip this box.

Activity	Ages of Children
1. Child employment	`8` [ ] [ ] `13` years years years
2. School sponsored activities or sports	`14` [ ] [ ] `19` years years years
3. Other sponsored activities (specify):	`20` [ ] [ ] `25` years years years

_____

56. How often have you changed child care arrangements in the past 3 months? `26` `27` times

57. Do you plan to change your child care arrangements in the near future? 1. Yes 2. No `28`

58. When one of their children is sick, employees often have to choose between going to work or staying home. When one of **your** children is sick, and you are able to **go to work**, which of the following is most likely to make it possible?

1. I can take my child to my regular child care arrangement.
2. My spouse or an older child can stay home with the sick child.
3. I bring someone in to care for the child.
4. The child can usually stay home alone.
5. I have another arrangement for emergencies.
6. I take the child to work with me. `29`
7. Other: _____

59. Similarly, when one of your children is sick, and you are able to **stay home**, which of the following is most likely to make it possible?

1. I use sick leave.
2. I have flexible hours.
3. I use emergency leave.
4. I take a day off without pay.
5. I use vacation or personal leave.
6. I do my work at home.
7. Other: _____ `30`
8. I am not able to stay at home.

60. To what extent do the personnel practices in your department make it easy or difficult for you to deal with child care problems during working hours?

1. Very easy
2. Easy
3. Somewhat easy
4. Somewhat difficult
5. Difficult `31`
6. Very difficult

61. About how much **extra time** does your travel for child care **add** to your daily round trip travel time to and from work? If none, put 0. `32` `33` minutes

62. In your experience, how easy or difficult has it been to **find** child care arrangements?

1. Very easy
2. Easy
3. Somewhat easy
4. Somewhat difficult
5. Difficult `34`
6. Very difficult

63. In your experience, how easy or difficult has it been to **continue with** child care arrangements?

1. Very easy
2. Easy
3. Somewhat easy
4. Somewhat difficult
5. Difficult `35`
6. Very difficult

64. Do you claim an income tax credit for child care? In other words, on your federal tax return, do you claim any expenses that you pay for child care? 1. Yes 2. No `36`

65. Any comments? Please write them on PAGE 6 →

Thank you for your participation. Please return this questionnaire in the envelope provided.

Figure A.1. Continued

Appendix B:
Expanded Tables, Chapters 3, 4, 5, and 6

TABLE 3.2B Effects of Personal Characteristics, Caregiving Demands, and Caregiving Resources on Absenteeism Variables Among Employees With Child-Care Responsibilities

	Absenteeism Variables								
	Days Missed			Late or Left Early			Interruptions		
Step entered regression:	1	2	3	1	2	3	1	2	3
Predictors									
Personal Characteristics									
Gender (female)	.13**	.11**	.10**	.14**	.10**	.07**	.08**	.07**	
Age of employee				-.11**	-.08**	-.08**			-.06*
Ethnicity (white)									.04*
Occupation (professional)			.04*	.05**	.04*				
Change in R^2 at Step 1	.02			.03			.01		
Demands									
Hours worked	-.06**							.07**	.05**
Shift (days)					.14**	.12**		.16**	.14**
Number of children under age 9									
Number of caregiving roles						.04*		.08**	.09**
Extra travel time for child care					.06**	.05*		.06**	.05*
Age of youngest child									
Child with disability		.04*	.04*						
Child-care cost as % of household income									
Total hours of out-of-home care		.07**	.08**					-.06*	
Change in R^2 at Step 2	.01			.03			.03		
Resources									
Household income			-.12**			.05*			.07**
Work schedule flexibility						.14**			.12**
Working partner			.06*			-.12**			-.06*
Nonworking partner						-.07**			
Number of children aged 9 to 17									.06**
Child has self-care arrangement									.07**
Informal support from kin									
Ease finding/continuing child care						-.08**			-.11**
Satisfaction with care						-.11**			-.10**
Change in R^2 at Step 3			.01			.04			.04
Total R^2/R^2 Adjusted		.04/.03			.10/.09			.09/.08	
Overall F		6.04**			16.35**			13.73**	
Df (reg./res.) 22,3179									

Note: Based on standardized betas; only significant betas reported.
* $p \le .05$; ** $p \le .01$.

TABLE 3.3B Effects of Personal Characteristics, Caregiving Demands, and Caregiving Resources on Stress Variables Among Employees With Child-Care Responsibilities

	Stress Variables								
	Personal Health Stress			Caregiving Stress			Difficulty Combining Work and Family		
Step entered regression:	1	2	3	1	2	3	1	2	3
Predictors									
Personal Characteristics									
Gender (female)	.13**	.12**	.09**	.08**	.09**		.23**	.24**	.16**
Age of employee	.05**	.06**	.08**	-.25**				-.08**	
Ethnicity									
Occupation (professional)				.08**	.06**	.06**			
Change in R^2 at Step 1	.02			.07			.06		
Demands									
Hours worked								.04*	
Shift (days)					-.04*				
Number of children under age 9					-.06*				
Number of caregiving roles		.06**	.05**		.05**	.04**		.07**	.05**
Extra travel time for child care					.11**	.05**		.11**	.05**
Age of youngest child					-.30**	-.24**		-.09**	
Child with disability								.04*	
Child-care cost as % of household income		.05*			.10**	.07**		.05*	
Total hours of out-of-home care								.06**	
Change in R^2 at Step 2	.01			.10			.04		
Resources									
Household income									
Work schedule flexibility			-.08**			-.09**			-.26**
Working partner									
Nonworking partner						-.10**			
Number of children aged 9 to 17									
Child has self-care arrangement						-.06**			-.07**
Informal support from kin						.04*			
Ease finding/continuing care			-.09**			-.21**			-.17**
Satisfaction with care			-.07**			-.27**			-.15**
Change in R^2 at Step 3			.03			.19			.18
Total R^2/R^2 Adjusted			.06/.05			.36/.36			.28/.28
Overall F			8.86**			82.06**			58.25**
Df (reg./res.) 22,3217									

Note: Based on standardized betas; only significant betas reported.

* $p \leq .05$; ** $p \leq .01$.

TABLE 4.1B Effects of Personal Characteristics, Caregiving Demands, and Caregiving Resources on Absenteeism Variables Among Employees With Adult-Care Responsibilities

	Absenteeism Variables								
	Days Missed			Late or Left Early			Interruptions		
Step entered regression:	1	2	3	1	2	3	1	2	3
Predictors									
Personal Characteristics									
Gender (female)							.21**	.18**	.17*
Age of employee				-.20*	-.18*	-.20*			
Ethnicity (white)									
Occupation (professional)	-.14*	-.14*							
Caring for parent									
Caring for spouse							.22**	.22**	.28**
Caring for child									
Change in R² at Step 1	.05			.07			.11		
Demands									
Hours worked									
Shift (day)		.15*	.16*		.13*			.18**	.20**
Number cared for									
Number of caregiving roles									
Distance from recipient									
Hours of care provided									
Special care needs									
Change in R² at Step 2	.04			.04			.06		
Resources									
Household income									
Work schedule flexibility									
Working partner									
Nonworking partner									
Informal support									
Formal support									
Ease finding/managing care									
Satisfaction with care									-.19**
Change in R² at Step 3	.02			.01			.07		
Total R²/R² Adjusted	.10/.01			.13/.04			.24/.16		
Overall F	1.14			1.43			3.04**		
Df (reg./res.) 22,213									

Note: Based on standardized betas; only significant betas reported.
* $p \le .05$; ** $p \le .01$.

TABLE 4.2B Effects of Personal Characteristics, Caregiving Demands, and Caregiving Resources on Stress Variables Among Employees With Adult-Care Responsibilities

	Stress Variables								
	Personal Health Stress			Caregiving Stress			Difficulty Combining Work and Family		
Step entered regression:	1	2	3	1	2	3	1	2	3
Predictors									
Personal Characteristics									
Gender (female)							.17**	.16*	
Age of employee	.17*	.20*	.18*						−.18*
Ethnicity (white)									
Occupation (professional)									
Caring for parent						.19*			
Caring for spouse				.24**	.22**	.25**			
Caring for child				.17*					
Change in R^2 at Step 1	.03			.07			.05		
Demands									
Hours worked									
Shift (day)									
Number cared for					.21**	.20**			
Number of caregiving roles								.16*	
Distance from recipient						−.16*			
Hours of care provided									
Special care needs		.18**	.15*		.34**	.20**		.20**	
Change in R^2 at Step 2		.05			.16			.06	
Resources									
Household income									
Work schedule flexibility									−.41**
Working partner									
Nonworking partner									.17*
Informal support									−.16**
Formal support									
Ease finding/managing care									
Satisfaction with care						−.14*			
Change in R^2 at Step 3			.05			.06			.25
Total R^2/R^2 Adjusted			.13/.04			.30/.23			.37/.31
Overall F			1.50			4.12**			5.82**
Df (reg./res.) 22,213									

Note: Based on significant betas; only significant betas reported.
* $p \le .05$; ** $p \le .01$.

TABLE 5.1B Effects of Personal Characteristics, Caregiving Demands, and Caregiving Resources on Absenteeism Variables Among Employees With Elder-Care Responsibilities

	Absenteeism Variables								
	Days Missed			Late or Left Early			Interruptions		
Step entered regression:	1	2	3	1	2	3	1	2	3
Predictors									
Personal Characteristics									
Gender (female)	.07**			.10**	.09**	.07**			
Age of employee	-.06*			-.18**	-.17**	-.15**	-.14**	-.09**	-.10**
Ethnicity (white)									
Occupation (professional)									
Caring for parent	.06*		.06*				.07**		
Caring for spouse							.07*	.05*	.05*
Change in R^2 at Step 1	.01			.05			.02		
Demands									
Hours worked							.10**	.08**	
Shift (day)					.09**	.08**	.13**	.11**	
Number cared for									
Number of caregiving roles					.11**	.13**	.20**	.21**	
Distance from recipient									
Hours of care provided								.05*	
Special care needs									
Change in R^2 at Step 2		.01			.02			.07	
Resources									
Household income			-.09**				.12**		
Work schedule flexibility						.07**			
Working partner						-.09**			
Nonworking partner						-.11**			
Informal support									
Formal support									
Ease finding/managing care			-.07*						
Satisfaction with care									-.10**
Change in R^2 at Step 3			.01			.01			.02
Total R^2/R^2 Adjusted			.03/.02			.08/.07			.11/.10
Overall F			2.42**			6.83**			9.07**
Df (reg./res.) 21,1544									

Note: Based on standardized betas; only significant betas reported.
* $p \le .05$; ** $p \le .01$.

TABLE 5.2B Effects of Personal Characteristics, Caregiving Demands, and Caregiving Resources on Stress Variables Among Employees With Elder-Care Responsibilities

| | Stress Variables | | | | | | | | |
| | Personal Health Stress | | | Elder-Care Stress | | | Difficulty Combining Work and Family | | |
Step entered regression:	1	2	3	1	2	3	1	2	3
Predictors									
Personal Characteristics									
Gender (female)	.09**	.09**	.06*	.09**	.06*		.09**	.12**	.07**
Age of employee						.07**	-.13**	-.08**	-.07**
Ethnicity (white)									
Occupation (professional)									-.05*
Caring for parent				.23**	.24**	.26**	.12**	.10**	.09**
Caring for spouse				.08**		.06*	.07**		.05*
Change in R² at Step 1	.01			.07			.04		
Demands									
Hours worked								.07**	.06*
Shift (day)									
Number cared for					.09**	.09**			
Number of caregiving roles					-.08**	-.08**		.17**	.15*
Distance from recipient					-.05*	-.09**			
Hours of care provided					.14**	.10**		.10**	.06*
Special care needs		.06*			.28**	.11**		.09**	
Change in R² at Step 2		.01			.12			.05	
Resources									
Household income			-.06*						
Work schedule flexibility			-.09**						-.29**
Working partner									
Nonworking partner									
Informal support									
Formal support						.08**			
Ease finding/managing care						-.19**			-.07*
Satisfaction with care			-.10**			-.14**			-.13**
Change in R² at Step 3			.03			.08			.13
Total R²/R² Adjusted			.05/.04			.27/.26			.22/.21
Overall F			4.16**			27.38**			20.97**
Df (reg./res.) 21,1544									

Note: Based on standardized betas; only significant betas reported.
* $p \leq .05$; ** $p \leq .01$.

TABLE 6.2B Effects of Personal Characteristics, Caregiving Demands, Caregiving Resources, and Multiple Roles on Dependent Variables

	Outcome Variables				
	Days Missed	Late or Left Early	Interruptions	Health Stress	Difficulty Combining Work and Family
Predictors					
Personal Characteristics					
Gender (female)	.08**	.07**	.05**	.08**	.12**
Age of employee		−.17**	−.10**	.03**	−.07**
Ethnicity (white)	−.02*		.02*	−.03*	
Occupation (professional)	.04**				.03**
Change in R^2 at Step 1	.01**	.04**	.01**	.01**	.02**
Demands					
Hours worked				.05**	.06**
Shift (day)	.04**	.11**	.12**		
Change in R^2 at Step 2	.00**	.02**	.02**		.00**
Resources					
Household income	−.10**	.03*	.05**	−.07**	−.04**
Work schedule flexibility		.09**	.08**	−.07**	−.26**
Working partner	.03*	−.08**			.06**
Nonworking partner	−.03*	−.05**		−.05**	
Change in R^2 at Step 3	.01**	.01**	.02**	.01**	.08**
Caregiving Roles					
Child care only	.05**	.10**	.22**	.02*	.28**
Adult care only			.04**	.03**	.03**
Elder care only	.03*	.03*	.09**	.04**	.10**
Child + adult care	.03*	.04**	.07**	.02*	.09**
Child + elder care	.04**	.08**	.19**	.05**	.19**
Adult + elder Care			.05**	.04**	.04**
Child, adult, elder	.03*		.06**		.05**
Change in R^2 at Step 4	.00*	.01**	.06**	.00**	.07**
Total R^2/R^2 Adjusted	.025/.023	.080/.079	.106/.104	.028/.027	.177/.176
Overall F	12.48**	43.10**	58.20**	14.52**	106.29**
DF (reg./res.) 17,8374					

Note: Based on standardized betas; only significant betas reported.
* $p \le .05$; ** $p \le .01$.

TABLE 6.3B Effects of Personal Characteristics, Caregiving Demands, Caregiving Resources, Multiple Roles, and Interaction Terms on Dependent Variables

Predictors	Days Missed	Late or Left Early	Interruptions	Personal Health Stress	Difficulty Combining Work and Family
			Outcome Variables		
Personal Characteristics					
Gender (female)	.06**	.04*		.06**	.05**
Age of employee		-.18**	-.11**	.04**	-.07**
Ethnicity (white)	-.04**				
Occupation (professional)	.05**	-.04*			
Change in R^2 at Step 1	.01**	.04**	.01**	.01**	.02**
Demands					
Hours worked					.08**
Shift (day)	.04*	.11**	.09**	.03*	
Change in R^2 at Step 2	.00**	.02**	.02**		.00**
Resources					
Household income	-.08**			-.09**	
Work schedule flexibility		.07**	.07**	-.06**	-.25**
Working partner		-.05*	.09**		.12**
Nonworking partner			.05**	-.09**	.04*
Change in R^2 at Step 3	.01**	.01**	.02**	.01**	.08**
Caregiving Roles					
Number caregiving roles					.45**
Change in R^2 at Step 4	.00**	.01**	.05**	.00**	.06**
Interaction Terms					
Roles by gender		.04*	.06**		.10**
Roles by age					-.15**
Roles by ethnicity		-.10*			
Roles by occupation		.07**			
Roles by hours worked					
Roles by shift			.10**		
Roles by income					
Roles by work flexibility		.09*			
Roles by working partner				-.10**	-.07**
Roles by nonworking partner		-.06*	-.06**	.05*	
Change in R^2 at Step 5		.00*	.00*		.01**
Total R^2/R^2 Adjusted	.025/.023	.082/.080	.106/.104	.028/.025	.170/.168
Overall F	10.33**	35.69**	47.20**	11.58**	81.64**
Df (reg./res.) 21,8370					

Note: Based on standardized betas; only significant betas reported.

* $p \leq .05$; ** $p \leq .01$.

Index

elder care and, 127, 129-137, 178
employee needs assessment, 248
employment effects on, 143-144
formal service use and, 126, 136
gender issues, 61-62, 81, 92, 116, 167
hours of work and, 120
informal support and, 125, 158
interaction effects, 53, 158-160, 166
measures, 46, 47
multiple caregiver roles, 15-16, 107-
108, 136, 146, 148-161, 173
schedule flexibility and, 18, 137
social class and, 124
spouse versus parent caregiving, 109-110
task types and, 121-122
Stride Rite, 226
Stroke victims, 93, 99
Support groups, 224
Survey:
cover letter, 269-270
employee needs assessment, 240-241
questionnaire, 271-275
response rate, 37, 182

Tardiness, 8. *See also* Absenteeism
Task forces, 241-242
Tax credits, 210-212
Technology, 8
Telecommunications, 8
Telecommuting, 198
Theoretical considerations, 30-36
Training, 203-204
Travelers Companies, 221

Turnover rates, 71, 101-103, 226

Unions, 200, 224-225

Voluntary reduced time, 195-196

Wages, 7
Work-family interactions, 3-7, 17-19, 184-
186
caregiver-noncaregiver comparisons, 53,
141-143, 150
care recipients and, 19-20
carryover effects, 17, 35
conceptual framework, 30-36, 179-184
emotional impacts, 15-20
research needs, 265
second world hypothesis, 11
study summary and implications, 184-
186
See also Absenteeism; Stress; *specific
caregiving roles*
Workplace resources. *See* Employer-supported programs; Resource(s)
Work scheduling, 70-71, 164, 173, 175, 264
caregivers of disabled adults, 110
caregivers of elders, 127, 137
caregiver stress and, 18
child care and, 64-65, 84, 86, 177, 258
compressed workweek, 199-201
flextime, 70, 201-203, 259
gender-related adaptability, 116

About the Authors

Nancy J. Chapman, Ph.D., is Professor and Chair of the Department of Urban Studies and Planning at Portland State University. She has been involved in research on informal helping networks and caregivers of the elderly for more than 12 years. Her related publications include *Helping Networks and Human Services,* with Charles Froland, Diane Pancoast, and Priscilla Kimboko, and an information synthesis of the literature, "Gender, Marital Status, and Childlessness of Older Persons and the Availability of Informal Assistance," in *Health Care for the Elderly: An Information Sourcebook,* edited by Marilyn Petersen and Diana White. Her other research has focused on housing and environment for the elderly (e.g., "Community and Neighborhood Issues" in *The Columbia Handbook on Retirement,* edited by Abraham Monk) and intergenerational relations.

Arthur C. Emlen, Ph.D., is Professor Emeritus of Social Work at Portland State University, where, for 16 years, he was Director of the Regional Research Institute for Human Services. His research interests have centered around child care and work-family issues, specifically the impact of employees' child-care needs on the workplace. Prior to that, he conducted research on informal family day-care arrangements, neighborhood referral services, family permanency, and planning for children who are in foster care or at risk of unnecessary placement. In 1987, he was awarded the Branford Price Millar Award for Faculty Excellence by his peers. Also in 1987, at the 75th anniversary of the United States Children's Bureau, he received the Secretary of Health and Human Services Award for pioneering work that assisted states to plan toward a permanent family status for children who receive public child welfare services. In "retirement," he continues to research work-family issues as President of Arthur Emlen & Associates, Inc.

Berit Ingersoll-Dayton, Ph.D., is an Associate Professor in the School of Social Work at the University of Michigan. She was formerly an Associate Professor in the Graduate School of Social Work and Department of Psychology at Portland State University. Much of her research has focused on the social supports of the elderly. She has recently published two articles in this area: "Reciprocal and Non-Reciprocal Social Support: Contrasting Sides of Intimate Relationships," coauthored with Toni Antonucci and published in the *Journal of Gerontology;* and "Supportive Relationships in Later Life," coauthored with Charlene Depner and published in *Psychology and Aging.* Another research focus is directed toward interventions with the elderly and their families. An article, "A Program for Caregivers in the Workplace," coauthored with Nancy J. Chapman and Margaret B. Neal, recently appeared in *The Gerontologist.*

Margaret B. Neal, Ph.D., is an Associate Professor in the Department of Urban Studies and Planning and the Institute on Aging at Portland State University. She has conducted research related to the development and evaluation of social and health programs and policies for the elderly and their families for the past 17 years. Her particular interests are in informal caregiving, terminal care, and assessment of quality of care. She was the principal investigator of "Work and Elder Care: Supporting Families in the Workplace," through which the data described here were gathered. She also coauthored, with Nancy J. Chapman, Berit Ingersoll-Dayton, Arthur C. Emlen, and Linda Boise, "Absenteeism and Stress Among Employed Caregivers of the Elderly, Disabled Adults, and Children" in *Aging and Caregiving: Theory, Research, and Policy,* edited by David E. Biegel and Arthur Blum.